DOMESDAY BOOK

Kent

History from the Sources

DOMESDAY BOOK

A Survey of the Counties of England

LIBER DE WINTONIA

Compiled by direction of

KING WILLIAM I

Winchester
1086

DOMESDAY BOOK

general editor

JOHN MORRIS

1

Kent

edited by

Philip Morgan

from a draft translation prepared by

Veronica Sankaran

PHILLIMORE
Chichester
1983

1983
Published by
PHILLIMORE & CO. LTD.
London and Chichester
Head Office: Shopwyke Hall,
Chichester, Sussex, England

ISBN 0 85033 153 6 (case)
ISBN 0 85033 154 4 (limp)

Printed in Great Britain by
Titus Wilson & Son Ltd.,
Kendal

KENT

Introduction

The Domesday Survey of Kent

Notes

Index of Persons

Index of Places

Map and Map Keys

Systems of Reference

Technical Terms

History from the Sources
General Editor: John Morris

The series aims to publish history
written directly from the sources
for all interested readers, both
specialists and others. The first
priority is to publish important
texts which should be widely
available, but are not.

DOMESDAY BOOK

The contents, with the folio on which each county begins, are:

Supplementary volume (35) **BOLDON BOOK**

Domesday Book is termed *Liber de Wintonia* (The Book of Winchester) in column 332c

INTRODUCTION

The Domesday Survey

In 1066 Duke William of Normandy conquered England. He was crowned King, and most of the lands of the English nobility were soon granted to his followers. Domesday Book was compiled 20 years later. The Saxon Chronicle records that in 1085

> at Gloucester at midwinter ... the King had deep speech with his counsellors ... and sent men all over England to each shire ... to find out ... what or how much each landholder held ... in land and livestock, and what it was worth ... The returns were brought to him.[1]

William was thorough. One of his Counsellors reports that he also sent a second set of Commissioners 'to shires they did not know, where they were themselves unknown, to check their predecessors' survey, and report culprits to the King.'[2]

The information was collected at Winchester, corrected, abridged, chiefly by omission of livestock and the 1066 population, and fair-copied by one writer into a single volume, now known as Domesday Book Volume I, or DB. The task of abridgement and codification was not complete by the time work stopped at the death of King William. The remaining material, the commissioners' circuit returns for Norfolk, Suffolk and Essex, which there had not been time to reduce, was left unabridged, copied by several writers, in a second volume, smaller than the first, usually now referred to as Domesday Book Volume II or Little Domesday Book or LDB, which states that 'the Survey was made in 1086'. The surveys of Durham and Northumberland, and of several towns, including London, were not transcribed, and most of Cumberland and Westmorland, not yet in England, was not surveyed. The whole undertaking was completed at speed, in less than 12 months, though the fair-copying of the main volume may have taken a little longer. Both volumes are now preserved at the Public Record Office. Some versions of regional returns also survive. One of them, from Ely Abbey,[3] copies out the Commissioners' brief. They were to ask

> The name of the place. Who held it, before 1066, and now?
> How many *hides*?[4] How many ploughs, both those in lordship and the men's?
> How many villagers, cottagers and slaves, how many free men and Freemen?[5]
> How much woodland, meadow and pasture? How many mills and fishponds?
> How much has been added or taken away? What the total value was and is?
> How much each free man or Freeman had or has? All threefold, before 1066,
> when King William gave it, and now; and if more can be had than at present.

The Ely volume also describes the procedure. The Commissioners took evidence on oath 'from the Sheriff; from all the barons and their Frenchmen; and from the whole Hundred, the priests, the reeves and six villagers from each village'. It also names four Frenchmen and four Englishmen from each Hundred, who were sworn to verify the detail.

---

[1]Before he left England for the last time, late in 1086. [2]Robert Losinga, Bishop of Hereford 1079-1095 (see *E.H.R.* 22, 1907, 74). [3]*Inquisitio Eliensis*, first paragraph. [4]A land unit, reckoned as 120 acres. [5]*Quot Sochemani*.

The King wanted to know what he had, and who held it. The Commissioners therefore listed lands in dispute, for Domesday Book was not only a tax-assessment. To the King's grandson, Bishop Henry of Winchester, its purpose was that every 'man should know his right and not usurp another's'; and because it was the final authoritative register of rightful possession 'the natives called it Domesday Book, by analogy from the Day of Judgement'; that was why it was carefully arranged by Counties, and by landholders within Counties, 'numbered consecutively ... for easy reference'.[6]

Domesday Book describes Old English society under new management, in minute statistical detail. Foreign lords had taken over, but little else had yet changed. The chief landholders and those who held from them are named, and the rest of the population was counted. Most of them lived in villages, whose houses might be clustered together, or dispersed among their fields. Villages were grouped in administrative districts called Hundreds, which formed regions within Shires, or Counties, which survive today with minor boundary changes; the recent deformation of some ancient county identities is here disregarded, as are various short-lived modern changes. The local assemblies, though overshadowed by lords great and small, gave men a voice, which the Commissioners heeded. Very many holdings were described by the Norman term *manerium* (manor), greatly varied in size and structure, from tiny farmsteads to vast holdings; and many lords exercised their own jurisdiction and other rights, termed *soca*, whose meaning still eludes exact definition.

The Survey was unmatched in Europe for many centuries, the product of a sophisticated and experienced English administration, fully exploited by the Conqueror's commanding energy. But its unique assemblage of facts and figures has been hard to study, because the text has not been easily available, and abounds in technicalities. Investigation has therefore been chiefly confined to specialists; many questions cannot be tackled adequately without a cheap text and uniform translation available to a wider range of students, including local historians.

Previous Editions

The text has been printed once, in 1783, in an edition by Abraham Farley, probably of 1250 copies, at Government expense, said to have been £38,000; its preparation took 16 years. It was set in a specially designed type, here reproduced photographically, which was destroyed by fire in 1808. In 1811 and 1816 the Records Commissioners added an introduction, indices, and associated texts, edited by Sir Henry Ellis; and in 1861-1863 the Ordnance Survey issued zincograph facsimiles of the whole. Texts of individual counties have appeared since 1673, separate translations in the Victoria County Histories and elsewhere.

[6]*Dialogus de Scaccario* 1,16.

This Edition

Farley's text is used, because of its excellence, and because any worthy alternative would prove astronomically expensive. His text has been checked against the facsimile, and discrepancies observed have been verified against the manuscript, by the kindness of Miss Daphne Gifford of the Public Record Office. Farley's few errors are indicated in the notes.

The editor is responsible for the translation and lay-out. It aims at what the compiler would have written if his language had been modern English; though no translation can be exact, for even a simple word like 'free' nowadays means freedom from different restrictions. Bishop Henry emphasized that his grandfather preferred 'ordinary words'; the nearest ordinary modern English is therefore chosen whenever possible. Words that are now obsolete, or have changed their meaning, are avoided, but measurements have to be transliterated, since their extent is often unknown or arguable, and varied regionally. The terse inventory form of the original has been retained, as have the ambiguities of the Latin.

Modern English commands two main devices unknown to 11th century Latin, standardised punctuation and paragraphs; in the Latin, *ibi* ('there are') often does duty for a modern full stop, *et* ('and') for a comma or semi-colon. The entries normally answer the Commissioners' questions, arranged in five main groups, (i) the place and its holder, its hides, ploughs and lordship; (ii) people; (iii) resources; (iv) value; and (v) additional notes. The groups are usually given as separate paragraphs.

In both volumes of the MS, chapters were numbered 'for easy reference'. In the larger volume, sections within chapters are commonly marked, usually by initial capitals, often edged in red. In LDB (representing an earlier stage of the Inquiry's codification) sections are at first usually introduced by a paragraph mark, while red edging is reserved for chapter and Hundred headings; further on, however, the system of paragraphing the text becomes more haphazard and it is thus not always followed in the present translation. Owing to the less tabulated nature of the entries in LDB for Norfolk and Suffolk it is not possible to maintain throughout the translation of these two counties the sub-paragraphing that the late John Morris employed in the translation of other counties in the series. Maps, indices and an explanation of technical terms are also given. Later, it is hoped to publish analytical and explanatory volumes, and associated texts.

The editor is deeply indebted to the advice of many scholars, too numerous to name, and especially to the Public Record Office, and to the publisher's patience. The draft translations are the work of a team; they have been co-ordinated and corrected by the editor, and each has been checked by several people. It is therefore hoped that mistakes may be fewer than in versions published by single fallible individuals. But it would be Utopian to hope that the translation is altogether free from error; the editor would like to be informed of mistakes observed.

The maps are the work of Nell Bowen.

The preparation of this volume has been greatly assisted by a generous grant from the Leverhulme Trust Fund.

This support, originally given to the late Dr. J. R. Morris, has been kindly extended to his successors. At the time of Dr. Morris's death in June 1977, he had completed volumes 2, 3, 11, 12, 19, 23, 24. He had more or less finished the preparation of volumes 13, 14, 20, 28. These and subsequent volumes in the series were brought out under the supervision of John Dodgson and Alison Hawkins, who have endeavoured to follow, as far as possible, the editorial principles established by John Morris.

Conventions

★   refers to note on discrepancy between MS and Farley text

[ ]   enclose words omitted in the MS   ( ) enclose editorial explanation

1 a

DOVERE Tēpore regis EDWARDI reddebat . xviii . libras . de quibus. denariis habebat rex . E . duas partes. 7 comes Goduin terciā. Contra hoc habebant canonici de ſco Martino medietatē aliam. Burgenſes dederᵗⁱ . xx . naues | una uice in anno ad . xv . dies. 7 in una quaq̚ naui erant hōēs . xx 7 uń. Hoc faciebant pro eo q̄d eis p̄donauerat ſaccā 7 ſocā. Quando miſſatici regis ueniebant ibi: dabant pro caballo tranſducendo . iii . denarios in hieme . 7 ii̊ . in eſtate. Burgenſes ũ inueniebā ſtiremannū 7 unū aliū adjutorē . 7 ſi plus opus . ēēt: de pecunia ej̄ conducebat. ꝉ A feſtiuitate S Michaelis uſq̚ ad feſtū Sci Andreæ: treuua regis erat in uilla. Siq̄s eam infregiſſet: inde p̄poſit regis accipiebat cō munē emendationē. ꝉ Quicunq̚ manens in uilla aſſiduus . reddebat regi c̄ſuetudinē: quietus erat de theloneo p̄ totā Angliā. Om̄s hæ conſuetudi nes erant ibi . quando Wills rex in Angliā uenit. In ipſo p̄mo Aduentu ej̄ in Angliā . fuit ipſa uilla cōbuſta. 7 idō p̄ciū ej̄ non potuit cōputari quantū ualebat quando ep̄s baiocenſis eā recepit . Modo app̄ciat . xl . lib̄ . 7 tam̄ p̄poſit inde reddit . l . iiii . lib̄. Regi qđē . xxiiii . lib̄ de denar̄ qui ſuᵗ xx . in ora: comiti ũ . xxx . lib̄ ad numerū.

KENT

D   **DOVER**

1   before 1066 paid £18, of which pence King Edward had two parts and Earl Godwin the third. Against this, the Canons of St. Martin's had the other half.

2   The burgesses gave 20 ships to the King once a year for 15 days. In each ship were 21 men. They did this because he had given over to them full jurisdiction.

3   When the King's messengers came there, they gave 3d in winter and 2d in summer for horse passage. The burgesses found a steersman and 1 other assistant. If there was more labour, it was hired with his own money.

4   From the Feast of St. Michael until the Feast of St. Andrew the King's truce, that is peace, was in the town. If anyone broke it, the King's reeve received the common fine for it.

5   Whoever lived permanently in the town and paid customary dues to the King was exempt from toll throughout the whole of England.

6   All these customs were there when King William came to England.

7   At his first arrival in England the town was burnt. Its valuation could not therefore be reckoned, what its value was when the Bishop of Bayeux acquired it. Now it is assessed at £40; however, the reeve pays £54, that is £24 of pence, which are 20 to the *ora,* to the King and £30 at face value to the Earl.

In Douere sux̄ . xxix . manſuræ . de q̄bᵹ rex p̄dit c̄ſue

tudinē . De his habet Roꝛt de romenel duas.

Radulf de curbeſpine . iii . Wiƚƚs fili Tedaldi . i .

Wiƚƚs fili Ogeri . i . Wiƚƚs fili Tedoldi ⁊ Roꝛtus

niger . vi . Wiƚƚs filius Goisfridi . iii . in q̄bᵹ erat

gihalla burgenſiū. Hugo de montfort . i . domū.

Durand . i . Rannulf de colūbels . i . Wadard . vi .

Filius Modꝛti unā. Et hi om̄s de his domibᵹ reuo

cant ep̄m baiocenſe ad ꝓtectorē ⁊ liberatorem.

ſ De illa maſura quā tenet Rannulf de colūbels quæ

fuit cujdā exuliſ:c̄cordant qđ dimidia t̄ra eſt

regis . ⁊ Rannulf ipſe habet utrunq̄ . Hunfridus

tenet . i . maſurā . de qua erat forisfactura dimidia

regis . Roger de Oſtrehā fecit quandā đomū ſup

aquā regis . ⁊ tenuit huc uſq̄ c̄ſuetudinē regis . Nec

dom fuit ibi T.R.E. ſ In introitu portus de Douere

eſt unū molendiñ . qđ om̄s pene naues confringit

ꝑ magnā turbationē maris . ⁊ maximū đānū fa

cit regi ⁊ hominibᵹ . ⁊ non fuit ibi . T.R.E. De hoc đicit

Nepos Herberti . qđ ep̄s baiocenſis conceſſit illū

fieri Auunculo ſuo Herberto filio Iuonis.

1 b

Has infra ſcriptas leges regis c̄cordant hōes

de . iiii . Leſtis . hoc . ē Boruuar Leſt . ⁊ Eſtreleſt.

⁊ Linuuartleſt . ⁊ Wiuuartleſt . Siq̄s fecerit

ſepē uel foſſatū pro quo ſtrictior fiat publica

uia regis . aut arborē ſtante extra uiā intra pro

ſtrauerit . ⁊ inde ramū uel frondē portauerit:

pro una quaq̄ harū forisfactur ſoluet regi . c . ſot.

8   In Dover are 29 dwellings whose customary dues the King
has lost. Of these, Robert of Romney has 2, Ralph of
Courbépine 3, William son of Theodwald 1, William son
of Odger 1, William son of Theodwald and Robert Black 6,
William son of Geoffrey 3, including the burgesses' guild-hall,
Hugh de Montfort 1 house, Durand 1, Ranulf of
Colombières 1, Wadard 6, and Modbert's son 1.
For these houses they all cite the Bishop of Bayeux as
protector and deliverer, that is donor.

9   For the dwelling which Ranulf of Colombières holds, which
was an exile's, that is an outlaw's, they agree that half the land
is the King's; Ranulf has both (halves) himself. Humphrey
Strapfoot holds 1 dwelling, half of which was forfeit to the
King. Roger of Westerham made a house on the King's
waterway, and has hitherto kept the King's customary dues.
The house was not there before 1066.

10   At the entrance to Dover harbour is a mill, which wrecks almost
all ships, through its great disturbance of the sea; it does very
great harm to the King and his men; it was not there before 1066.
Of this, Herbert's nephew says that the Bishop of Bayeux gave
permission for it to be made by his uncle, Herbert son of Ivo.

11   The men of four Lathes, that is Borough Lathe, Eastry Lathe,   1 b
Lympne Lathe and Wye Lathe, agree upon the following
royal laws.

12   If anyone has made a fence or ditch whereby the King's
public road is narrowed, or has felled into the road a tree
that stood outside the road, and has carried off branch or
foliage from it; for each of these offences he shall pay 100s
to the King.

Et fi abierit domū non apphenfus uel diuadi
atus ꞏ/ tamen minifter regis eū fequeꞇ . 7 c . foliꝺ
emdabit. De gribrige ū fiꝗs eā fecerit 7 calū
niat | aut diuadiat fuerit ꞏ/ viii . liꝭ regi emda
bit. Sin autē ꞏ/ quieꞇ erit erga regē . non erga
dñm cuꞁ homo fuerit . de aliis forisfacturis ficuti
de gribrige . fed ꝑ . c . foꞏꞇ emdabit. Has forisfac
turas hꞇ rex fuꝑ oms alodiarios totiꞌ comitatus
de Chent . 7 fuꝑ hōes ipfoꝝ . Et quando moriꞇ
alodiarius ꞏ/ rex inde habet releuationē trǣ.
excepta tra S̄ ꝀINITATIS 7 S̄ Auguftini . 7 S̄ mar
tini . 7 Exceptis his . Godric de Burnes . 7 Godric
carlefone . 7 Alnod cilt . 7 Efber biga . 7 Siret de
cillehā . 7 Turgis 7 Norman . 7 Azor. Suꝑ iftos
hꞇ rex forisfacturā . de capitibꝛ eoꝝ tantū m̊.
7 de terris eoꝝ hꞇ releuamen . qui hñt fuā facā
7 focā. Et de his tris fcilicet Goflaches . 7 Boche
land . 7 aliū Bocheland . 7 tciū Bocheland . 7 Herfte .
. i . jugū de ora . 7 i . jugū de Herte.
Schildrichehā . Macheheue . Ernulfitone . Ofla
chintone . Piria . 7 alia Piria . Brulege . Ofpringes.
Hortone . hꞇ rex . has forisfacturas . Handfocā.
Gribrige . Foriftel. De Adulterio ū ꝑ totū cheꞃ
hꞇ rex hominē . 7 Archieꝑs mulierē . excepta
tra S̄ ꝀINITATIS . 7 S̄ Auguftini . 7 S̄ Martini . de
quibꝛ rex nichil hꞇ. De latrone qui judicaꞇ eft ad
morte . hꞇ rex medietatē pecuniæ eꞁ . Et qui exulē re
cepit fine licentia regis ꞏ/ inde hꞇ rex forisfacturā.

13   If he has gone away from home without being apprehended or attached, nevertheless the King's officer should follow him and he shall be fined 100s.

14   On breach of the peace, if anyone commits it and is charged on the road or attached he shall pay a fine of £8 to the King. But if he is exempt towards the King he shall not be so for the Lord whose man he is.

15   For other offences it as for breach of the peace, but he shall pay a fine of 100s.

16   The King has (the fines for) these penalties over all freeholders of the whole of the County of Kent.

17   When a freeholder dies then the King has the death duty on the land, apart from the land of Holy Trinity, of St. Augustine's and of St. Martin's, and with these exceptions; Godric of Bishopsbourne, Godric Karlson, Young Alnoth, Esbern Big, Sired of Chilham, Thorgils, Norman and Azor. Over these the King has only the capital penalty even now, and he has the death duty on the lands of those who have full jurisdiction.

18   And over these lands, namely *Goslaches,* Buckland, the other Buckland, the third Buckland, Hurst, 1 yoke of Oare, 1 yoke of Harty, *Schildricheham,* Macknade, Arnolton, *Oslachintone,* Perry, the other Perry, Throwley, Ospringe and Horton the King has these penalties: house-breaking, breach of the peace, highway robbery.

19   On adultery, over the whole of Kent the King has the (fine from) the man and the Archbishop (from) the woman, apart from the land of Holy Trinity, of St. Augustine's and of St. Martin's, from which the King has nothing.

20   On theft, the King has half the goods of whoever is condemned to death.

21   Whoever receives an exile without the King's permission, the King has the fine from him.

De terris ſu|pra nominatis Alnodi 7 ſimiliũ ej̄: h̄t rex
cuſtodiã . vi . diebȝ apud cantuariã . uel apud Sanuuic ꝛ
7 ibi h̄nt de rege cibũ 7 potũ . Si non habuerint ꝛ ſine
forisfactura recedunt . Si fuerint p̄moniti ut c̄ueniaꝸ
ad ſcirã ꝛ ibunt uſqȝ ad pinnedennã . non longius . Et ſi
non uenerint꞉ de hac forisfactura 7 de aliis om̄ibȝ rex
. c . ſol habebit . excepta Gribrige quæ . viii . lib em̄dat.
7 de callibȝ ſic ſupius ſcriptũ . ē.

In Linuuartleſt in briſeuuei h̄t rex c̄ſuetudinē . ſcilicet.
. ii꞉caretas . 7 ii . ſticas anguillaꝛ ꝑ uno Ineuuardo . 7 in
tra ſophis h̄t xii . den ꝑ uno Ineuuardo . 7 de uno jugo
de northburg . xii . den aut unũ Ineuuard . 7 de dena
xviii . den . 7 de Gara unũ Ineuuard . He træ jacent in Wi꞉
7 h̄oes de his tris cuſtodiebaꝸ regē apud cantuariã
t̄ apud Sanuuic ꝑ . iii . dies . ſi rex illuc u̇eniſſet .

¹ c
In Leſt de Sudtone 7 in Leſt de Ailesford habueꝛ
iſti ſachã 7 Socã . Brixi cilt . Adelold de Elteh̄ã.
Anſchil de Becheh̄ã . Azor de Leſneis . Aluuinus hor
Wluuard Wit . Ordinc de hortone . Eſbern de
cillesſelle . Leuenot de Sudtone . Eduuard de Eſtan.
Vleſtan 7 Leuric de Otrinberge . Oſuuard de Nord
tone . Edid de Aiſiholte . Alret de Ellinges.

Terra Canonicoȝ s̄ Martini de Dovre.

In Lest de Eſtrede habebant canonici de ſco
Martino . T . R . E . xxi . ſolin In hunḋ de Cornely
7 in hunḋ de Beuſberge . In Leſt de Linuuarlet
habebant . iii . ſolins . unũ in Eſtret hunḋ . aliũ in
Beliſſolt hunḋ . 7 tciũ in Blacheborn hunḋ.
T . R . E . eraꝸ p̄bendæ cõmunes . 7 reddeb̄ . lxi . lib.
int totũ . Modo ſunt diuiſæ ꝑ ſingulos . ꝑ ep̄m Baioc.

22 From the aforenamed lands of Young Alnoth and others like him, the King has a body-guard for 6 days at Canterbury or at Sandwich. They have food and drink from the King; if they have not had it they withdraw without penalty.

23 If they are summoned to meet at the Shire they go as far as Pennenden, not further. If they do not come, the King has 100s for this offence and for all others, with the exception of breach of the peace for which the fine is £8; and from the roads, as written above.

24 In Lympne Lathe, in *Briseuuei* the King has a customary due, namely 2 carts and 2 sticks of eels, for one Escort; and in the land of *Sophis* he has 12d for one Escort; and from 1 yoke of 'Northborough' 12d for one Escort; and from Dean 18d, and from *Gara* one Escort. These lands lie in Wye. Men from these lands guard the King at Canterbury or at Sandwich for 3 days if the King comes there.

25 In the Lathe of Sutton and in the Lathe of Aylesford, these had   1 c
full jurisdiction: Young Brictsi, Aethelwold of Eltham, Askell of Beckenham, Azor of Lessness, Alwin Horn, Wulfward White, Ording of Horton, Esbern of Chelsfield, Leofnoth of Sutton, Edward of Stone, Wulfstan and Leofric of Wateringbury, Osward of Norton, Edith of Asholt and Alfred of Yalding.

M   LAND OF THE CANONS OF ST. MARTIN'S OF DOVER

1 In the Lathe of Eastry the Canons of St Martin's had 21 sulungs before 1066 in Cornilo Hundred and Bewsborough Hundred. In the Lathe of Lympne they had 3 sulungs, one in Street Hundred, another in Bircholt Hundred, and a third in Blackburn Hundred. Before 1066 they were prebends in common; and paid £61 in total. Now they have been distributed individually by the Bishop of Bayeux.

Radulf de S Sanſone ten . i . ꝏ in p̄benda . Cerlen
tone uocat . 7 defd ſe p . i . ſolin . Ibi hȓ . iii . uittos
7 iiii . bord cū . i . car . Int tot ual lxx . ſot . T.R.E.
c . ſot . Leuuin tenuit in p̄benda.

In ead uilla ten Witts fili Ogerii . i . ſolin . 7 ibi hȓ
i . uitt 7 . vii . bord cū dim car . 7 i . molin de . xl . ſot .
Ibi qdā francig hȓ . i . car . Iſd Witts ten . i . monaſt
in Dovere de epo . 7 redd ei . xi . ſot . Canonici calūn .
Hoc tot ual . vi . lib . T.R.E. xii . lib . Sired tenuit.

In Bochelande ten Aluui . i . ſolin . 7 ibi hȓ . vi . uitt
7 . x . bord cū . i . car 7 dimid . Int tot ual . iiii . lib .
T.R.E. c . ſot . Iſte idē tenuit in p̄benda.

In Gociſtone ten Vlric . i . jug . 7 ibi hȓ . ii . uittos
7 i . bord cū . i . car . Ad hanc trā ptin . xxv . ac træ
in Corneli hund . 7 ibi ſunt . v . bord cū dim car .
Int tot ual . xx . ſot . T.R.E. x . ſot . Elric tenuit in

IN HOC EOD HVND Jacet S *Margarita.* p̄benda.
Ibi hȓ Sired . i . ſolin . 7 i . car in dnio . 7 vi . bord
cū . iiii . ſeruis . Val . c . ſot . T.R.E. iiii . lib . Pat ejd
Sired tenuit in p̄benda.

Ibidē ten Radulf . i . ſolin . 7 hȓ . i . car in dnio .
7 vii . bord . Val . lx 7 ix . ſot . 7 ii . den . T.R.E:
iiii . lib . Alric tenuit in p̄benda ſimilit .

Ibidē ten Alred . i . ſolin . 7 hȓ in dnio . i . car .
7 ii . uitt 7 ii . bord cū dim car . Val . lx . ſot . T.R.E.
xx . ſot . Pat huj tenuit in p̄benda.

In BEWSBOROUGH Hundred

2   Ralph of St. Samson holds 1 manor in prebend. It is called
CHARLTON, and answers for 1 sulung. He has
    3 villagers and 4 smallholders with 1 plough.
In total, value 70s; before 1066, 100s.
    Leofwin held it in prebend.

3   In the same village William son of Odger holds 1 sulung. He has
    1 villager and 7 smallholders with ½ plough.
    1 mill at 40s.
    A Frenchman has 1 plough.
    William also holds 1 monastery in Dover from the Bishop; it
      pays him 11s; the Canons claim it.
Value of all this £6; before 1066, £12.
    Sired held it.

4   In BUCKLAND Alwin holds 1 sulung. He has
    6 villagers and 10 smallholders with 1½ ploughs.
In total, value £4; before 1066, 100s.
    He held it himself in prebend.

5   In GUSTON Wulfric holds 1 yoke. He has
    2 villagers and 1 smallholder with 1 plough.
To this land belongs 25 acres of land in Cornilo Hundred;
    5 smallholders with ½ plough.
In total, value 20s; before 1066, 10s.
    Alric held it in prebend.

6   In this same Hundred lies ST. MARGARET'S (at Cliffe). Sired
has 1 sulung and 1 plough in lordship and
    6 smallholders with 4 slaves.
Value 100s; before 1066, £4.
    Sired's father held it in prebend.

7   There Ralph also holds 1 sulung. He has 1 plough in lordship
and
    7 smallholders.
Value 60s and 9s 2d; before 1066, £4.
    Alric held it in prebend likewise.

8   There Alfred also holds 1 sulung. He has 1 plough in lordship
and
    2 villagers and 2 smallholders with ½ plough.
Value 60s; before 1066, 20s.
    His father held it in prebend.

Ibid ten Roɓt niger . 1 . folin . 7 hɾ ibi . III . uiłłos

7 VI . borđ cū . 1 . car . Vał . xxx . fol . T . R . E ⁒ xx . fol.

Efmellt tenuit capellan . R . E.

Ibid ten Walter . 1 . folin . 7 ibi hɾ . III . uiłł . 7 v . borđ.

cū . 1 . car 7 dim . Vał . LX . fol . T . R . E ⁒ LXX . folid.

Sigar tenuit in ꝓbenda.

Ibid ten Turbat dimiđ folin . 7 ibi hɾ . II . uiłłos 7 I . borđ

cū dimiđ car . 7 ifđē Roɓt haɓ dimiđ folin in *CORNILAI HĐ*.

7 ibi dimiđ car in dn̄io . 7 v . borđ . Inɼ toɼ uał . III . liɓ.

T . R . E ⁒ IIII . liɓ . Goldftan tenuit.

Ibidē ten Eduuine dimiđ folin . 7 adhuc . xxv . aĉs . træ.

In dn̄io Lɾ dimiđ car . 7 I . uiłłm cū dimiđ car . *IN CORNILAI HĐ*

hɾ ifđ Eduin qt xx . 7 v . aĉs . 7 ibi . 1 . uiłłm cū . 1 . car.

Vał . III . liɓ . T . R . E ⁒ IIII . liɓ . Ipfemet tenuit . T . R . E . De hac

ꝓbenda fūpfit eꝑs Baioĉ . VIII . aĉs . 7 dedit Alan clerico fuo.

Modo hɾ Vlric de Oxeneford . *IN CORNELAI HVNĐ*.

In Addelā ten Anfchitil . 1 . folin . 7 ibi hɾ in dn̄io . II . car.

cū . VI . borđ . hanc trā tenuit Stigand Archieꝑs.

Huic eiđ Anfchitillo deđ eꝑs baioĉ . L . aĉs træ Ad delā.

7 alias . L . aĉs aꝑ fcām Margaritā . ubi hɾ . 1 . uiłłm

7 dim car . Hæ . c . acræ erant de ꝓbendis ut teftificant.

Inɼ totū ualet . VIII . liɓ . T . R . E ⁒ VII . liɓ . *IN BEVSBERG HĐ*.

9   There Robert Black also holds 1 sulung. He has
       3 villagers and 6 smallholders with 1 plough.
    Value 30s; before 1066, 20s.
    Smelt, King Edward's Chaplain, held it.

10   There Walter also holds 1 sulung. He has
       3 villagers and 5 smallholders with 1½ ploughs.
    Value 60s; before 1066, 70s.
    Sigar held it in prebend.

11   There Thorbert also holds ½ sulung. He has   1 d
       2 villagers and 1 smallholder with ½ plough.

    In Cornilo hundred Robert also has ½ sulung and ½ plough
       in lordship, and 5 smallholders.
    In total, value £3; before 1066, £4.
    Goldstan held it.

12   There Edwin also holds ½ sulung and a further 25 acres of land.
    He has ½ plough in lordship, and
       1 villager with ½ plough.

In CORNILO Hundred
13   Edwin also has 85 acres, and
       1 villager with 1 plough.
    Value £3; before 1066, £4.
    He held it himself before 1066. The Bishop of Bayeux took
    8 acres from this prebend and gave them to his clerk Alan.
    Now Wulfric of Oxford has it.

In CORNILO Hundred
14   In DEAL Archdeacon Ansketel holds 1 sulung.
       He has 2 ploughs in lordship, with
       6 smallholders.
       Archbishop Stigand held this land. The Bishop of Bayeux also
    gave Ansketel 50 acres of land at Deal and another 50 acres
    at St. Margaret's (at Cliffe), where he has
       1 villager and ½ plough.
    These 100 acres were from the prebends, as they testify.
    In total, value £8; before 1066, £7.

In Sibertefuualt ten Witts pictau dimid folin
7 xii . acs . 7 in Addela dimid folin . xii . acs min . 7 ibi
ht . ii . uittos 7 iii . bord . cu . i . car 7 dim . Totu hoc valet
lv . fot . T.R.E. iiii . lib .   *IN CORNELAI HVND.*

☞ In Addelam ten Adelold . iii . uirg . 7 ibi ht . iii . uittos
7 viii . bord cu . i . car . Vat 7 ualuit fep . lx . fot . Iftemet
tenuit T.R.E.   *IN BEVSBERG HD 7 IN CORNELAI HD.*
In Addela ten abb S Auguftini . i . folin . 7 ibi ht . iii . uittos
7 vii . bord cu . i . car 7 dimid . Vat . xxx . fot . T.R.E. xl . fot .
Anteceffor ej tenuit in pbenda fimilit .

In Addela ten Witts filius Tedaldi dimid folin 7 dimid
jugu . 7 ibi ht in dnio . i . car . 7 ii . uittos 7 ii .. bord . Vat
lx . fot . T.R.E. xl . fot . Derinc tenuit .

In Sibertefuualt ten Sigar . i . jugu 7 dimid . 7 ibi ht
in dnio dimid car . 7 ii . uittos 7 i . bord . Vat . xxv . fot .
T.R.E. xxxv . fot . Pat ipfius tenuit in pbenda .

Nigellus medicus ap fcam Margarita ten . i . jugu .
7 dimid . 7 ibi ht . i . uittm cu . ii . bobz . Vat . xx . fot . T.R.E.
xxv . fot . Spirites tenuit in pbenda .   *IN BEVSBERG HD.*
In Ferlingelai ten Witts fili Gaufridi . i . folin . 7 ibi ht
in dnio . i . car . 7 iiii . uittos cu . i . car . Vat . iiii . lib . T.R.E.
vi . lib . Sired tenuit in pbenda .

In BEWSBOROUGH Hundred

15 In SIBERTSWOLD William of Poitou holds ½ sulung and 12 acres,
and in DEAL ½ sulung less 12 acres. He has
2 villagers and 3 smallholders with 1½ ploughs.
Value of the whole, 55s; before 1066 £4.

16 *Added at the foot of the column and directed to its proper place by transposition signs.*

In CORNILO Hundred

17 In DEAL Aethelwold holds 3 virgates. He has
3 villagers and 8 smallholders with 1 plough.
The value is and always was 60s.
He held it himself before 1066.

In BEWSBOROUGH Hundred and in CORNILO Hundred

18 In DEAL the Abbot of St Augustine's holds 1 sulung. He has
3 villagers and 7 smallholders with 1½ ploughs.
Value 30s; before 1066, 40s.
His predecesssor held it in prebend likewise.

19 In DEAL William son of Theodwold holds ½ sulung and ½ yoke.
He has in lordship 1 plough, and
2 villagers and 2 smallholders.
Value 60s; before 1066, 40s.
Dering son of Sired held it.

20 In SIBERTSWOLD Sigar holds 1½ yokes. He has in lordship ½
plough, and
2 villagers and 1 smallholder.
Value 25s; before 1066, 35s.
His father held it in prebend.

21 Nigel the Doctor holds 1½ yokes at St. Margaret's (at Cliffe).
He has 1 villager with 2 oxen.
Value 20s; before 1066, 25s.
Spirites held it in prebend.

In BEWSBOROUGH Hundred

22 In FARTHINGLOE William son of Geoffrey holds 1 sulung.
He has in lordship 1 plough, and
4 villagers with 1 plough.
Value £4; before 1066, £6.
Sired held it in prebend.

In Hichā ten̄ Balduin̄ . i . ſolin . 7 ibi hт̄ . iiii . uiłłos . 7 v .

borđ cū . ii . car̄ . Vał . iiii . liƀ . T . R . E : o . ſoł . Eduin̄ tenuit .

In Bocheland ten̄ Godric̄ . i . ſolin . 7 ibi hт̄ . ii . car̄ in dn̄io .

7 iii . uiłłos 7 iiii . borđ cū . i . car̄ . 7 una ӕccła . Vał . vi . liƀ .

T . R . E : viii . liƀ .

☞ In Siƀteſuuald ten̄ Vłſtan . f . Vluuin . i . ſolin 7 ibi hт̄ dimiđ car̄ .

7 iii . uiłłos 7 ix . borđ cū, i . car̄ . T . R . E . ualƀ . c . ſoł . modo . lx . ſoł .

Pat ej tenuit .

2 a

In Civitate Cantvaria habuit Rex Edward

l . 7 i . burgens̄ . reddentes gablū . 7 alios . cc 7 xii .

ſup quos habebat ſacā 7 ſocā . 7 iii . molenđ de . xl . ſoł .

Modo burgens̄ gablū reddentes ſunt . xix . De . xxxii .

alijs qui fueraɴ : ſunt uaſtati . xi . in foſſato ciuitatis .

7 archieps hт̄ ex eis . vii . 7 aƀƀ S Auguſtini alios . xiiii .

ꝑ excābio caſtelli . 7 adhuc ſunt . cc . 7 xii . burḡs̄ . ſup .

quos hт̄ rex ſacā 7 ſocā . 7 molenđ redđ . c 7 viii . ſoł .

7 theloneū redđ . lxviii . ſoł . Ibi . viii . acrӕ ꝓti quӕ

ſolebant . ēē . legátoᵹ regis . m̄ redđ de cenſu . xv . ſoł .

7 mille acrӕ ſiluӕ infructuoſӕ . de qua exeuɴ . xxiiii .

ſolidi . Int totū . T . R . E . ualuit . li . liƀ . 7 tn̄tđ qdo uicec

receꝑ . 7 m̄ . l . liƀ apꝑciat̄ . Tam qui ten̄ n̄c reddit . xxx .

liƀ arſas 7 penſatas . 7 xxiiii . liƀ ad numerū . Sup h̄ om̄a

hт̄ uicecom̄ . c 7 x . ſoł .

Duas dom duoᵹ burgſiū . unā foris aliā int̄ ciuitatē . qđa

monachus ӕcclӕ cantuar̄ abſtulit . Hӕ eraɴ poſitӕ in caſſe

23   In HOUGHAM Baldwin holds 1 sulung. He has
      4 villagers and 5 smallholders with 2 ploughs.
Value £4; before 1066, 100s.
      Edwin held it.

24   In BUCKLAND Godric holds 1 sulung. He has 2 ploughs in
lordship, and
      3 villagers and 4 smallholders with 1 plough.
      A church.
Value £6; before 1066, £8.

Directed to its proper place by transposition signs.

16   In SIBERTSWOLD Wulfstan son of Wulfwin holds 1 sulung.
He has ½ plough, and
      3 villagers and 9 smallholders with 1 plough.
Value before 1066, 100s; now 60s.
      His father held it.

C 1   In the City of Canterbury King Edward had 51 burgesses   2 a
who paid tribute and another 212 over whom he had full
jurisdiction; and 3 mills at 40s. Now there are 19 burgesses
who pay tribute. (The houses) of 32 others who were there
have been destroyed, 11 in the city ditch, the Archbishop has
7 of them, the Abbot of St. Augustine's another 14 in exchange
for the castle. There are still 212 burgesses over whom the
King has full jurisdiction; and the 3 mills pay 108s. The toll
pays 68s; 8 acres of meadow which used to be the King's
messengers' now pay 15s in tribute; 1000 acres of unproductive
woodland which produce 24s.
In total, value before 1066, £51; as much when Hamo the Sheriff
acquired it; now assessed at £50. However the present holder pays
£30 assayed and weighed, and £24 at face value. Over and above
all this the Sheriff has 110s.

2   A monk of Canterbury Church took away two houses of two
burgesses, one outside, the other inside, the City. These were
situated on the King's road.

¶ Burgſcs habuer̄ . XLV . manſur̄ ext̄ ciuitatē . de q̄b;
ipſi habeb̄ gablū 7 c̄ſuetud̄ :· rex aut̄ hab̄ ſacā 7 ſocā.
Ipſi q̄q; burgſes habebant de rege . XXX . III . ac̄s træ
in gildā ſuā. Has dom̄ 7 hanc trā ten̄ Rannulf̄ de Colū
bels . Habet etiā q̄t XX . ac̄s træ ſup̄ hæc . quas tenebāt
burgens̄ in alodia de rege. Tenet quoq; . V . ac̄s træ.
quæ juſte p̄tinent uni æcclæ. De his om̄ib; reuocat
iſdē Rannulf̄ ad p̄tectorē ep̄m Baiocenſem.
¶ Radulf̄ de Curbeſpine h̄t . IIII . manſuras in ciuitate.
quas tenuit quædā c̄cubina heraldi . de quib; eſt ſaca
7 ſoca regis. ſed uſq; n̄c non habuit.
Iſdē Radulf̄ ten̄ alias . XI . maſuras de ep̄o baioc' in ipſa ciuitate.
Que fuer̄ Sbern biga . 7 reddt̄ XI . ſolid̄ 7 II . den̄ . 7 I . obolū
Per totā ciuitatē cantuariæ h̄t rex ſacā 7 ſocā . excepta
trā æcclæ S̄ TRIN . 7 S̄ Auguſtini . 7 Eddeuæ reginæ . 7 Alnod
cild . 7 Esber biga . 7 Siret de Cillehā.
Corcordatū eſt de rectis callib; quæ habēt p̄ ciuitatē
introitū 7 exitū . quicunq; in illis forisfecerit :· regi
em̄dabit . Similit̄ de callib; rectis extra ciuitatē :·
uſq; ad unā leugā . 7 III . p̄ticas . 7 III . pedes. Siq̄s g̊
infra has publicas uias intus ciuitatē uel ext̄ foderit
uel palū fixerit :· ſequit̄ illū p̄poſit̄ regis ubicunq; abierit.
7 emendā accipiet ad opus regis.
Archiep̄s calūniat̄ forisfacturā in uiis ext̄ ciuitatē ex utq; parte.
ubi terra ſua . ē . ¶ Quidā p̄poſit̄ Brumann̄ n̄oe T . R . E . cepit c̄ſue
tudines de extraneis mercatorib; in trā S̄ TRINITATIS 7 S̄ Auguſtini.
Qui poſtea T . R . W . ante archiep̄m Lanfranc̄ 7 ep̄m baiocenſē recog
nouit ſe injuſte accepiſſe . 7 ſacram̄to facto jurauit qd̄ ipſæ æcclæ
ſuas c̄ſuetudines q̄etas habuer̄ . R . E . tēpore. Et exinde utreq; æcclæ
in ſua trā habuer̄ c̄ſuetud̄ ſuas . judicio baronū regis q̄ placitū tenuer̄.

3 The burgesses had 45 dwellings outside the City, from which they had tribute and customary dues; the King however had full jurisdiction. These burgesses also had from the King 33 acres of land for their tax. Ranulf of Colombières holds these houses and this land. He also has 80 acres of land over and above these, which the burgesses held in freehold from the King. He also holds 5 acres of land which rightly belong to a church. For all these Ranulf appeals to the Bishop of Bayeux as his protector.

4 Ralph of Courbépine has 4 dwellings in the City, which Harold's concubine held; of which the full jurisdiction is the King's, but up to the present he has not had it.

5 Ralph also holds another 11 dwellings from the Bishop of Bayeux in the City itself; they belonged to Esbern Big, and paid 11s 2½d.

6 The King has full jurisdiction throughout the whole City of Canterbury, apart from the land of Holy Trinity Church, of St. Augustine's, of Queen Edith, of Young Alnoth, of Esbern Big and of Sired of Chilham. It was agreed about the straight roads which have entry and exit through the City, that whoever does wrong on them shall pay the fine to the King; likewise regarding the straight roads outside the City as far as 1 league, 3 perches and 3 feet. If anyone digs or fixes a post within these public roads within the City or outside it, the King's reeve follows him wherever he has gone, and receives the fine for the King's works.

7 The Archbishop claims the fine on roads outside the City on both sides where the land is his.

8 A reeve, named Brunman, took the customs from foreign merchants before 1066 in the land of Holy Trinity and of St. Augustine's; after 1066 he acknowledged before Archbishop Lanfranc and the Bishop of Bayeux that he had received them wrongfully; he swore on the sacrament that these Churches had their customs exempt before 1066. From then on both Churches had their customs in their land, by the judgement of the King's barons, who tried the case.

Ciuitas *ROVECESTRE* T.R.E. ualebat . c . folid . Qdo recep̄ fimilit̄.
Modo ual . xx . liɓ . tamen ille qui ten reddit . xL . liɓ.

ITEM POSSESSIO S̄ MARTINI.

De cōmunitate Sc̄i *MARTINI* hn̄t fimul iii . canonici
unū folin 7 xvi . acras . ideſt Sired . Godric 7 Seuuen.
In hac tra funt . iiii . uilli 7 ix . borɗ cū una car . Reddunt
. xxii . folid . ꝼ De Leſt *LIMWARLET* . unū folin In Blache
burne hunɗ . 7 ibi funt . ix . uilli cū . ii . car . Reddt̄ . xvi . fol
7 viii . den . ꝼ In *STRET* hunɗ jacet un̄ folin de Stanetdeſte.
Ibi . vii . uilli hn̄t . ii . car 7 dimiɗ . 7 vii . borɗ . 7 un̄ pratū reddt̄
xvi . fol 7 viii . den . ꝼ In *BILESOLD* hunɗ un̄ folin de
Staneſtede . ibi funt . vii . uilli 7 vii . borɗ 7 hn̄t . iiii . car .
7 Reddt̄ . xx fol . ii den min . Ad iſta . iii . folina funt
. v . denæ . 7 vi . uilli 7 v . borɗ . 7 reddt̄ . ix . fol . iii . denar
min . hn̄t . iii . car 7 dimiɗ . In *BRenfete* paululū terræ
funt . ii . uilli 7 iii . borɗ 7 hn̄t dim car . Reddunt . L . denar.
Illa . iiii . folina fupɗicta hn̄t canonici S̄ Martini in cōmu
nitate int nemi 7 planū . T.R.E. ualb̄ . x . liɓ . modo fimilit̄.
Terra Nordeuuode 7 tra Ripe . 7 tra Brandet reddt̄ xx . fol.
7 vi . den ad S̄ Martin̄ in elemofina.
In inland S̄ Martini manerı . vii . borɗ . cū dimiɗ car . Redɗ
LX . folid ad calciamta canonicoꝛ . S̄ Margarita redɗ . viii . liɓ.
Theloneū de doure T.R.E. ualb̄ . viii . liɓ . modo xxii . liɓ.
Tres æcclæ ap̄ Douerā reddt̄ . xxxvi . folid . 7 viii . denar.

R

1 The City of Rochester was valued at 100s before 1066; when the Bishop acquired it, the same; value now £20; however the holder pays £40.

P   **LIKEWISE THE POSSESSIONS OF ST. MARTIN'S**   2 b

1 Three Canons of the community of St. Martin's together have 1 sulung and 16 acres, that is Sired, Godric and Sewen. In this land are
    4 villagers and 9 smallholders with 1 plough.
They pay 22s.

2 Of the Lathe of Lympne, 1 sulung in Blackburn Hundred.
    9 villagers with 2 ploughs.
They pay 16s 8d.

3 In Street hundred lies 1 sulung of STANSTED.
    7 villagers have 2½ ploughs and 7 smallholders.
    A meadow which pays 16s 8d.

4 In Bircholt hundred 1 sulung of STANSTED.
    7 villagers and 7 smallholders have 4 ploughs.
They pay 20s less 2d.
    To these 3 sulungs belong 5 pig pastures, and
    6 villagers and 5 smallholders.
They pay 9s less 3d. They have 3½ ploughs.

5 In BRENZETT a small piece of land.
    2 villagers and 3 smallholders have ½ plough.
They pay 50d.
    The Canons of St. Martin's have those 4 said sulungs in common, wood and open land.
Value before 1066, £10; now the same.

6 The land of NORWOOD, the land of RIPE and the land of BRENZETT pay 20s 6d to St. Martin's in alms.

7 In the *inland* of St. Martin's live 7 smallholders with ½ plough; they pay 60s for the Canon's footwear.

8 St. Margaret's (at Cliffe) pays £8. 1 countryman there.

9 Value of the tolls from Dover before 1066, £8; now £22.

10 Three churches at Dover pay 36s 8d.

De paſtura Medrediue 7 de hortis douere exeuɴ . ix . ſoł

7 iiii . denar̄ . Vna paſtura in Siberteſuualt ꞉ xvi . den̄ redd̄.

Sc̄s Martin ht̄ . x . molend̄ 7 dimid̄ . redd̄ vii . lib̄ . T.R.E.

tantd̄ reddider̄ . Modo app̄ciant̄ . xii . lib̄ . ſed n̄ ad ꝓſicuũ

canonicoꝛ . Sub illis molinis manent . viii . hōes . Apud

ſcortebroc una paſtura redd̄ . ii . ſolid̄.

De hac cōmunitate ht̄ Archieps̄ ſingulis annis . lv . ſoł.

Ibi ſunt . vi . hōes cū . i car 7 dimid̄.

In cōmuni tra S̄ Martini ſunt . cccc . acræ . 7 dimid̄ . quæ

fiunt . ii . ſolinos 7 dimid̄. H̄ tra nunꝗ reddid̄ aliꝙd c̄ſue

tudinis uel ſcoti . ꝗa . xx.iiii . ſolini H̄ ōmia adꝙetant.

Ap̄ Ripā ſunt . c . acræ . quæ ſe adꝙetat ubi T.R.E . ſe

adꝙetabat . Ap̄ Nordeude ſunt . l . acræ . 7 c . ap̄ Brand.

que adꝙetant ſe ubi 7 ſupiora . In hac tra ſunt . iii . uiłłi

7 ix . bord̄ . hn̄t . i . car 7 dimid̄. H̄ ōma ſi canonici ha

berent ſicuti jus . ēet ꞊ ualeret iłł . lx . lib̄ ſinguł annis.

modo n̄ hn̄t niſi . xlvii . lib̄ . 7 vi . ſoł . 7 iiii . denar̄.

Rannulſ de Colūbels aufert eis uñ p̄tū . Rotb̄t de rome

nel aufert eis ſinguł annis . xx . denar̄ . 7 unā ſalinā 7 unā

piſcariā Herb̄tus fili Juonis ded̄ ep̄o baioc̄ſi mark auri

ꝓ uno molino eoꝛ . nolentibꝛ illis . Lanb̄t uñ . Wadard . uñ.

Radulſ de curbeſpine uñ.

Alnod p̄ uiolentiā Heraldi abſtulit S̄ Martino Mercleſhā.

7 Hauocheſten . ꝓ quibꝛ ded̄ canonicis iniquā cōmutatıonē.

Modo teñ Rob̄tus de Romenel . qd̄ ei canonici calūni

antur ſemp.

11   From the pasture at MEDERCLIVE and from the gardens in DOVER come 9s 4d.

12   A pasture in SIBERTSWOLD pays 16d.

13   St. Martin's has 10½ mills; they pay £7; before 1066 they paid as much; now they are assessed at £12, but not for the Canon's profit. Under those mills 8 men live.

14   At *SCORTESBROC* a pasture pays 2s.

15   From this community the Archbishop has every year 55s.
     6 men with 1½ ploughs.

16   In the community of St. Martin's are 400½ acres, which make 2½ sulungs. This land never paid any customary due or levy because 24 sulungs meet the tax for the whole.

17   At RIPE are 100 acres which meet their tax where they did before 1066.

18   At NORWOOD are 50 acres and 100 at BRENZETT which meet their tax as the above do. In this land are 3 villagers and 9 smallholders. They have 1½ ploughs. If the Canons had all these as rightly they should, the value would be £60 each year; now they have only £47 6s 4d.

19   Ranulf of Colombières takes away from them a meadow and Robert of Romney takes away from them each year 20d, a salt-house and a fishery. Herbert son of Ivo gave the Bishop of Bayeux a mark of gold for 1 of their mills, against their will; Lambert 1 mill, Wadard 1 mill, and Ralph of Courbépine 1 [mill].

20   Young Alnoth, through Harold's violence took away from St. Martin's *MERCLESHAM* and HAWKHURST, for which he granted the Canons an unfair exchange. Now Robert of Romney holds them; the Canons continue to claim it from him.

.I. REX WILLELMVS.

.II. Archieps Cantuar.

.III. 7 Monachi 7 hões ej.

.IIII Eps Rofeceſtrens.

.V. Eps Baiocenſis.

.VI. Abbatia de Batailge.

.VII. Abbatia S Auguſtini.

.VIII. Abbatia de Gand.

.IX. Hugo de montford.

.X. Comes Euſtachius.

.XI. Ricardus de Tonebrige.

.XII. Haimo uicecomes.

.XIII. Albertus capellanus.

2 c ## TERRA REGIS.

IN DIMIDIO LEST DE SVDTONE. *IN ACHESTAN HD.*

.I. REX WILLELMVS ten *TARENTEFORT.*

ꝑ uno ſolino 7 dimidio ſe defd. Tra.ē.xL.

caruc. In dñio ſunt .II. car. 7 cxLII . uilli

cũ .x. bord hñt. LIII. car. Ibi ſunt .III. ſerui . 7 I. mold.

pti .xx.II. acræ.paſturæ.xL.ac. De ſilua.vIII. denæ

paruæ . 7 III. magnæ. Ibi .II. hedæ. id eſt .II. port.

T.R.E. ualuit . Lx . lib. 7 tntd qdo haimo recepit.

Modo apꝑciat ab anglis . Lx . lib .Ppoſit û francig

qui ten ad firmã . dicit qa ual qt xx. lib. 7 x .lib.

Ipſe tam reddit de iſto ꝋ . Lxx . lib penſatas . 7 cxI.

ſolid de den.xx. in ora. 7 vII . lib 7 xxvI . den ad numer.

Sup hæc reddit uicec.c.ſol.

LIST OF LANDHOLDERS IN KENT

1 King William

2 The Archbishop of Canterbury

3 His monks and his men

4 The Bishop of Rochester

5 The Bishop of Bayeux

6 Battle Abbey

7 St. Augustine's Abbey

8 Ghent Abbey

9 Hugh de Montfort

10 Count Eustace

11 Richard of Tonbridge

12 Hamo the Sheriff

13 Albert the Chaplain

LAND OF THE KING

1   In the Half-Lathe of SUTTON   2 c

   In AXTON Hundred
1   King William holds DARTFORD. It answers for 1½ sulungs.
     Land for 40 ploughs. In lordship 2 ploughs.
          142 villagers with 10 smallholders have 53 ploughs.
          3 slaves; a mill; meadow, 22 acres; pasture, 40 acres;
               from the woodland 8 small and 3 large pig pastures;
               2 hythes, that is 2 harbours.
     Value before 1066, £60; as much when Hamo the Sheriff
     acquired it; now it is assessed by the English at £60; but
     the French reeve who holds at a revenue says that its value
     is £90. However, he pays from this manor £70 weighed
     and 111s of pence at 20d to the *ora*, and £7 and 26d at
     face value. In addition to this it pays the Sheriff 100s.

Homines de hund teſtificant. qđ de iſto ⵘ regis
ablatū.ē unū p̄tū. 7 uñ alnetū. 7 uñ molđ. 7 xx. acræ
træ. 7 adhuc tant p̄ti quantū p̄tiñ ad . x . ac̄s træ.
quæ oīa eraꝜ in firma regis. E. dū uiueret . ħ ual̄ . xx.
ſol.   Dicunt aut qđ Oſuuard īc uicecom præſtitit ea
Aleſtan p̄poſito Lundoñ. 7 m̄ ten helt dapifer 7 nepos ej.
Teſtant quoꝗ qđ HAGELEI de iſto ⵘ ablata . ē.
quæ ſe defđ ꝓ dim ſolin . Hanc trā tenebat uicecom.
7 qdo uicecomitatū amittebat: in firma regis remaneb̄.
Ita ꝑmanſit 7 poſt mortē R.E.Modo ten Hugo de
port. cū . L.IIII. acris træ plus. Totū hoc ual̄ . xv . lib̄.
De eođ ⵘ regis adhuc ſunt ablatæ.vi. acræ træ.
7 quædā ſilua quā iſđ Oſuuard poſuit ext̄ ⵘ.
ꝑ qđđā uadimoñ.XL . ſolidoꝛ.
Æcclam huj ⵘ ten eps de Roueceſtre . 7 ual̄ . LX . ſol.
Extra hanc ſuꝜ adhuc ibi . III . æccleſiolæ.

IN LEST DE ELESFORD .IN LAVROCHESFEL HVND.

Rex.W. ten *ELESFORD* . ꝓ uno ſolin ſe defđ . Tra
ē . xv . car̄. In dñio ſunt . III . car̄. 7 XL . uilli cū
.v. borđ hñt .xv. car̄. Ibi . VIII . ſerui . 7 I . molđ .XL.
deñ. 7 XLIII . ac̄ p̄ti . Silua . LXX . porc̄.
Int tot ualeb̄ . T.R.E.xv . lib̄ . 7 tñtđ qdo haimo recep̄.
m̄ ual̄ . xx . lib̄ . Tam redđ .XXXI.lib̄. 7 uicec̄ inde hꝵ
III . lib̄. De hoc ⵘ ten Anſgot juxta roueceſtre
tantū træ. qđ apꝓciat̄ . VII . lib̄.
Eps etiā de Roueceſt ꝓ excābio tre in qua caſtellū
ſedet . tantū de hac tra ten. qđ . XVII . ſol 7 IIII . deñ ual̄.

The men of the Hundred testify that from this manor of
the King's have been taken 1 meadow, 1 alder grove, 1 mill
and 20 acres of land and furthermore as much meadow as
belongs to 10 acres of land. All of these were in King Edward's
revenue while he was alive. Value of this, 20s. However,
they say that Osward, then Sheriff, leased them to Alstan,
Reeve of London. Now Helto the Steward and his nephew
hold them.

They also testify that Hawley has been taken from this manor.
It answered for ½ sulung. The Sheriff held this land. When he lost
the Sheriffdom, it stayed in the King's revenue. It remained so
after King Edward's death. Now Hugh of Port holds it with 54
acres of land more.
Value of the whole, £15.

Further from the same manor of the King 6 acres of land
have been taken and a wood which Osward the Sheriff also
placed outside the manor through a pledge of 40s.

The Bishop of Rochester holds the church of this manor.
Value 60s.

As well as this there are a further 3 small churches.

In AYLESFORD Lathe
In LARKFIELD Hundred

2   King William holds AYLESFORD. It answers for 1 sulung. Land
for 15 ploughs. In lordship 3 ploughs.
     40 villagers with 5 smallholders have 15 ploughs.
     8 slaves; a mill at 40d; meadow, 43 acres;
       woodland, 70 pigs.
Total value before 1066, £15; as much when Hamo the Sheriff
acquired it; value now £20; however it pays £31; the Sheriff
has £3 from it. Ansgot holds as much of the land of this
manor as is assessed at £7 near Rochester. The Bishop of Rochester also
holds as much of this land as is valued at 17s 4d in exchange
for the land on which the castle is situated.

In Lest de Middeltvne. In Middeltvn Hvnd.

Rex . W . ten Middeltvne . p quat . xx . solins se
defd. Extra hos ꝉ sunt in dnio . IIII . solins . 7 ibi . III .
car in dnio. In hoc M . ccc . 7 ix . uilti cu . lxxi:ii . bord.
hnt . clx.vii . car. Ibi sunt . vi . mold de . xxx . solid.
7 xviii . ac pti. Ibi . xxvii . salinæ de . xxvii . solidis.

2 d

Ibi . xxxii . piscariæ de . xxii . sol 7 viii . den. De theloneo
xl . sol. De pastura . xiii . sol 7 iiii . den. Silua . cc.xx . porc.
7 hões de Walt reddunt . l . sol pro Ineuuard 7 Aueris.
In hoc M sunt . x . serui. Int totu . T.R.E. ualeb . cc . lib
ad numeru . 7 tntd qdo Haimo recep . 7 m similiter.

De hoc M ten hugo de port . viii . solins 7 unu jugu.
qui T.R.E. erant cu alijs solins in csuetudine. Ibi ht . iii . car
in dnio.

H tra qua ten Hugo de port . ual . xx . lib . q coputant in . cc . lib
toti M Middeltvn . qui ten reddit . cxl . lib ad igne
7 ad pensa . 7 insup . xv . lib 7 vi . sol . ii . denar min ad nu
meru. Haimoni dat pposit . xii . lib.

De silua regis ht Wadard tant qd redd xvi . den p ann.
7 dimidia dena tenet qua T.R.E. qda uillan tenuit. 7 Alnod
cild duas partes cuida uitto p uim abstulit.

Æcctas 7 decimas huj M ten abb S Augustini . 7 xl.
sol de . iiii . solins regis exeunt ei.

In Lest de Wiwarlet. In Favreshant Hvnd.

Rex . W . ten Favreshant . p . vii . solins de defd . Tra . e
xvii . car. In dnio sunt . ii. Ibi . xxx . uilti cu . xl . bord.
hnt . xxiiii . car. Ibi . v . serui . 7 i . molin de . xx . sol . 7 ii . ac
pti. Silua . c . porc. 7 de pastura siluæ . xxxi sol . 7 ii . den.

In the Half-Lathe of MILTON

In MILTON Hundred

3 King William holds MILTON (Regis). It answers for 80 sulungs. As well as these, there are 4 sulungs in lordship. In lordship 3 ploughs. In this manor

    309 villagers with 74 smallholders have 167 ploughs.

    6 mills at 30s; meadow, 18 acres. 27 salt-houses at 27s.

        32 fisheries at 22s 8d; from the tolls, 40s; from the 2 d pasture, 13s 4d; woodland, 220 pigs.

        Walter's men pay 50s for Escorts and cartage.

        In this manor, 10 slaves.

Total value before 1066, £200 at face value; as much when Hamo the Sheriff acquired it; now the same.

Hugh of Port holds 8 sulungs and 1 yoke of this manor, which were with the other sulungs before 1066 in customary payment. He has 3 ploughs in lordship. Value of this land which Hugh of Port holds, £20, which are accounted in the £200 of the whole manor of Milton. Its holder pays £140 fired and weighed, and in addition £15 6s less 2d at face value. The reeve gives Hamo the Sheriff £12.

Wadard has as much of the King's woodland as pays 16d a year. He holds ½ a pig pasture which a villager held before 1066. Young Alnoth took away 2 parts from a villager by force.

The Abbot of St. Augustine's holds the churches and tithes of this manor; 40s from 4 sulungs of the King go to him.

In WYE Lathe

In FAVERSHAM Hundred

4 King William holds FAVERSHAM. It answers for 7 sulungs. Land for 17 ploughs. In lordship 2.

    30 villagers with 40 smallholders have 24 ploughs.

    5 slaves; a mill at 20s; meadow, 2 acres; woodland, 100 pigs;

        from woodland pasture, 31s 2d;

        a market at £4.

Mercatū . de . iiii . lib . 7 ĩ . ſalinæ de . iii . ſolid 7 ii .den. 7 in
cantuar̅ ciuitate· . iii . hagæ|ad hoc ꝋ ꝑtiñ . In totis ualent
T . R . E . ualeb . lx . lib . v . ſolid min. 7 poſt: ́ix . lib . Modo uat
q̃ter . xx . lib.

TERRA ARCHIEPI CANTVARIENSIS.

.II. *IN CIVITATE CANTVARIA* habet Archieps.xii . bur
genſes. 7 xxxii . manſuras quas tenent clerici de uilla
in gildā ſuā . 7 reddunt . xxxv . ſot . 7 uñ mold de . v . ſot.

SANDWICE jacet in ſuo ꝓprio *HVND* . hoc burgū ten
archieps . 7 eſt de ueſtitu monachoꝝ . 7 reddit ſimile
ſeruitiū regi ſicut *DOVERE* . 7 hoc teſtificant homin:s
de iſto burgo . qd̅ antequā rex EDW dediſſet illū Ꞩ *KIN*.
reddeb regi . xv . lib.Tēpore | R.E: ́ non erat ad firmam.
Q̣do recep̃ archieps: ́ reddeb . xl . lib . de firma . 7 xl .
milia allecibꝫ ad uictū monachoꝝ . In anno quo facta
eſt hæc deſcriptio: ́ reddidit | l. lib de firma . 7 alleces
ſicut prius . T.R.E: ́ erant ibi .ccc. 7 vii . manſuræ hos
pitatæ . modo ſunt plus . lxxvi . ideſt ſimul.ccc.lxxx.iii.

IN ACHESTAN HVND.

Archieps cantuar̅ ten̅ in dn̅io. *TARENT* . ꝑ . ii . ſolins
ſe defd . Tra . ē̅   In dn̅io . ē̅ una car . 7 xxii . uiłłi
cū . vii . cot hn̅t. vii . car̅. Ibi. vi . ſerui . 7 ii . mold de . l . ſot.
Ad hoc ꝋ ꝑtiñ . v . burgſes in rouecest̅. redd̅ . vi . ſot 7 viii . den.
Ibi . viii . ac pti. Silua . xx . porc̅. In totis ualent T.R.E. ualuit
xiiii. lib. Q̣do recep̃: ́ x. lib . m̊ .xv. lib 7 x . ſot . Tam̅ qui
tenet ꝋ redd̅ .xviii . lib.

2 salt-houses at 3s 2d; in the City of
Canterbury 3 sites at 20d belong to this manor.
Total value before 1066, £60 less 5s; later £60; now £80.

2   LAND OF THE ARCHBISHOP OF CANTERBURY   3 a

1   In the City of CANTERBURY the Archbishop has 12 burgesses
and 32 dwellings which the clergy of the town hold in their
guild; they pay 35s.
    A mill at 5s.

2   SANDWICH lies in its own Hundred. The Archbishop holds
this Borough. It is for the clothing of the monks. It pays the
same service to the King as Dover. The men of this borough
testify this, that before King Edward gave it to Holy Trinity,
it paid £15 to the King. In 1066 it was not in the revenue.
When the Archbishop acquired it, it paid £40 in revenue and
40,000 herrings for the supplies of the monks. In the year in
which this Survey was made Sandwich paid £50 in revenue and
herrings as before. Before 1066 there were 307 habitable
dwellings; now there are 76 more; that is, 383 altogether.

In AXTON Hundred
3   The Archbishop of Canterbury holds DARENTH, in lordship.
It answers for 2 sulungs. Land for ... In lordship 1 plough.
    22 villagers with 7 cottagers have 7 ploughs.
    6 slaves; 2 mills at 50s.
    To this manor belong 5 burgesses in Rochester who
    pay 6s 8d.
    Meadow, 8 acres; woodland, 20 pigs.
Total value before 1066, £14; when acquired, £10; now
£15 10s. However the holder of the manor pays £18.

Ipfe Archiepf ten̅ OTEFORT in dn̅io .p .VIII. | ſolins ſe defd̅ . Tra. e̅

XL.II. car̅. In dn̅io ſunt .VI. car̅. Ibi .c. 7 un̅ uiłłs cū .XVIII.

bord̅ hn̅t .XLV. car̅. Ibi .VIII. ſerui . 7 .VI. molini de .LXXII.

ſolid̅ . 7 L. ac̅ p̅ti. Silua .c.L. porc̅.

De hoc m̅ ten̅. III. teigni .I. ſolin 7 dimid̅ . 7 ibi hn̅t in dn̅io

.III. car̅. 7 XVI. uiłłos cū .XI. bord̅ hn̅tes .IIII. car̅. Ibi . V. ſerui

7 II. mold̅ de .XXIIII. ſoł. 7 XXVIII. ac̅s p̅ti. Silua .XXX. porc̅.

In totis ualent̅ T.R.E. 7 poſt uałeb̅   Modo

ap̅pciat̅ dn̅iū arch̅ .LX. lib̅. Teignoȝ .' XII. lib̅. Ricard̅ de

Tonebrige qd̅ in ſua leuga ten̅.' ap̅pciat̅ .X. lib̅.

Ipſe archiepf ten̅ SONDRESSE .p uno ſolin 7 dim̅ ſe defd̅.

Tra. e̅   In dn̅io ſunt .III. car̅. 7 XXVII. uiłti cū .IX.

bord̅ hn̅t .VIII. car̅. Ibi .VIII. ſerui. 7 III. mold̅ 7 dim̅ de

.XIII. ſolid̅ 7 dim̅. Ibi .VIII. ac̅ p̅ti. Silua .LX. porc̅. Ibi æcc̅ła.

In totis ualent̅ T.R.E. uał .XII. lib̅. Qd̅o recep̅.' XVI. lib̅. 7 modo

XVIII. lib̅. Tam̅ reddit .XXIII. lib̅ . 7 unū militē in ſeruitio Arch̅.

IN HELMESTREI HVND̅.

Ipſe Archiepf ten̅. BIX .p .iiił ſolins ſe defd̅ T.R.E. 7 m̅ .p .iił

Tra. e̅   In dn̅io ſunt .II. car̅. 7 XLI. uiłt cū .XV. bord̅

hn̅t .X. car̅. Ibi æcc̅ła. 7 III. mold̅ de .XLVIII. ſolid̅ . 7 VIII. ac̅

p̅ti. Silua .c. porc̅. In totis ualent̅ T.R.E. 7 poſt uał .XII. lib̅

7 m̅ .XX. lib̅ . 7 tam̅ reddit .XXX. lib̅ . 7 VIII. ſoł.

IN LITELAI HVND̅.

Ipſe archiepf ten̅ ERHEDE .p .IIII. ſolins ſe defd̅ . Tra. e̅ .VIII.

car̅. In dn̅io ſunt .II. 7 XXVII. uiłti cū .II. bord̅ hn̅t .VIII. car̅.

3 b

Ibi æcc̅ła. 7 III : mold̅ de .L. ſolid̅ 7 VI. den̅. Ibi .V. ſeruił

7 X. ac̅ p̅ti. Silua .XL. porc̅. In totis ualent̅ T.R.E. uał

XII. lib̅. 7 tn̅td̅ qdo recep̅. Modo .XVI. lib̅ . 7 tam̅ redd̅

XXI. lib̅.

The Archbishop himself holds

4   OTFORD, in lordship. It answers for 8 sulungs. Land for
42 ploughs. In lordship 6 ploughs.
> 101 villagers with 18 smallholders have 45 ploughs.
> 8 slaves; 6 mills at 72s; meadow, 50 acres; woodland,
> 150 pigs.
> Of this manor 3 thanes hold 1½ sulungs. They have 3 ploughs
in lordship, and
> 16 villagers with 11 smallholders, who have 4 ploughs.
> 5 slaves; 2 mills at 24s; meadow, 28 acres; woodland, 30 pigs.
Total value before 1066 and later ...; now the Archbishop's
lordship is assessed at £60; the thanes' at £12.
What Richard of Tonbridge holds in his territory is assessed at £10.

5   SUNDRIDGE. It answers for 1½ sulungs. Land for ... In lordship
3 ploughs.
> 27 villagers with 9 smallholders have 8 ploughs.
> 8 slaves; 3½ mills at 13s 6d; meadow, 8 acres;
> woodland, 60 pigs. A church.
Total value before 1066 £12; when acquired, £16; now £18;
however, it pays £23 and a man-at-arms for the Archbishop's
service.

in RUXLEY Hundred

6   BEXLEY.   It answered for 3 sulungs before 1066; now for 2.
Land for ... In lordship 2 ploughs.
> 41 villagers with 15 smallholders have 10 ploughs.
> A church; 3 mills at 48s; meadow, 8 acres; woodland,
> 100 pigs.
Total value before 1066 and later £12; now £20; however it
pays £30 8s.

in LITTLE Hundred

7   CRAYFORD. It answered for 4 sulungs. Land for 8 ploughs.
In lordship 2.
> 27 villagers with 2 smallholders have 8 ploughs.
> A church; 3 mills at 50s 6d; 5 slaves; meadow, 10 acres;   3 b
> woodland, 40 pigs.
Total value before 1066 £12; as much when acquired; now £16;
however, it pays £21.

Ipſe archieps ten in dñio *Metlinges* . ꝑ . ii . ſolins

ſe defd . Tra . ē . vii . car. In dñio ſunt . iii . car. 7 xxx.viii.

uitti cū . xii . bord hñt . v . car. Ibi æccła 7 v . ſerui . 7 ii .

mold de . x . ſoł . 7 xxi . ać ꝓti . Silua . lx . porc. In totis

ualent . T . R . E . uał . ix . liƀ. Similit qdo receꝑ . 7 m̊ tntd

7 tam redd . xv . liƀ.   *In Tollentrev Hvnd.*

Ipſe archieps ten in dñio *Norflvet* . ꝑ . vi . ſolins

defd ſe . T . R . E . 7 m̊ ꝑ . v . Tra . ē . xiiii . car. In dñio ſuꝴ

.ii . 7 xxxvi . uitti hñt . x . car. Ibi æccła 7 vii . ſerui

7 i . moliñ de x . ſoł cū una piſcar . 7 xx . ać ꝓti . Silua

xx . porc. In totis ualent. T . R . E . uał . x . liƀ. Qdo receꝑ

xii . liƀ . 7 m̊ . xxvii . liƀ . 7 tam redd xxxvii . liƀ 7 x . ſoł.

Ricard de tonebrige qd ten in ſua leuga de hoc Ⓜ . uał

        In Broteħā Hvnd.   ᚠxxx . ſoł.

Ipſe archieps ten *Broteham* . ꝑ . viii . ſolins ſe defd.

Tra . ē . xx . car. In dñio ſunt . iii . car. 7 lxxvi . uitti

cū . xviii . bord hñt . xiiii . car. Ibi æccła 7 x . ſerui.

7 iii . mold de . xv . ſolid . 7 . ix̅ . ać ꝓti . Silua qdo fructific.

q̅ngent porc.

De hoc Ⓜ ten Witts diſpenſat . i . ſolin . 7 ibi h̅t .i . car

in dñio . 7 ii . uittos cū dim car.

De eod Ⓜ ten Goiſfr de archiepo .i . ſolin . 7 ibi h̅t .i . car.

7 vi . uittos cū .i . bord hñtes . ii . car.

De ipſo Ⓜ ten Farman .i . jug 7 dim de archiepo . 7 ibi h̅t

iii . car . 7 vi uittos cū xii . cot hñtes . ii . car Ibi .x . ſerui.

In totis ualent. T . R . E . uał hoc Ⓜ .xv . liƀ. 7 poſt .xvi.

liƀ . Modo apꝓciat dñiu arch. xxiiii . liƀ . 7 tam redd

xxxv . liƀ . Militū. xi . liƀ . Ricard de Tonebrige

qd ten in ſua leuga. apꝓciat xv . liƀ.

in the Lathe of AYLESFORD
in LARKFIELD Hundred

8 (? East) MALLING in lordship. It answers for 2 sulungs. Land
for 7 ploughs. In lordship 3 ploughs.
   38 villagers with 12 smallholders have 5 ploughs.
   A church; 5 slaves; 2 mills at 10s; meadow, 21 acres;
      woodland, 60 pigs.
Total value before 1066 £9; the same when acquired; now as much;
however, it pays £15.

in TOLTINGTROUGH Hundred

9 NORTHFLEET, in lordship. It answered for 6 sulungs before 1066;
now for 5. Land for 14 ploughs. In lordship 2.
   36 villagers have 10 ploughs.
   A church; 7 slaves; 1 mill at 10s, with a fishery;
      meadow, 20 acres; woodland, 20 pigs.
Total value before 1066 £10; when acquired, £12; now £27;
however, it pays £37 10s. What Richard of Tonbridge holds in
his territory from this manor, value 30s.

in WROTHAM Hundred

10 WROTHAM. It answers for 8 sulungs. Land for 20 ploughs.
In lordship 3 ploughs.
   76 villagers with 18 smallholders have 14 ploughs.
   A church; 10 slaves; 3 mills at 15s; meadow, 9 acres;
      woodland, when fruitful, 500 pigs.
   William the Bursar holds 1 sulung of this manor; he has
1 plough in lordship, and
   2 villagers with ½ plough.
   Geoffrey holds 1 sulung of the same manor from the
Archbishop; he has 1 plough, and
   6 villagers with 1 smallholder who have 2 ploughs.
   Farman holds 1½ yokes of this manor from the Archbishop;
he has 3 ploughs, and
   6 villagers with 12 cottagers who have 2 ploughs.
   10 slaves.
The total value of this manor before 1066 £15; later £16; now the
Archbishop's lordship is assessed at £24; however, it pays £35;
the men-at-arms' £11; what Richard of Tonbridge holds in his
territory is assessed at £15.

Ipſe archieps ten̄ *MEDDESTANE* . ꝑ x . ſolins ſe defđ.
Tra . ē . xxx . car̄. In dn̄io ſunt . iii . car̄. 7 xxv . uiłłi cū
xxi . borđ hn̄t . xxv . car̄. Ibi æccła 7 x . ſerui . 7 v . molin̄
de . xxxvi . ſolid 7 viii . den̄. Ibi . ii . piſcariæ . de cclxx . anguiłł.
Ibi . x . ac̄ p̄ti . Silua . xxx . porc̄.

De hoc ꝏ ten̄ de archiepo . iii . milit . iiii . ſolins . 7 ibî
hn̄t . iii . car̄ 7 dim in dn̄io . 7 xxxii . uiłłos cū . x . borđ
hn̄tes . vi . car̄. 7 x . ſerū. 7 hn̄t . i . molin̄ de . v . ſolid . 7 xiii.
ac̄s p̄ti . 7 ii . piſcar̄ 7 dimid de . clxxx . anguiłł 7 . ii . ſalin̄.
Siluā . xxiii . porc̄.

In totis ualent T . R . E ual hoc ꝏ . xiiii . lib̄ . Qdo recep̄.
xii . lib̄ . 7 m̄ dn̄iū archiepi ual . xx . lib̄ . Militū . xv.
lib̄ 7 x . ſoł. Monachi cantuar̄ hn̄t om̄i anno de
duobʒ hōibʒ huj ꝏ . xx . ſoł.

Ipſe archieps ten̄ *GELINGEHĀ* . ꝑ . vi . ſolins ſe defđ.
Tra . ē . xv . car̄. In dn̄io ſunt . ii . car̄. 7 xlii . uiłłi cū
xvi . borđ hn̄t . xv . car̄. Ibi æccła . 7 iii . ſerui . 7 iii . pis
cariæ de . xl.ii . ſolid 7 viii . den̄. 7 i . molin̄ de . xvi.
ſolid 7 viii . den̄. 7 xiiii . ac̄ p̄ti . Silua . xx . porc̄.
De hoc ꝏ ten̄ qđa franciḡ trā ad . i . car̄. 7 ibi h̄t
ii . borđ. In totis ualent T . R . E . ual hoc ꝏ . xv . lib̄.
Qdo recep̄. xii . lib̄. 7 m̄ xxiii . lib̄. 7 tam̄ redđ
xxvi . lib̄ . xii . den̄ min̄. Qđ ten̄ franciḡ . xl . ſoł.

Ipſe Archieps ten̄ *ROCVLF* . ꝑ . viii . ſolins ſe
defđ.Tra . ē . xxx . car̄. In dn̄io ſunt . iii . car̄.
7 q̄t xx . 7 x . uiłłi cū . xxv . borđ hn̄t . xxvii . car̄.

in MAIDSTONE Hundred

11 MAIDSTONE. It anwers for 10 sulungs. Land for 30 ploughs.
In lordship 3 ploughs.
  25 villagers with 21 smallholders have 25 ploughs.
  A church; 10 slaves; 5 mills at 36s 8d; 2 fisheries at
    270 eels. Meadow, 10 acres; woodland, 30 pigs.
  Of this manor 3 men-at-arms hold 4 sulungs from the
Archbishop; they have 3½ ploughs in lordship, and
  32 villagers with 10 smallholders who have 6 ploughs.
  10 slaves. They (also) have 1 mill at 5s; meadow, 13 acres;
    2½ fisheries at 180 eels; 2 salt-houses; woodland, 23 pigs.
Total value of this manor before 1066 £14; when acquired £12;
now the value Archbishop's lordship £20; the men-at-arms' £15 10s.
The monks of Canterbury have 20s from 2 men of this manor
every year.

in CHATHAM Hundred   3 c

12 GILLINGHAM. It answers for 6 sulungs. Land for 15 ploughs.
In lordship 2 ploughs.
  42 villagers with 16 smallholders have 15 ploughs.
  A church; 3 slaves; 3 fisheries at 42s 8d; 1 mill at 16s 8d;
    meadow, 14 acres; woodland, 20 pigs.
  Of this manor a Frenchman holds land for 1 plough. He
    has 2 smallholders.
Total value of this manor before 1066 £15; when acquired, £12;
now £23; however, it pays £26 less 12d; what the Frenchman
holds 40s.

in RECULVER Hundred

13 RECULVER. It answers for 8 sulungs. Land for 30 ploughs.
In lordship 3 ploughs.
  90 villagers with 25 smallholders have 27 ploughs.

Ibi æccła 7 1 . molin de xxv . deñ . 7 xxx.iii. ač p̄ti.
Silua . xx . porč . 7 v . ſalinæ de lxiiii . deñ . 7 una
piſcaria . In totis ualent . T.R.E. ualuit hoc ⊙ . xiiii .
liƀ . Q̇do recep̄ꝰ ſimilit . 7 m̄ .xxxv. liƀ . Sup̄ hæc
h̄t archiep̄s . vii . liƀ 7 vii . ſoliꝺ.

Ipſe Archiep̄s teñ *Nortone* in dñio . ꝑ xiii . ſo
lins ſe deſꝺ . Tra . ē . xxvi . car̄ . In dñio ſunt . ii.
car̄ . 7 q̇t xx . 7 xii . uiłłi cū . xl borꝺ . h̄nt . lix .
car̄ 7 dimiꝺ . Ibi æccła . 7 x . ač p̄ti . Silua . l . porč .
In totis ualent . T.R.E. ualuit hoc ⊙ . xxiiii . liƀ
7 v . ſoł . 7 poſt tn̄tꝺ . 7 m̄ redꝺ archiep̄o . l . liƀ .
7 xiiii . ſoł 7 ii . deñ . 7 archidiacono . xx . ſoł.
De hoc ⊙ teñ Vitalis de archiep̄o . iii . ſolins .
7 uñ juḡ 7 xii . ač s træ . 7 ibi h̄t . v . car̄ . 7 xxix .
borꝺ 7 v . ſeruos . 7 vii . ſalinas de . xxv . ſoł 7 iiii . deñ .
Ibi . ē æccła 7 una parua dena ſiluæ . Int totū ual
xiiii . liƀ . 7 vi . ſoł 7 vi . deñ .

In Borowart Lest . *In Piteh̄a hvnd*.
Ipſe archiep̄s teñ *Piteham* . ꝑ . vii . ſolins ſe deſꝺ .
Tra . ē ad xx . car̄ . In dñio ſunt . iii . car̄ . 7 xxxii .
uiłłi cū xxi . borꝺ h̄nt . xix . car̄ . Ibi . ii ꞏ æcclæ .
Ibi . ii ° . ſerui . 7 xiii . ač p̄ti . Silua . xx ꞏ porč .
In totis ualent T.R.E. ualuit hoc ⊙ . xvii . liƀ .
7 vi . ſoł 7 iii . deñ . 7 poſt tn̄tꝺ . 7 m̄ uał . xx . liƀ .
De hoc ⊙ teñ Godefrid 7 Nigelℓ de archiep̄o
uñ ſolin 7 dim̄ . 7 juḡu . 7 ibi h̄nt . iiii . car̄ .
7 iiii . uiłłos cū . viii . borꝺ h̄ntes . iii . car̄ . Int tot
uał . ix . liƀ . De his h̄nt monachi . viii . ſoł ꝑ an̄n .

A church; a mill at 25d; meadow, 33 acres; woodland
20 pigs; 5 salt-houses at 64d; a fishery.
Total value of this manor before 1066 £14; when acquired,
the same; now £35. In addition to these the Archbishop
has £7 7s.

14 WHITSTABLE, in lordship. It answers for 13 sulungs. Land for
26 ploughs. In lordship 2 ploughs.
92 villagers with 40 smallholders have 59½ ploughs.
A church; meadow, 10 acres; woodland, 50 pigs.
Total value of this manor before 1066 £24 5s; later as much;
now it pays £50 14s 2d to the Archbishop and 20s to the
Archdeacon.
Vitalis holds 3 sulungs 1 yoke and 12 acres of land of this
manor from the Archbishop. He has 5 ploughs and
29 smallholders and 5 slaves.
7 salt-houses at 25s 4d. A church; a small pig pasture
of woodland.
In total, value £14 6s 6d.

in BOROUGH Lathe
in PETHAM Hundred
15 PETHAM. It answers for 7 sulungs.. Land for 20 ploughs.
In lordship 3 ploughs.
32 villagers with 21 smallholders have 19 ploughs.
2 churches. 2 slaves; meadow, 13 acres; woodland, 20 pigs.
Total value of this manor before 1066 £17 6s 3d; later as much;
value now £20.
Godfrey and Nigel hold 1½ sulungs and 1 yoke of this manor
from the Archbishop. They have 4 ploughs and
4 villagers with 8 smallholders who have 3 ploughs.
In total, value £9. Of these the monks have 8s a year.

Ipſe archieps teñ *ESTVRSETE* in dñio . ꝑ VII . ſo

lins ſe defđ . Tra . ē . xx . caꝛ . In dñio ſunt . IIII . caꝛ .

7 XVII . uiłłi cū q̃t xx . 7 III . borđ hñt . XVI . caꝛ .

Ibi . XII . molins de . IIII . liƀ 7 v . ſoł . 7 c . ãc p̃ti . Silua

. L . porc̃ . Ad hoc ꟽ ꝑtinueꝛ T . R . E . iñ ciuitate

LII . maſuræ . 7 m̃ non ſunt niſi . xxv . q̃a aliæ

ſunt deſtruc̃tæ Iñoua hoſpitatione archie p̃i.

3 d

In totis ualent T . R . E . 7 poſt ualeƀ XXIIII . liƀ . 7 XII . ſoł 7 VI .

deñ . Modo uał XL . liƀ .

De hoc ꟽ hñt . v . hões archiep̃i . unū ſolin 7 VI . juga.

7 ibi hñt . v . caꝛ 7 dimiđ in dñio . 7 VIII . uiłłos cū . XXVI .

borđ hñtes . II . caꝛ . 7 III . molđ 7 XXXIIII . ãcs p̃ti . Silua . x .

porc̃ . Int totū uał . IX . liƀ .

De ipſo ꟽ teñ Haimo uicec̃ . dimiđ ſolin de arcħ . 7 ibi hꝛ

II . caꝛ . cū . v . borđ 7 uno ſeruo . 7 II . molđ de . xv . ſoł . Vał

Ꞔ c . ſolid.

Ipſe archieps teñ in dñio *BVRNES* . ꝑ . VI . ſolins ſe defđ .

Tra . ē . L . caꝛ . In dñio ſunt . v . caꝛ . 7 LXIIII . uiłłi cū . LIII . ƀ

borđ hñt xxx caꝛ 7 dim . Ibi æccła 7 II . molđ de . VIII . ſoł

7 VI . deñ . 7 xx ãc p̃ti . Silua . xv . porc̃ . De herbagio . XXVII .

deñ . In totis ualent . T . R . E . 7 poſt ualeƀ . xx . liƀ . m̃ . xxx . liƀ .

Ipſe archieps teñ in dñio *BOLTVNE* . ꝑ . v . ſolins 7 dim

ſe defđ . Tra . ē   In dñio ſunt . II . caꝛ . 7 xxxI . uiłłs

cū . xxxI . borđ hñtes xv . caꝛ . Ibi . IIII . ãc p̃ti . 7 piſcaria

de . x . deñ . Salina de . xvI . deñ . Silua . XLV . porc̃ . In

totis ualent T . R . E . 7 poſt ualeƀ . xv . liƀ 7 xvI . ſoł 7 III . deñ .

7 I . obolū . Modo uał xxx . liƀ . 7 xvI . ſoł 7 III . deñ 7 I . obolū.

2

in WESTGATE Hundred

16   WESTGATE in lordship. It answers for 7 sulungs. Land for 20
ploughs. In lordship 4 ploughs.
   17 villagers with 83 smallholders have 16 ploughs.
   A church; 12 mills at £4 5s; meadow, 100 acres;
      woodland, 50 pigs.
   To this manor belonged 52 dwellings before 1066; now there
are only 25 because the rest were destroyed for the Archbishop's
new lodging.
Total value before 1066 and later £24 12s 6d; value now £40.   3 d
   Of this manor 5 of the Archbishop's men have 1 sulung
and 6 yokes. They have 5½ ploughs in lordship, and
   8 villagers with 26 smallholders who have 2 ploughs.
   3 mills; meadow, 34 acres; woodland 10 pigs.
In total, value £9.
   Hamo the Sheriff holds ½ sulung of this manor from the
Archbishop. He has 2 ploughs, with
   5 smallholders and 1 slave.
   2 mills at 15s.
Value 100s.

in BARHAM Hundred

17   BISHOPSBOURNE in lordship. It answers for 6 sulungs. Land
for 50 ploughs. In lordship 5 ploughs.
   64 villagers with 53 smallholders have 30½ ploughs.
   A church; 2 mills at 8s 6d; meadow, 20 acres; woodland,
      15 pigs; from grazing, 27d.
Total value before 1066 and later £20; now £30.

in BOUGHTON Hundred

18   BOUGHTON [under Blean] in lordship. It answers for 5 sulungs.
Land for ... In lordship 2 ploughs, and
   31 villagers with 31 smallholders who have 15 ploughs.
   Meadow, 4 acres; a fishery at 10d; a salt-house at 16d;
      woodland, 45 pigs.
Total value before 1066 and later £15 16 3½d; value now
£30 16 3½d.

2

Ipſe archieps teñ in dñio *Cheringes* . p . viii . ſot ſe defð.

Tra . ē . xl . car . In dñio . ē uñ ſolin 7 ibi . iiii . car 7 dim . Ibi . xxvi .

uitti cū . xxvii . borð hñt . xxvii . car . Ibi . xii . ſerui . 7 uñ

moliñ de xl . deñ . Ibi . xxv . ãc p̃ti . Silua . xxvi . porc .

In totis ualent T.R.E. ualeð . xxiiii . liɓ . Q̇do recep̃: tñtð.

Modo ap̃ciat. xxxiiii . liɓ . 7 tam reddit . lx . liɓ.

Ipſe archieps teñ in dñio *Plvchelei* . p uno ſolin ſe defð.

Tra . ē . xii . car . In dñio . ii . car 7 dim . 7 xvi . uitti cū . vii .

borð hñt . xi . car . Ibi . viii . ſerui . 7 xii . ãc p̃ti 7 dim . Silua

cxl . porc . Int tot T.R.E. ualeð xii . liɓ . Q̇do recep̃:

viii . liɓ . 7 modo . xv . liɓ . 7 tam redd . xx . liɓ.

In Lest De Estrei.   *In Wingehā hvnd.*

Ipſe archieps teñ . *Wingehā* . in dñio . p . xl . ſolins ſe

defð . T.R.E. 7 m̃ p xxxv . Tra . ē   In dñio ſunt

viii . car . 7 q̃ter xx̃ . 7 v . uitti cū . xx . borð . hñtes . lvii .

car . Ibi . viii . ſerui . 7 ii . molð de . xxx.iiii . ſot . Silua . v .

porc . 7 ī. ſiluulæ ad clauſurā . In totis ualent T.R.E. uat

lxxvii . liɓ . Q̇do recep̃: ſimilit . 7 m̃ . c . liɓ.

De hoc m̃ teñ Witts de arcis . i . ſolin In Fletes . 7 ibi h̃t in

dñio . i . car . 7 iiii . uittos 7 uñ militē cū . i . car . 7 unā piſcar

cū ſalina de . xxx . deñ . Tot uat . xl . ſot.

De ipſo m̃ teñ . v . hões archiep̃i . v . ſolins 7 dim . 7 iiij . juga .

7 ibi hñt in dñio . viii . car . 7 xxii . borð 7 viii . ſeru . Int tot

uat xxi . liɓ .   *In Langebrige hvnd.*

Ipſe archieps teñ in dñio *Merseham* . p vii . ſolins ſe defð.

T.R.E. 7 m̃ p . iii . Tra . ē . xii . car . In dñio ſunt . iii . car,

7 xxxix . uitti cū . ix . borð hñtes . xvi . car . Ibi æccɫa . 7 ji . molð

de v . ſot . 7 ii . ſalinæ de . v . ſot . 7 xiii . ãc p̃ti . Silua . xxx . porc .

4 a

In totis ualent T.R.E. uat 7 poſt . x . liɓ . Modo . xx . liɓ.

in CALEHILL Hundred

19 CHARING in lordship. It answers for 8 sulungs. Land for 40
ploughs. In lordship 1 sulung. 4½ ploughs.
   26 villagers with 27 smallholders have 27 ploughs.
   12 slaves; a mill at 40d. Meadow, 25 acres; woodland,
      26 pigs.
Total value before 1066 £24; when acquired, as much; now it
is assessed at £34; however, it pays £60.

20 PLUCKLEY in lordship. It answers for 1 sulung. Land for 12
ploughs. In lordship 2½ ploughs.
   16 villagers with 7 smallholders have 11 ploughs.
   8 slaves; meadow, 12½ acres; woodland, 140 pigs.
Total value before 1066 £12; when acquired, £8; now £15;
however, it pays £20.

in the Lathe of EASTRY
in WINGHAM Hundred

21 WINGHAM in lordship. It answered for 40 sulungs before 1066;
now for 35. Land for ... In lordship 8 ploughs, and
   85 villagers with 20 smallholders who have 57 ploughs.
   8 slaves; 2 mills at 34s; woodland, 5 pigs; 2 small woods
      for fencing.
Total value before 1066 £77; when acquired the same; now £100.
   William of Arques holds 1 sulung of this manor in Fleet. He
has 1 plough in lordship, and
   4 villagers and 1 man-at-arms with 1 plough.
   A fishery with a salt-house at 30d.
Value of the whole 40s.
   Of the manor itself 5 of the Archbishop's men hold 5½ sulungs
and 3 yokes. In lordship they have 8 ploughs.
   22 smallholders and 8 slaves.
In total, value £21.

in LONGBRIDGE Hundred

22 MERSHAM in lordship. Before 1066 it answered for 6 sulungs;
now for 3. Land for 12 ploughs. In lordship 3 ploughs.
   39 villagers with 9 smallholders who have 16 ploughs.
   A church. 2 mills at 5s; 2 salt-houses at 5s; meadow, 13
      acres; woodland, 30 pigs.
Total value before 1066 and later £10; now £20.   4 a

Ipfe archieps ten ALDINTONE in dnĩo . p̄ xxi . folin fe

defđ .T.R.E. 7 m̃ p̄ . xv . folins . Tra . c . car̃. In dnĩo funt . xiii .

car̃ . 7 ducenti uiłłi x . min cũ . L . borđ h̃nt Lxx . car̃ .

Ibi æccła . 7 xiii . fcrui . 7 iii . mołđ de xvi . foł . 7 iii . pifcar̃

de . xxi . den̄ . Ibi . cLxx . ac̃ p̃ti . Silua . Lx . porc̃ .

In totis ualent T . R . E . ualeb̄ . Lxii . lib̄ . 7 tñtđ q̄do recep̄ .

Modo redđ . c . lib̄ 7 . xx . foł .

Ipfe archieps ten uillā quæ uocat S̃ Martin 7 p̃tin ad

Efturfete . 7 jacet in ipfo hund . 7 defđ | p̄ uno folin 7 dim̃

Tra . ē   In dnĩo funt . ii . car̃ . 7 xxxvi . borđ .

Ad hanc trā p̃tin . vii . burḡfes in cantuaria . redđtes

viii . foł 7 iiii . den̄ . Ibi . v . mołđ de . xx . foł . 7 parua filua .

In hac uilla ten Radulf dim̃ folin de archiep̄o . 7 ibi h̃t

ii . car̃ in dnĩo . 7 v . uiłłos cũ . iii . borđ h̃ntes . ii . car̃ 7 dimiđ .

T . R . E . ualeb̄ . vii . lib̄ dim̃ folin S̃ Mart . 7 aliud dim̃ folin

uał femp̄ . iiii . lib̄ .

IN ROMENEL funt q̃t xx . 7 v . burḡfes qui p̃tin ad *ALDINT*

m̃ archiep̄i . 7 ualuer̄ 7 m̃ ualent dnõ . vi . lib̄ .

De ipfo m̃ Aldinton jacet in Limes dimiđ jugũ 7 dimiđ

uirga . Archieps ten in dnĩo . 7 ibi h̃t . i . car̃ . 7 uñ uiłłm

cũ xviii . borđ h̃ntes . i . car̃ . 7 dimiđ . Ibi funt . vii . p̄ri qui

reddunt . vii . lib̄ 7 v . foł . Tra . ē . ii . car̃ . Vał 7 ualuit . xii . lib̄ .

7 tam̃ reddit . xv . lib̄ .

De eođ m̃ ten comes de Ow. Eftotinghes p̄ . i . m̃ .

p̄ uno folin 7 dim̃ fe defđ T . R . E . 7 m̃ p̄ uno folin tantũ .

Tra . ē . viii . car̃ . In dnĩo funt . ii . 7 xxvii . uiłłi cũ . xiii . borđ .

h̃ntes . vii . car̃ . 7 i . molĩn de . xxv . den̄ . Ibi æccła . 7 xx . ac̃ p̃ti .

Silua . x . porc̃ . 7 viii . ferui . T . R . E . 7 poft . uał . viii . lib̄ . M̃ . x . lib̄ .

in LYMPNE Lathe
in BIRCHOLT Hundred

23 ALDINGTON, in lordship. Before 1066 it answered for 21 sulungs; now for 15 sulungs. Land for 100 ploughs. In lordship 13 ploughs.
   200 villagers less 10 with 50 smallholders have 70 ploughs.
   A church; 13 slaves; 3 mills at 16s; 3 fisheries at 21d.
     Meadow, 170 acres; woodland, 60 pigs.
Total value before 1066 £62; as much when acquired; now it pays £100 20s.

24 the village which is called ST. MARTINS. It belongs to Westgate; lies in this Hundred and answers for 1½ sulungs. Land for ...
In lordship 2 ploughs;
   36 smallholders.
   To this land belong 7 burgesses in Canterbury who pay 8s 4d.
   5 mills at 20s; a small wood.
   In this village Ralph holds ½ sulung from the Archbishop. He has 2 ploughs in lordship, and
   5 villagers with 3 smallholders who have 2½ ploughs.
Value before 1066 of ½ sulung of St. Martins' £7; value of another ½ sulung always £4.

25 In ROMNEY 85 burgesses who belong to Aldington, the Archbishop's manor. The value to the lordship was and now is £6.
   Of this manor of Aldington ½ yoke and ½ virgate lie in Lympne. The Archbishop holds in lordship. He has 1 plough, and
   1 villager with 18 smallholders who have 1½ ploughs.
   7 priests who pay £7 5s.
   Land for 2 ploughs.
The value is and was £12; however, it pays £15.
   Of this manor the Count of Eu held Stowting as 1 manor
Before 1066 it answered for 1½ sulungs; now for only 1 sulung.
Land for 8 ploughs. In lordship 2, and
   27 villagers with 13 smallholders who have 7 ploughs.
   1 mill at 25d; a church; meadow, 20 acres; woodland.
     10 pigs; 8 slaves.
Value before 1066 and later £8; now £10.

Ipſe Archieps ten in dñio *Leminges* . p .vii. ſolins ſe defđ.

Tra . e .lx. cař . In dñio ſunt . iiii . 7 c. 7 uñ uilłs cũ . xvi . borđ

hñtes .lv. cař . Ibi æcclʸa 7 x. ſerui . 7 i. moliñ de . xxx . den.

7 i. piſcař de xl. anguilł . 7 xxx. ač p̃ti . Silua . c . porc.

Ibi p̃tiñ . vi. burgens in *Hede* . T.R.E. ualeb . xxiiii. lib.

7 poſtea . xl. lib . 7 m̃ ſimilit . 7 tam̃ reddit . lx . lib.

De hoc m̃ ten . iii. hões archiep̃i . ii. ſolins 7 dim̃ . 7 dimiđ

jugũ . 7 ibi hñt . v . cař in dñio . 7 xx . uilłos cũ . xvi . borđ.

hñtes . v . cař 7 dimiđ . 7 i. ſeruũ . 7 ii. moliñ de . vii. ſoł 7 vi. den.

7 xl . ač s p̃ti . Silua . xi. porc . Ibi . ii. æcclæ. Inł toł ual . xi. lib.

Ipſe Archieps ten *Newedene* . p uno ſolin ſe defđ . Tra . e

Ibi ſunt . xxv. uilłi cũ . iiii. borđ . hñtes . v . cař . Ibi . e mer

catũ de xl . ſoł . v . den min. Silua . xl. porc . Inł totũ

T.R.E. ualeb . c . ſoł . Q̣do recep̃ xii. lib . 7 m̃ . x . lib . 7 tam̃

p̃poſit redđ . xviii. lib . 7 x . ſoliđ.

4 b TERRA MILITVM EJUS. *In Achestan Hvnd.*

Anſgotus ten de archiep̃o . *Forningeham* .

p uno ſolino ſe defđ . Tra . e   In dñio ſunt

ii . cař . 7 xiii. uilłi cũ . v . borđ hñtes . iii. cař 7 dim̃.

Ibi . vi. ač p̃ti . Silua . xx. porc . 7 Ricarđ de Tonebrige

de eađ ſilua tntđ hł in ſua leuua . T.R.E. ualebat

hoc m̃ . vii. lib . 7 m̃ . xi. lib . De his hñt monachi

cantuař . iiii. lib . ad ueſtitũ ſuũ . 7

In LONINGBOROUGH Hundred

26   The Archbishop holds LYMINGE himself, in lordship. It answers
for 7 sulungs. Land for 60 ploughs. In lordship 4, and
   101 villagers with 16 smallholders who have 55 ploughs.
   A church; 10 slaves; a mill at 30d; a fishery at 40 eels;
     meadow, 30 acres; woodland, 100 pigs.
   6 burgesses belong in Hythe.
Value before 1066 £24; later £40, now the same; however,
it pays £60.
   Of this manor 3 of the Archbishop's men hold 2½ sulungs and
½ yoke. They have 5 ploughs in lordship, and
   20 villagers with 16 smallholders who have 5½ ploughs.
   1 slave; 2 mills at 7s 6d; meadow, 40 acres; woodland, 11 pigs.
   2 churches.
In total, value £11.

In SELBRITTENDEN Hundred

27   The Archbishop holds NEWENDEN himself. It answers for 1 sulung.
Land for ...
   25 villagers with 4 smallholders who have 5 ploughs.
   A market at 40s less 5d; woodland, 40 pigs.
In total, value before 1066, 100s; when acquired, £12; now £10;
however, the reeve pays £18 10s.

2   LAND OF HIS MEN-AT-ARMS   4 b

In AXTON Hundred

28   Ansgot holds FARNINGHAM from the Archbishop. It answers for
1 sulung. Land for ... In lordship 2 ploughs, and
   13 villagers with 5 smallholders who have 3½ ploughs.
   Meadow, 6 acres; woodland, 20 pigs.
   Richard of Tonbridge has as much of the same woodland
in his territory.
Value of this manor before 1066 £7; now £11; of these the
monks of Canterbury have £4 for their clothing.

Radulf fili Vnſpac ten̄ Elesford de archiepo.

p̄ . vi . ſolins ſe defđ . Tra . ē   In dn̄io ſunt

.v. car̄ . 7 xxix . uilti cū . ix . borđ hn̄t . xv . car̄ . Ibi

ii . æcctæ. 7 ix . ſerui . 7 ii . molđ de . xl.iii . ſot . 7 xxix . ac̄

p̄ti . Silua . xx . porc̄ . T.R.E. ualeƀ . xvi . liƀ . 7 m̄ uat

. xx . liƀ . De hoc m̄ ten̄ Ricarđ de Tonebrige . tantū

ſiluæ unde exire poſſ. xx . porc̄ . 7 i . molin̄ de . v . ſoliđ.

7 unā piſcariā in ſua leuua.

Malgeri ten̄ de archiepo . iii . juga . in Orpinton.

7 pro tanto ſe defđ ext̄ Orpinton . T.R.E. Modo ſun̄

ii . juga int̄ Orpint̄ . 7 tciū extra . Tra . ē   In dn̄io

.i. car̄ . 7 iiii . uilti cū . i . borđ . 7 iiii . ſeru̇ . 7 dimiđ car̄ . 7 iii .

ac̄ p̄ti . 7 ſilua . xi . porc̄ . T.R.E. ualeƀ xl . ſot . Qdo

recep̄. xx . ſot . 7 m̄ . l . ſot.

Haimo uicec̄ ten̄ de archiepo BRIESTEDE . p̄ uno

ſolin 7 dimiđ ſe defđ . Tra . ē . x . car̄ . In dn̄io ſunt . ii.

7 xxiiii . uilti cū . xvi . borđ hn̄t xii . car̄ . Ibi æccta 7 xv.

ſerui . 7 ii . molđ de xxiiii . ſot . Silua q̇t xx . porc̄ . 7 de

herbagio . ix . ſoliđ 7 . vi . den̄ . Int toł T.R.E. ualebat

x . liƀ . 7 tn̄tđ qdo recep̄. 7 m̄ xvii. liƀ. Hoc m̄ tenuit

Alnod aƀƀ de archiepo cantuar̄.

Comes de Ow ten̄ de Archiepo OLECVBE . p̄ . ii.

ſolins | ſe defđ . T.R.E. 7 m̄ p̄ . ii . tant̄ . Tra . ē . ix . car̄ In dn̄io

ſunt . ii . car̄ . 7 xxiii . uilti cū . viii . borđ hn̄t . vii . car̄.

Ibi . æccta 7 un̄ molđ de . iiii . ſot . 7 viii . ac̄ p̄ti . Silua

quat xx . porc̄ . Int toł . T.R.E. ualeƀ . x . liƀ . Qdo recep̄.

viii. lib . Modo . xi . liƀ . Hoc m̄ tenuit Alfer de arch.

29   Ralph son of Ospak holds EYNSFORD from the Archbishop. It
answers for 6 sulungs. Land for ... In lordship 5 ploughs.
   29 villagers with 9 smallholders have 15 ploughs.
   2 churches; 9 slaves; 2 mills at 43s; meadow, 29 acres;
      woodland, 20 pigs.
Value before 1066 £16; value now £20.
   Of this manor Richard of Tonbridge holds as much woodland
as can support 20 pigs; 1 mill at 5s and 1 fishery in his territory.

30   Mauger holds 3 yokes in ORPINGTON from the Archbishop. Before
1066 it answered for as much outside Orpington. Now there are
2 yokes inside Orpington and a third outside. Land for ...
In lordship 1 plough.
   4 villagers with 1 smallholder and 4 slaves; ½ plough.
   Meadow, 3 acres; woodland, 11 pigs.
Value before 1066, 40s; when acquired, 20s; now 50s.

31   Hamo the Sheriff holds BRASTED from the Archbishop. It answers
for 1½ sulungs. Land for 10 ploughs. In lordship 2.
   24 villagers with 16 smallholders have 12 ploughs.
   A church; 15 slaves; 2 mills at 24s; woodland, 80 pigs;
      from grazing, 9s 6d.
In total, value before 1066 £10; as much when acquired; now £17.
   Abbot Alnoth held this manor from the Archbishop of Canterbury.

32   The Count of Eu holds ULCOMBE from the Archbishop. It answered
for 2½ sulungs before 1066; now for only 2. Land for 9 ploughs.
In lordship 2 ploughs.
   23 villagers with 8 smallholders have 7 ploughs.
   A church; a mill at 4s; meadow, 8 acres; woodland, 80 pigs.
In total, value before 1066 £10; when acquired, £8; now £9.
   Alfhere held this manor from the Archbishop.

Radulf filius turaldi ten *Boltone* de archiepo.

.p dimid solin se defd 7 jacet in . vi . solins de Holinge

borne . Tra . e . i . car 7 dim . Idnio . e una car . 7 iii . uilli

cu . ii . bord hnt . i . car . Ibi æccla . 7 ii . ac pti . 7 silua

xvi . porc . Int totu ual 7 ualuit sep . xl . solid.

In Faversha Hvnd.

Ricard ho archiepi ten de eo *Levelant* . p uno solin

se defd . Tra . e   In dnio . i . car . 7 ii . uilli cu . i . bord

hnt . i . car . Silua . v . porc . T.R.E. 7 post ual . xxx . sol.

Isde Ricard ten de arch *In Boltone Hvnd* . ℔ m̄ . xx . sot.

Gravenel . p uno solin se defd . Tra . e

In dnio . e . i . car . 7 viii . uilli cu . x . bord . hnt . ii . car.

Ibi . v . serui . 7 x . ac pti . 7 iiii . salinæ de . iiii . sot . T.R.E.

7 post: ualuit . c . sot . m̄ . vi . lib . De his hnt monachi cant

℔ xx . sot.

Godefrid dapifer ten de archiepo . *Lerha* . p . ii . solin

se defd . Tra . e   In dnio sunt . ii . car . 7 xv . uilli

cu . ii . bord . hnt . iiii . car . Ibi . iiii . serui . 7 vi . ac pti . 7 i . molin

de . vii . sot . 7 silua de . x . porc . Int tot ual . viii . lib . 7 tam

reddit . xii . lib 7 x . sot.   *In Therha Hvnd.*

Isde Godefrid ten de archiepo in *Scape* . dimid solin . Tra . e

In dnio . i . car . cu . ii . bord 7 iiii . serui . T.R.E. 7 post:

ualuit . xxx . sot . Modo: iiii . lib . 7 tam reddit . c . sot.

Osbn filius Letard ten . i . jugu   *In Estrei Hvnd.*

de archiepo in *Bocoland* . 7 ibi ht in dnio . i . car . 7 ual . x . sot.

In EYHORNE Hundred

33 Ralph son of Thorold holds BOUGHTON (Malherbe) from the
Archbishop. It answers for ½ sulung, and lies in 6 sulungs of
Hollingbourne. Land for 1½ ploughs. In lordship 1 plough.
   3 villagers with 2 smallholders have 1 plough.
   A church; meadow, 2 acres; woodland, 16 pigs.
In total, the value is and always was 40s.

In FAVERSHAM Hundred

34 Richard, one of the Archbishop's men, holds LEAVELAND (Court)
from him. It answers for 1 sulung. Land for ... In lordship 1 plough.
   2 villagers with 1 smallholder have 1 plough.
   Woodland, 5 pigs.
Value before 1066 and later 30s; now 20s.

In BOUGHTON Hundred

35 Richard also holds GRAVENEY from the Archbishop. It answers for
1 sulung. Land for ... In lordship 1 plough.
   8 villagers with 10 smallholders have 2 ploughs.
   5 slaves; meadow, 10 acres; 4 salt-houses at 4s.
Value before 1066 and later 100s; now £6; of these the monks of
Canterbury have 20s.

In CALEHILL Hundred

36 Godfrey the Steward holds (East) LENHAM from the Archbishop.
It answers for 2 sulungs. Land for ... In lordship 2 ploughs.
   15 villagers with 2 smallholders have 4 ploughs.
   4 slaves; meadow, 6 acres; 1 mill at 7s; woodland at 10 pigs.
In total, value £8; however, it pays £12 10s.

4 c

In TEYNHAM Hundred

37 Godfrey also holds ½ sulung in SHEPPEY from the Archbishop.
Land for ... In lordship 1 plough, with
   2 smallholders and 4 slaves.
Value before 1066 and later 30s; now £4; however it pays 100s.

In EASTRY Hundred

38 Osbern son of Ledhard holds 1 yoke in BUCKLAND from the
Archbishop. He has 1 plough in lordship.
Value 10s.

☞ Wilts Folet ten de Archiepo *FLENGVESSA*. p dim̄ solin
se defd. Ibi h̄t. vi. uilt. cū. i. car 7 dim̄.

Iſd Wilts ten Eſtenberge de Archiepo. 7 p dim̄ solin se
defd. 7 ibi h̄t. xii. uillos cū. i. car 7 dimid.   ⨍ xxx. ſot.
He træ ualeb̄ T.R.E. xl. ſot. Q̄do arch recep: x. ſot. Modo

Hugo de Montfort ten de Archiepo *IN HEN HVND.*
SALTEODE. p. vii. solins se defd T.R.E. 7 m̄ p. iii. solins.
Tra. ē. xv. car̄. In dn̄io ſunt. ii. car̄. 7 xxxiii. uilti cū. xii. bord
hn̄tes. ix. car̄. 7 dimid. Ibi æccta 7 ii. ſerui. 7 ix. mold de. xx.
ſolid. 7 xxxiii. ac̄ pti. Silua q̄t xx. porc̄.
Ad hoc m̄ ptin̄. cc. xxv. burgſes in Burgo hedæ
Int burgū 7 m̄ uat T.R.E. xvi. lib̄. Q̄do recep: viii. lib̄.
m̄ int totū xxix. lib̄. 7 vi. ſot 7 iiii. den. *IN ESKAITES HD.*

Wilts de Eddeſhā ten de Archiepo *BEREWIC* p uno m̄.
p dimid solin se defd. Tra. ē. iii. car̄. In dn̄io ſunt. ii. 7 ix.
uilti cū. ix. bord hn̄t. i. car̄ 7 dim̄. Ibi. xviii. ac̄ pti. 7 Silua
xx. porc̄. T.R.E. ualeb̄. lx. ſot. 7 poſt: xx. ſot. Modo. vii.
lib̄. 7 tam̄ redd xi. lib̄.   *IN LAMPORT HVND.*

Robt de Romenel ten de Archiepo *LAMPORT.*
p uno solin 7 dim̄ se defd. Tra. ē. vi. car̄. In dn̄io ſunt. ii.
7 xxix. uilti cū. ix. bord. hn̄t. ix. car̄. Ibi. vii. ſalinæ
de. viii. ſot 7 ix. den.
Ad hoc m̄ ptin̄. xxi. burgſ. qui ſunt in Romenel. de
quib̄ h̄t archieps. iii. forisfactas. Latrocniū. pace
fracta. foriſtellū. Rex ū h̄t ome ſeruitiū ab eis. 7 ipſi
hn̄t oms c̄ſuetudines 7 alias forisfactas p ſeruitio ma
ris. 7 ſunt in manu regis. T.R.E. 7 poſt ualuit. x. lib̄.
7 m̄. xvi. lib̄.

39 William Follet holds FINGLESHAM from the Archbishop. It
answers for ½ sulung. He has
    6 villagers with 1½ ploughs.
    William also holds Statenborough from the Archbishop.
It answers for ½ sulung. He has
    12 villagers with 1½ ploughs.
Value of these lands before 1066, 40s; when the Archbishop
acquired them 10s; now 30s.
(40 entered after 2,43 and directed to its proper place by transpositions signs.)

In HAYNE Hundred

41 Hugh de Montfort holds SALTWOOD from the Archbishop. Before
1066 it answered for 7 sulungs; now for 3 sulungs. Land for 15
ploughs. In lordship 2 ploughs, and
    33 villagers with 12 smallholders who have 9½ ploughs.
    A church; 2 slaves; 9 mills at 20s; meadow, 33 acres;
      woodland, 80 pigs.
    To this manor belong 225 burgesses in the Borough of Hythe.
Between the Borough and manor, value before 1066 £16; when
acquired, £8; in total, now £29 6s 4d.

In STREET Hundred

42 William of Adisham holds BERWICK from the Archbishop as 1 manor.
It answers for ½ sulung. Land for 3 ploughs. In lordship 2.
    9 villagers with 9 smallholders have 1½ ploughs.
    Meadow, 18 acres; woodland, 20 pigs.
Value before 1066, 60s; later 20s; now £7; however, it pays £11.

In LANGPORT Hundred

43 Robert of Romney holds LANGPORT from the Archbishop. It
answers for 1½ sulungs. Land for 6 ploughs. In lordship 2.
    29 villagers with 9 smallholders have 9 ploughs.
    7 salt-houses at 8s 9d.
    To this manor belong 21 burgesses who are in Romney from whom
the Archbishop has 3 forfeitures; robbery, breach of the peace and
highway robbery. But the King has all the service from them; they
themselves have all the customary dues and other forfeitures for
service at sea; they are in the hands of the King.
Value before 1066 and later £10; now £16.

☞ Wilts ten de Archiepo *TILEMANESTONE* . p uno folin fe
fe defend . In dnio st . ii . car . 7 v . bord.
Oli . xx . fol . Modo ual . xxx . folid.

.III.   TERRA MONACHOʒ ARCHIEPI *IN HELMESTREI HVND.*

Archieps cantuar ten *ORPINTVN* . p . iii . folins fe defd.
T.R.E . 7 m p . ii . folins 7 dim . Tra . e   In dnio funt
ii . car . 7 XLVI . uilli cu . xxv . bord hntes . xxiii . car . Ibi . iii.
mold de xvi . folid 7 iiii . den . 7 x . ac pti . 7 v denæ filuæ de . L.
porc . In totis ualent . T.R.E . ualeb . xv . lib . Qdo recep. viii . lib.
7 modo . xxv . lib . 7 tam reddit . xxviii . lib . Ibi funt . ii . æcclæ.

IN LEST DE ELESFORD.   *IN LITEFELLE HVND.*

Ipfe Archieps ten *PECHEHA* . p . vi . folins fe defd . T.R.E . 7 m
p . v . folins 7 uno jugo . Tra . e . x . car . In dnio . funt . ii . 7 xvi . uilli
cu . xiiii . bord hnt . iiii . car . 7 dim . Ibi | . x . serui . 7 i . mold 7 vi.
ac pti . Silua . x . porc.

De tra huj M ten un ho archiepi dimid folin . 7 cu his . vi . folins
geldabat . T.R.E . quis n ptineret M nifi de fcoto . qa liba tra erat.
De eod M ten Ricard de Tonebrige . ii . folins 7 un jugu . 7 ibi ht
xxvii . uillos hntes . vii . car . 7 filua . x . porc . 7 tot ual . iiii . lib.
T.R.E . ualeb M . xii . lib . Qdo recep archieps. viii . lib . 7 m qd
habet ualet . viii . lib .   *IN AIHORDE HVND.*

Ipfe Archieps ten *HOILINGEBORDE* . p . vi . folins fe defd . Tra . e
xxiiii . car . In dnio funt . ii . 7 LXI . uilts cu . xvi . bord hnt . xxiii.
car . Ibi æccla 7 xii . serui . 7 ii . mold . 7 viii . ac pti . Silua . xL . porc.
Int tot T.R.E . 7 post . ualeb . xx . lib . 7 m ual xxx . lib.

40 William holds TILMANSTONE from the Archbishop. It answers
for 1 sulung. In lordship 2 ploughs.
    5 smallholders.
Value formerly 20s; now 30s.

3   LAND OF THE ARCHBISHOP'S MONKS   4 d

In RUXLEY Hundred
1   The Archbishop of Canterbury holds ORPINGTON. Before 1066 it
answered for 3 sulungs; now for 2½ sulungs. Land for ...
In lordship 2 ploughs, and
    46 villagers with 25 smallholders who have 23 ploughs.
    3 mills at 16s 4d; meadow, 10 acres; 5 pig pastures of woodland
        at 50 pigs.
Total value before 1066 £15; when acquired, £8; now £25;
however, it pays £28.
    2 churches.

  The Archbishop himself holds
   in AYLESFORD Lathe
   in LITTLEFIELD Hundred
2   (East) PECKHAM. Before 1066 it answered for 6 sulungs; now for 5
sulungs and 1 yoke. Land for 10 ploughs. In lordship 2.
    16 villagers with 14 smallholders have 4½ ploughs.
    A church; 10 slaves; 1 mill; meadow, 6 acres; woodland, 10 pigs.
    One of the Archbishop's men holds ½ sulung of the land of this
manor; before 1066 it paid tax with these 6 sulungs although it did
not belong to the manor except for (payment of) a levy, because it
was free land.
    Richard of Tonbridge holds 2 sulungs and 1 yoke of this manor.
He has
    27 villagers who have 7 ploughs.
    Woodland, 10 pigs.
Value of the whole £4.
Value of the manor before 1066 £12; when the Archbishop
acquired it £8; value of what he now has £8.

   in EYHORNE Hundred.
3   HOLLINGBOURNE. It answers for 6 sulungs. Land for 24 ploughs.
In lordship 2.
    61 villagers with 16 smallholders have 23 ploughs.
    A church; 12 slaves; 2 mills; meadow, 8 acres; woodland, 40 pigs.
In total, value before 1066 and later £20; now £30.

Huic m̄ adjacet dimid̄ folin . q̇d̄ nunq̇ reddid̄ ſcot . Hunc
ten eps baioc̄ de archiepo ad gablū.   *IN TOLLENTREV HD̄.*
Ipſe Archieps ten̄ *MEPEHĀ* . ꝑ . x . ſolins ſe defd̄ T.R.E. m̂ ꝑ . vii.
Tra ē . xxx . car̄ . In dn̄io ſunt . iiii . 7 xxv . uiłłi cū . lxxi . bord̄
hn̄t . xxv . car̄ . Ibi æcc̄ła 7 xvii . ſerui . 7 xvi . ac̄ ꝑti . Silua
x . porc̄ . In totis ualen̄t T.R.E. ualeƀ xv . liƀ 7 x . ſoł . Q̇do
recep̄:ͻxv . liƀ . Modo:ͻxxvi . liƀ . Ricard̄ de Tonebrige ht̄
in ſua leuga q̇d̄ uał . xviii . ſoł 7 vi . den̄ . Siluā . xx . porc̄.
Ipſe Archieps ten̄ *FERLAGA.*   *IN MEDESTAN HVND̄.*
ꝑ . vi . ſolins ſe defd̄ . Tra . ē . xxvi . car̄ . In dn̄io ſunt . iiii . 7 xxxv.ta
uiłłi cū . lvi . bord̄ hn̄t . xxx . car̄ . Ibi æcc̄ła . 7 iii . mołd̄ de
xxvii . ſolid̄ 7 viii . den̄ . Ibi . viii . ſerui . 7 vi . piſcarie . de mille
cc . anguiłł . Ibi . xii . ac̄ ꝑti . Silua . c . xv . porc̄.
De tra huj m̄ ten̄ Godefrid̄ in feuo dimid̄ ſolin . 7 ibi ht̄ . ii.
car̄ . 7 vii . uiłłos cū x . bord̄ hn̄tes . iii . car̄ . 7 iiii . ſeruos . 7 i . mołd̄
de . xx . den̄ . 7 iiii . ac̄s ꝑti . 7 Siluā . xxx . porc̄.
Totū m̄ T.R.E. ualeƀ xvi . liƀ . 7 poſt tn̄td̄ . 7 m̂:ͻxxii . liƀ.
Q̇d̄ abel m̂ ten̄:ͻvi . liƀ . Q̇d̄ Godefrid̄:ͻix . liƀ . Q̇d̄ Ricard̄
in ſua leuga:ͻiiii . liƀ.   *IN ESSAMELE HVND̄.*
Ipſe Archieps ten̄ *CLIVE* . ꝑ iii . ſolins 7 dimid̄ ſe defd̄ . Tra . ē
vi . car̄ . In dn̄io . ē una car̄ 7 dim̄ . 7 xx . uiłłi cū . xviii . bord̄
hn̄t . v . car̄ 7 dim̄ . Ibi æcc̄ła . 7 ii . ſerui . 7 xxxvi . ac̄ ꝑti.
Silua de . xii . den̄ . T.R.E. ualeƀ tot m̄ . vi . liƀ . 7 poſt:ͻvii . liƀ.
IN BOROWART LEST . *IN TANET HVND̄.* ƒ 7 m̂ . xvi . liƀ.
Ipſe Archieps ten̄ *MONOCSTVNE* . T.R.E. ꝑ xx . ſolins
ſe defd̄ . 7 m̂ ꝑ . xviii . Tra . ē . xxxi . car̄ . In dn̄io ſunt . iiii.
7 q̇t xx . 7 ix . uiłłi cū . xxi . bord̄ hn̄t . xxvii . car̄ . Ibi
ii . æcc̄łæ . 7 unū mołd̄ de . x . ſolid̄ . Ibi noua piſcaria . 7 una
ſalina de . xv . denar̄ . Silua . x . porc̄.
In totis ualen̄t ualeƀ T.R.E. 7 poſt:ͻxx . liƀ . 7 m̂ . xl . liƀ.

To this manor is attached ½ sulung which has never paid a levy. The Bishop of Bayeux holds this from the Archbishop on payment of tribute.

in TOLTINGTROUGH Hundred

4   MEOPHAM. Before 1066 it answered for 10 sulungs; now for 7.
Land for 30 ploughs. In lordship 4.
    25 villagers with 71 smallholders have 25 ploughs.
    A church; 17 slaves; meadow, 16 acres; woodland, 10 pigs.
Total value before 1066 £15 10s; when acquired, £15; now £26.
    Richard of Tonbridge has in his territory what is valued at 18s 6d.
    Woodland, 20 pigs.

in MAIDSTONE Hundred

5   (East) FARLEIGH. It answers for 6 sulungs. Land for 26 ploughs.
In lordship 4.
    35 villagers with 56 smallholders have 30 ploughs.
    A church; 3 mills at 27s 8d. 8 slaves; 6 fisheries at 1,200 eels.
      Meadow, 12 acres; woodland, 115 pigs.
    Godfrey holds ½ sulung of the land of this manor as a holding. He
has 2 ploughs, and
    7 villagers with 10 smallholders who have 3 ploughs and 4 slaves.
    1 mill at 20d; meadow, 4 acres; woodland, 30 pigs.
Value of the whole manor before 1066 £16; later as much; now £22.
What Abel now holds £6; what Godfrey (holds) £9; what Richard
(holds) in his territory £4.

in SHAMWELL Hundred

6   CLIFFE. It answers for 3½ sulungs. Land for 6 ploughs. In lordship
1½ ploughs.
    20 villagers with 18 smallholders have 5½ ploughs.
    A church; 2 slaves; meadow, 36 acres; woodland at 12d.
Value of the whole manor before 1066 £6; later £7; now £16.

in BOROUGH Lathe
in THANET Hundred

7   MONKTON. Before 1066 it answered for 20 sulungs; now for 18.
Land for 31 ploughs. In lordship 4.
    89 villagers with 21 smallholders have 27 ploughs.
    2 churches; a mill at 10s. A new fishery; 1 salt-house at 15d;   5 a
      woodland, 10 pigs.
Total value before 1066 and later £20; now £40.

Ipſe archieps ten̄ GECHAM   IN DVNEHĀFORT HD̄.

p̄ . IIII . ſolins ſe defd̄ . Tra . ē . XII . car̄ . In dn̄io ſunt . III .

7 XXIX . uiłłi cū . LX . cot hn̄t XVI . car̄ 7 dim̄ . Ibi æcc̄ła .

7 IIII . mold̄ de . c . ſolid̄ . 7 XXXV . ac̄ pti . 7 Silua . XXX . porc̄ .

Toī M̄ ualeb̄ T.R.E. 7 poſt : XXII . lib̄ . Modo : XXXII . lib̄ .

De tra huj M̄ ten̄ Wiłłs hō ſuus tantū qd̄ uał . VII . lib̄ .

Ipſe archieps ten̄ NORDEVDE.   IN CANTVARIE HVND̄ .

p̄ uno ſolin ſe defd̄ . Tra . ē .   In dn̄io . I . car̄ 7 dim̄ .

7 VII . uiłłi cū . XXVI . bord̄ hn̄t . II . car̄ . Huic M̄ ptinent

in ciuitate cantuaria . c . burgſes . III . min . reddentes

VIII . lib̄ 7 IIII . ſoł . Ibi . VIII . mold̄ de . LXXI . ſoł . XXIIII .

ac̄ pti . Silua . XXX . porc̄ . Int toī uał 7 ualuit . XVII . lib̄ .

In eod̄ BOROWART LEST . jacet paruū burgū nōe

SESELTRE qd̄ ppe ptin coq̄næ archiepi . Quidā nōe

Blize ten̄ de monachis . In dn̄io . ē una car̄ . 7 XLVIII .

bord̄ cū . I . car̄ . Ibi æcc̄ła . 7 VIII . piſcariæ de XXV . ſoł .

Silua . X . porc̄ . T.R.E. 7 poſt : ualuit . XX . V . ſoł .

IN WIWARLET LEST . IN FAVRESHANT HD̄ ſ 7 m̄ . c . ſoł .

Ipſe archieps ten̄ PRESTETONE . p̄ uno ſolin de defd̄ .

Tra . ē . VI . car̄ . In dn̄io ſunt . III . 7 XIII uiłłi cū XIIII . bord̄

hn̄t . III . car̄ . Ibi æcc̄ła 7 I . ſeruus . 7 I . mold̄ ſine cenſu . 7 una

piſcaria de . CC . L . anguillis . Ibi . II . ac̄ pti . Silua . V . porc̄ .

T.R.E. 7 poſt : ualuit . X . lib̄ . Modo : XV . lib̄ .

Ipſe archieps ten̄ CERTEHAM . IN FELEBERG HVND̄ .

p̄ . IIII . ſolins ſe defd̄ . Tra . ē . XIIII . car̄ . In dn̄io ſunt . II .

in DOWNHAMFORD Hundred

8   ICKHAM. It answers for 4 sulungs. Land for 12 ploughs. In lordship 3.
29 villagers with 60 cottagers have 16½ ploughs.
A church; 4 mills at 100s; meadow, 35 acres; woodland, 30 pigs.
Value of the whole manor before 1066 and later £22; now £32.
William, one of his men, holds as much of the land of this manor as is valued at £7.

in CANTERBURY Hundred

9   NORTHGATE. It answers for 1 sulung. Land for ... In lordship 1½ ploughs.
7 villagers with 26 smallholders have 2 ploughs.
To this manor belong 100 burgesses less 3 in the City of Canterbury who pay £8 4s.
8 mills at 71s; meadow, 24 acres; woodland, 30 pigs.
In total, the value is and was £17.

10   In the same Borough Lathe lies a small Borough called SEASALTER, which belongs to the Archbishop's own kitchen. A man called Blize holds from the monks. In lordship 1 plough;
48 smallholders with 1 plough.
A church; 8 fisheries with (payment of) tribute at 25s;
woodland, 10 pigs.
Value before 1066 and later 25s; now 100s.

The Archbishop himself holds
in WYE Lathe
in FAVERSHAM Hundred

1   (South) PRESTON.   It answers for 1 sulung. Land for 6 ploughs.
In lordship 3.
13 villagers with 14 smallholders have 3 ploughs.
A church; 1 slave; 1 mill without dues; a fishery at 250 eels.
Meadow, 2 acres; woodland, 5 pigs.
Value before 1066 and later £10; now £15.

in FELBOROUGH Hundred

12   CHARTHAM. It answers for 4 sulungs. Land for 14 ploughs.
In lordship 2.

⁊ LX . uilli cū . xv . cot hn̄t xv . car ⁊ dim . Ibi æccła ⁊ i . seru.

⁊ v . molđ ⁊ dim de . LXX . soł . ⁊ xxx . ac̄ p̄ti . ⁊ silua . xxv.

porc̄ . T . R . E . ⁊ qdo recep̄: ualuit xii . lib̄ . Modo: xxv . lib̄.

⁊ tam̄ reddit . xxx . lib̄.

Ipse archieps ten̄ GOMERSHAM . p . viii . solins se defđ.

Tra . ē . xii . car̄ . In dn̄io sunt . ii . ⁊ LX . uilli cū . viii . cot

hn̄t . xvii . car̄ . Ibi æccła ⁊ ii . serui . ⁊ i . molđ de . xxv . soł.

⁊ xii . ac̄ p̄ti . Silua . XL . porc̄ . T . R . E . ⁊ qdo recep̄: ualuit

xii . lib̄ . Modo: xx . lib̄ . ⁊ tam̄ reddit . xxx . lib̄.

Ipse archieps ten̄ CERTH . p . iii . solins IN CERT HVND.

se defđ . Tra . ē . xii . car̄ . In dn̄io sunt . ii . ⁊ xxxvi . uilli cū

xi . cot hn̄t . xxii . car̄ ⁊ dim . Ibi . v . serui . ⁊ ii . molđ de . vi.

soliđ . ⁊ salina de . vi . den̄ . ⁊ xxvii . ac̄ p̄ti . ⁊ Silua . c . porc̄.

T . R . E . ⁊ qdo recep̄: ualuit . xii . lib̄ . Modo . xx . lib . ⁊ tam̄ redđ

Ipse archieps ten̄ IN CALEHELLE HVND. ſxxvii . lib̄.

LITELCERT . T . R . E . se defđ p . iii . solins . ⁊ m̄ p . ii . hiđ ⁊ dim̄.

Tra . ē   In dn̄io sunt . ii . ⁊ xix . uilli cū . v . borđ hn̄t

vii . car̄ . Ibi . ii . molđ de . v . soł ⁊ x . den̄ . ⁊ xi . ac̄ p̄ti . ⁊ silua

xv . porc̄.

De tra huj̄ m̄ ten̄ Wilłs de archiep̄o dimiđ solin . ⁊ ibi ht̄

in dn̄io . i . car̄ . cū . iiii . seruis . ⁊ x . ac̄s p̄ti . ⁊ siluā . xx . porc̄.

Totū m̄ ualeb̄ T . R . E . ⁊ post: c . soł . Modo . viii . lib̄ . ⁊ viii . soł

⁊ iiii . den̄ . Qđ Wilłs ten̄: app̄ciat . XL . soł.

5 b

Ipse archieps ten̄ WELLE . T . R . E . se defđ p . vii . solins.

⁊ m̄ p . v . Tra . ē . xviii . car̄ . In dn̄io sunt . iiii . ⁊ q̄t xx.

⁊ un uilłs cū . v . borđ hn̄t . xii . car̄ ⁊ dim . Ibi . vii . serui.

⁊ un̄ molđ de xxx . den̄ . ⁊ xx . ac̄ p̄ti . Silua . q̄t xx . porc̄.

T . R . E: ualeb̄ xvii . lib̄ ⁊ xi . soł ⁊ iiii . den̄ . Qdo recep̄:

tn̄tđ . Modo: xxiiii . lib̄ . ⁊ iiii . den̄ . ⁊ tam̄ redđ . XL . lib̄.

60 villagers with 15 cottagers have 15½ ploughs.
A church; 1 slave; 5½ mills at 70s; meadow, 30 acres;
    woodland, 25 pigs.
Value before 1066 and when acquired £12; now £25; however,
it pays £30.

13   GODMERSHAM. It answers for 8 sulungs. Land for 12 ploughs.
In lordship 2.
    60 villagers with 8 cottagers have 17 ploughs.
    A church; 2 slaves; 1 mill at 25s; meadow, 12 acres;
        woodland, 40 pigs.
Value before 1066 and when acquired £12; now £20; however it
pays £30.

in CHART Hundred
14   (Great) CHART. It answers for 3 sulungs. Land for 12 ploughs.
In lordship 2.
    36 villagers with 11 cottagers have 22½ ploughs.
    5 slaves; 2 mills at 6s; a salt-house at 6d; meadow, 27 acres;
        woodland, 100 pigs.
Value before 1066 and when acquired £12; now £20; however
it pays £27.

in CALEHILL Hundred
15   (Little) CHART. Before 1066 it answered for 3 sulungs; now for 2½
hides. Land for ... In lordship 2.
    19 villagers with 5 smallholders have 7 ploughs.
    2 mills at 5s 10d; meadow, 11 acres; woodland, 15 pigs.
    William holds ½ sulung of the land of this manor from the
Archbishop. He has 1 plough in lordship, with 4 slaves.
    Meadow, 10 acres; woodland, 20 pigs.
Value of the whole manor before 1066 and later 100s; now £8 8s 4d;
what William holds is assessed at 40s.

16   WESTWELL. Before 1066 it answered for 7 sulungs; now for 5.   5 b
Land for 18 ploughs. In lordship 4.
    81 villagers with 5 smallholders have 12½ ploughs.
    7 slaves; a mill at 30d; meadow, 20 acres; woodland, 80 pigs.
Value before 1066 £17 11s 4d; when acquired, as much;
now £24 4d; however, it pays £40.

Ipſe archieps̃ ten̄ *Estrei* . p̄ . vii . ſolins ſe defd̃.

Tra . ē.   In dn̄io ſunt . iii . car̃ . 7 lxxii . uilĺi

cū . xxii . bord̃ hn̄t . xxiiii . car̃ . Ibi . i . molin̄ 7 dimid̃

de . xxx . ſolid̃ . 7 iii . ſalinæ de . iiii . ſolid̃ . 7 xviii . ac̄ p̃ti.

Silua ꞉ x . porc̃.

Et in Getinge ten̄ monachi cantuar̃ dimid̃ ſolin

7 unū jugū . 7 v . ac̄s . 7 ibi hn̄t . vi . uilĺos cū . ii . car̃ 7 dim̃.

Int totū T.R.E. 7 poſt ualeb̃ . xxvi . lib̃ 7 x . ſol

7 iiii . den̄ . 7 i . ferding . Modo ꞉ xxxvi . lib̃ . 7 x . ſolid̃

7 iiii . den̄ 7 i . ferding.

Ipſe Archieps̃ ten̄ *Edesham* . p̄ xvii . ſolins ſe deſd̃.

Tra . ē   In dn̄io . ii . car̃ ſunt 7 dim̃ . 7 c . uilĺi cū

xiiii . bord̃ hn̄t . xxxvi . car̃ . Ibi . xiii . ac̄ p̃ti . 7 iii . ſerui.

Silua ad clauſurā.

De tra huj⁹ ꝏ ten̄ . ii . milites de archiepo . iii . ſolins . 7 ibi

hn̄t in dn̄io . iiii . car̃ . 7 xviii . uilĺi cū . v . bord̃ hn̄t . i . car̃.

Totū ꝏ . T.R.E. ualeb̃ . xl . lib̃ . Q̃do recep̃ ꞉ ſimiliter.

Modo redd̃ xlvi . lib̃ 7 xvi . ſolid̃ 7 iiii . den̄ . 7 archiepo

. c . ſoł de Garſūnne.

Qd̃ milites ten̄ uał . xi . lib̃ . 7 tam̄ redd̃ . xiii . lib̃.

Ipſe Archieps̃ ten̄ *Werahorne* .   *In Hame Hvnd.*

p̄ uno ſolin ſe defd̃ . Tra . ē . ii . car̃ . In dn̄io . ē . i . car̃.

7 vi . uilĺi cū . iii . bord̃ hn̄t . i . car̃ . Ibi xii . ac̄ p̃ti . 7 ſilua

vi . porc̃ . T.R.E. ꞉ 7 poſt . uał . xx . ſoł . 7 m̊ . lx . ſoł.

In Limowart Lest .   *In Blacheborne Hvnd.*

Ipſe Archieps̃ ten̄ *Apeldres* . T.R.E. ſe defd̃ p̄ . ii . ſolins.

7 m̊ p̄ uno . Tra . ē . viii . car̃ . In dn̄io ſunt . iii . car̃ . 7 xxxvii.

uilĺi cū . xli . bord̃ hn̄t . xi . car̃ . Ibi æccła . 7 vi . piſcariæ

de . iii . ſoł . 7 iiii . den̄ . Ibi . ii . ac̄ p̃ti . 7 ſilua . vi . porc̃.

T.R.E. 7 poſt ꞉ ualeb̃ . vi . lib̃ . Modo ꞉ xvi . lib̃ 7 xvii . ſoł

in EASTRY Lathe
in EASTRY Hundred

17   EASTRY.   It answers for 7 sulungs. Land for ... In lordship 3 ploughs.
     72 villagers with 22 smallholders have 24 ploughs.
     1½ mills at 30s; 3 salt-houses at 4s; meadow, 18 acres;
          woodland, 10 pigs.
     The monks of Canterbury also hold ½ sulung, 1 yoke and 5 acres
in Giddinge. They have
     6 villagers with 2½ ploughs.
In total, value before 1066 and later £26 10s 4¼d; now £36 10s 4¼d.

18   ADISHAM.   It answers for 17 sulungs. Land for ... In lordship
     2½ ploughs.
     100 villagers with 14 smallholders have 36 ploughs.
     Meadow, 13 acres; 3 slaves; woodland for fencing.
     2 men-at-arms hold 3 sulungs of the land of this manor from the
Archbishop. They have 4 ploughs in lordship.
     18 villagers with 5 smallholders have 1 plough.
Value of the whole manor before 1066 £40; when acquired, the same;
now it pays £46 16s 4d; and 100s as a premium to the Archbishop.
Value of what the men-at-arms hold £11; however it pays £13.

in HAM Hundred

19   WAREHORNE.   It answers for 1 sulung. Land for 2 ploughs.
     In lordship 1 plough.
     6 villagers with 3 smallholders have 1 plough.
     Meadow, 12 acres; woodland, 6 pigs.
     Value before 1066 and later 20s; now 60s.

in LYMPNE Lathe
in BLACKBURN Hundred

20   APPLEDORE.   Before 1066 it answered for 2 sulungs; now for 1.
     Land for 8 ploughs. In lordship 3 ploughs.
     37 villagers with 41 smallholders have 11 ploughs.
     A church; 6 fisheries at 3s 4d. Meadow, 2 acres; woodland, 6 pigs.
     Value before 1066 and later £6; now £16 17s 6d.

Ipſe Archieps ten̄ *IN HVND DE WI*   £ 7 vi . den̄.

unū ōō qđ ſe defđ ꝓ uno ſolin T.R.E. 7 m̄ ꝓ dimidio.

Tra . ii . car̄ . In dn̄io . ē una . 7 iii . uilti cū . iiii . borđ hn̄t

ii . car̄ 7 dimid . Ibi æccła . 7 i . molin̄ de . ii . ſoł . 7 ii . ſerui.

7 vii . ãc p̄ti . Silua . x . porc̄ . T.R.E . 7 poſt.́ l . ſoł . m̄ . iiii . lib̄.

Ipſe archieps ten̄ *ASMESLANT* . *IN MARESC DE ROMEN̄*.

ꝓ uno ſolin ſe defđ . Tra . ē . iii . car̄ . Ibi ſunt xxi . uilts.

hn̄tes vii . car̄ . Vał 7 ualuit ſep̄ . liii . ſoł.

De hac tra hт̄ Wilts ſolet . i . jugū . 7 uał ei p annū . x . ſoł.

SANDWIC ſup̄ſcript eſt . p̄tin ad dn̄iū monachoꝝ.

.iiii. ## TERRA EP̄I ROVECESTRE.

Ep̄s Roſenſis ten̄ *SVDFLETA* . ꝓ . vi . ſolins ſe

defđ . Tra . ē . xiii . car̄ . In dn̄io . ē una car̄ . 7 xxv . uilti

cū ix . borđ hn̄tes . xii . car̄ . Ibi vii . ſerui . 7 xx . ãc p̄ti.

Silua . x . porc̄ . Modo ſe defđ ꝓ . v . ſolins . Ibi . ē æccła.

T.R.E . 7 poſt ualuit . xi . lib̄ . Modo . xxi . lib̄ . 7 tam̄ redđ

xxiiii . lib̄ 7 unciā auri .   £ ap̄pciatᵗⁱ . xx . ſoł.

De iſto ōō eſt in Tonebrige tantū de ſilua 7 de tra . qđ

Iſdem ep̄s ten̄ *ESTANES* . T.R.E.ſᵉ defđ ꝓ vi . ſolins . 7 m̄

ꝓ . iiii . ſolins . Tra . ē . xi . car̄ . In dn̄io ſunt . iiᵃᵉ . 7 xx . uilti

cū . xii . borđ hn̄t . xi . car̄ . Ibi . æccła 7 iiii . ſerui . 7 lxxiiᵗᵃ ᵃᵉ.

ãc p̄ti . 7 uñ molđ de . vi . ſoliđ 7 viii . den̄ . 7 una piſcaria

de . iii . ſoł 7 iiii . den̄ . Silua . lx . porc̄ . T.R.E . 7 poſt.

ualeb̄ . xiii . lib̄ . 7 m̄ xvi . lib̄ . 7 tam̄ redđ . xx . lib̄.

7 unā unciā Auri . 7 uñ Marſum . Ricarđ de Tonebrige

ten̄ de iſto ōō tanт̄ ſiluæ qđ uał . xv . ſoł.

in WYE Hundred

21 One manor which answered for 1 sulung before 1066; now for ½.
Land for 2 ploughs. In lordship 1.
   3 villagers with 4 smallholders have 2½ ploughs.
   A church; 1 mill at 2s, 2 slaves; meadow, 7 acres; woodland, 10 pigs.
[Value] before 1066 and later 50s; now £4.

in ROMNEY MARSH

22 Alms-land. It answers for 1 sulung. Land for 3 ploughs.
   21 villagers who have 7 ploughs.
The value is and always was 53s.
   Of this land William Follet has 1 yoke.
Value to him 10s a year.

23 SANDWICH has been entered above. It belongs to the lordship of
the monks.

4   LAND OF THE BISHOP OF ROCHESTER

5 c

1 The Bishop of Rochester holds SOUTHFLEET. It answered for 6
sulungs. Land for 13 ploughs. In lordship 1 plough, and
   25 villagers with 9 smallholders who have 12 ploughs.
   7 slaves; meadow, 20 acres; woodland, 10 pigs. ·
Now it answers for 5 sulungs.
   A church.
Value before 1066 and later £11; now £21; however, it pays £24
and an ounce of gold.
   In Tonbridge there is as much woodland and land from this
manor as is assessed at 20s.
The Bishop also holds

2 STONE. Before 1066 it answered for 6 sulungs; now for 4 sulungs.
Land for 11 ploughs. In lordship 2.
   20 villagers with 12 smallholders have 11 ploughs.
   A church; 4 slaves; meadow, 72 acres; a mill at 6s 8d;
      a fishery at 3s 4d; woodland, 60 pigs.
Value before 1066 and later £13; now £16; however it pays £20,
an ounce of gold and a porpoise.
   Richard of Tonbridge holds as much woodland from this manor
as is valued at 15s.

Isdē eps ten̄ *FACHESHAM* . ᵽ . ii . ſolins ſe defđ . T̄ra . ē

   In dn̄io . ē una car̄ . 7 xv . uiłłi cū . iii . borđ

hn̄t . iiii . car̄ . Ibi æccła 7 iii . ſerui . 7 ii . molini de . xv .

ſoł . 7 iiii . ac̄ ṗti . Silua . xxx . porc̄ . T.R.E . 7 poſt꞉ ua

lebat . vii . liƀ . Modo . viii . liƀ .

Isdē eps ten̄ *LANGAFEL* . 7 Anchitill ᵽbr de eo . ᵽ uno

ſolin ſe defđ . T̄ra . ē   In dn̄io . ē una car̄ . 7 ix . uiłłi

cū . vii . borđ hn̄t . ii . car̄ . Valuit . lxx . ſoł . 7 m̄ . c . ſoliđ .

Isdē eps ten̄ *BRONLEI* . ᵽ . vi .   *IN BRONLEI HVND.*

ſolins ſe defđ . T.R.E . 7 m̄ ᵽ . iii . T̄ra . ē . xiii . car̄ . In dn̄io

ſunt . ii . car̄ . 7 xxx . uiłłi cū . xxvi . borđ hn̄t . xi . car̄ .

Ibi . i . molđ de . iiii . ſoliđ . 7 ii . ac̄ ṗti . Silua . c . porc̄ .

T.R.E . 7 poſt꞉ ualuit . xii . liƀ 7 x . ſoł . Modo . xviii .

liƀ . 7 tam̄ reddit . xxi . liƀ . ii . ſoliđ minus .

Isdē eps ten̄ *OLDEHAM* . ᵽ . vi . ſolins ſe defđ . T.R.E .

7 m̄ ᵽ tribȝ . T̄ra . ē . v . car̄ . In dn̄io ſunt . ii . 7 xviii . uiłłi

cū xvi . borđ hn̄t . vi . car̄ . Ibi . vi . ſerui . 7 i . piſcaria .

7 lx . ac̄ ṗti . Silua . xx . porc̄ . Ibi æccła . T.R.E . 7 poſt꞉

ualuit . viii . liƀ . Modo . xii . liƀ .

Isdē eps ten̄ *MELLINGETES* . ᵽ . iii . ſolins ſe defđ

T.R.E . 7 m̄ ᵽ uno 7 dimiđ . T̄ra . ē . iii . car̄ . In dn̄io . ē

una . 7 v . uiłłi cū . vi . borđ hn̄t . ii . car̄ . Ibi æccła .

7 un̄ molđ de . ii . ſoliđ . Silua . xx . porc̄ . T.R.E . 7 poſt꞉

ualuit . xl . ſoł . 7 m̄ . iiii . liƀ .

Isdē eps ten̄ *TOTESCLIVE* . T.R.E . ᵽ . iii . ſolins ſe

defđ . 7 m̄ ᵽ uno ſolin . T̄ra . ē . iii . car̄ . In dn̄io . ē un̄

ſolin 7 una car̄ ibi . 7 x . uiłłi cū . ii . car̄ . Ibi æccła .

7 i . ſeruus . 7 . ii . ac̄ ṗti . 7 Silua . x . porc̄ . T.R.E . 7 poſt꞉

ualuit . lx . ſoł . 7 m̄ . vii . liƀ .

3   FAWKHAM.   It answers for 2 sulungs. Land for ...
In lordship 1 plough
     15 villagers with 3 smallholders have 4 ploughs.
     A church; 3 slaves; 2 mills at 15s; meadow, 4 acres; woodland, 30
       pigs.
Value before 1066 and later £7; now £8.

4   LONGFIELD and Ansketel the priest from him. It answers for 1 sulung.
Land for ... In lordship 1 plough.
     9 villagers with 7 smallholders have 2 ploughs.
The value was 70s; now 100s.

   in BROMLEY Hundred
5   BROMLEY.   Before 1066 it answered for 6 sulungs; now for 3.
Land for 13 ploughs. In lordship 2 ploughs.
     30 villagers with 26 smallholders have 11 ploughs.
     A mill at 4s; meadow, 2 acres; woodland, 100 pigs.
Value before 1066 and later £12 10s; now £18; however,
       it pays £21 less 2s.

6   WOULDHAM. Before 1066 it answered for 6 sulungs; now for 3.
Land for 5 ploughs. In lordship 2.
     18 villagers with 16 smallholders have 6 ploughs.
     6 slaves; 1 fishery, meadow, 60 acres; woodland, 20 pigs.
     A church.
Value before 1066 and later £8; now £12.

7   (? West) MALLING. Before 1066 it answered for 3 sulungs; now for
1½. Land for 3 ploughs. In lordship 1.
     5 villagers with 6 smallholders have 2 ploughs.
     A church; a mill at 2s; woodland, 20 pigs.
Value before 1066 and later 40s; now £4.

8   TROTTISCLIFFE.   Before 1066 it answered for 3 sulungs; now for 1
sulung. Land for 3 ploughs. In lordship 1 sulung; 1 plough.
     10 villagers with 2 ploughs.
     A church; 1 slave; meadow, 2 acres; woodland, 10 pigs.
Value before 1066 and later 60s; now £7.

Isdē eps ten̄ ESNOILAND . T.R.E. ſe defđ ɹp . vɪ . ſolins.

7 m̄ ɹp . ɪɪɪ. Tra . ē . vɪ . car̄ . In dn̄io ſunt . ɪɪ . car̄ . 7 x.

uiłłi cū . vɪ . borđ hn̄t . vɪ . car̄ . Ibi æccła 7 v . ſerui.

7 ɪɪɪ . molđ de . xL . ſoliđ . 7 xxx . ac̄ p̄ti . Silua . ɪɪɪɪ , porc̄.

T.R.E. 7 poſt. ualeb̄ . vɪ . lib̄ , 7 m̄ . ɪx . lib̄.

5 d

Isdē eps ten̄ COCLESTANE . IN ESSAMELE HVND.

ɹp . ɪɪ . ſolins 7 dimiđ ſe defđ T.R.E. 7 m̄ ɹp . ɪɪ. tan̄t . Tra . ē

vɪ . car̄ . In dn̄io ſunt . ɪɪ . 7 xv . uiłłi cū . ɪx . borđ hn̄t v . car̄.

Ibi æccła 7 ɪɪ . ſerui . 7 ɪ . molin̄ de xxx . den̄ . 7 xx . ac̄ p̄ti.

T.R.E. 7 poſt. ualeb̄ . ɪɪɪɪ . lib̄ 7 x . ſoł . 7 m̄ x . lib̄ 7 x . ſoliđ.

Isdē eps ten̄ DANITONE . ɹp . ɪɪ . ſolins ſe defđ T.R.E. 7 m̄

ɹp dimiđ ſolin . Tra . ē . ɪɪ . car̄ . In dn̄io . ē una . 7 vɪ . uiłłi hn̄t

ibi . ɪ . car̄ . Ibi æccła 7 ɪɪɪɪ . ſerui . 7 ɪɪɪɪ . ac̄ p̄ti . Silua . xv . porc̄.

T.R.E. 7 poſt. ualeb̄ . c . ſoł . 7 m̄ . vɪɪ . lib̄ 7 xv . ſoliđ.

Isdē eps ten̄ HALLINGES . T.R.E. ſe defđ ɹp . vɪ . ſolins . 7 m̄

ɹp . ɪɪ. 7 dimiđ . Tra . ē . vɪɪ . car̄ . In dn̄io ſunt . ɪɪɪ . car̄ . 7 xv . uiłłi

cū . ɪx . borđ hn̄t . vɪ . car̄ . Ibi æccła 7 ɪɪ . ſerui . 7 xxx . ac̄ p̄ti.

7 ſilua . v . porc̄ . T.R.E. 7 poſt ualeb̄ . vɪɪ . lib̄ . M̄ xvɪ . lib̄ . Qđ Ricard ten in ſua leu: ual.vɪɪ.ſot.

Isdē eps ten̄ FRANDESBERIE . ɹp . x . ſolins ſe defđ T.R.E.

7 m̄ ɹp . vɪɪ . Tra . ē . xv . car̄ . In dn̄io ſunt . v . car̄ . 7 xL . uiłłi cū

xxvɪɪɪ . borđ hn̄t . xɪ . car̄ . Ibi æccła 7 ɪx . ſerui . 7 un̄ molin̄ de

xɪɪ . ſoł . 7 xL . ac̄ p̄ti . Silua . v . porc̄ . T.R.E. 7 poſt ualeb̄ . vɪɪɪ.

lib̄ . 7 m̄ . xxv . lib̄ . Qđ Ricard ten in ſua Leuua: ual . x . ſoł.

Isdē eps ten̄ BORCHETELLE . IN HVND DE ROVECESTRE..

T.R.E. ɹp . ɪɪ . ſolins ſe defđ . 7 m̄ ɹp uno ſolin 7 dimiđ . Tra . ē . ɪɪɪɪ.

car̄ . In dn̄io ſunt . ɪɪ . car̄ . 7 vɪ . uiłłi cū . ɪɪɪ . car̄ . Ibi . L . ac̄ p̄ti.

7 ɪɪ . molini de . xx . ſoliđ . T.R.E. 7 poſt. ualeb̄ . vɪ . lib̄ . 7 modo

x . lib̄.

9   SNODLAND. Before 1066 it answered for 6 sulungs; now for 3.
Land for 6 ploughs. In lordship 2 ploughs.
   10 villagers with 6 smallholders have 6 ploughs.
    A church; 5 slaves; 3 mills at 40s; meadow, 30 acres;
      woodland, 4 pigs.
Value before 1066 and later £6; now £9.

5 d

in SHAMWELL Hundred

10   CUXTON. Before 1066 it answered for 2½ sulungs; now for only 2.
Land for 6 ploughs. In lordship 2.
   15 villagers with 9 smallholders have 5 ploughs.
    A church; 2 slaves; 1 mill at 30d; meadow, 20 acres.
Value before 1066 and later £4 10s; now £10 10s.

11   DENTON. Before 1066 it answered for 2 sulungs; now for ½ sulung.
Land for 2 ploughs. In lordship 1.
   6 villagers have 1 plough.
    A church; 4 slaves; meadow, 4 acres; woodland, 15 pigs.
Value before 1066 and later 100s; now £7 15s.

12   HALLING. Before 1066 it answered for 6 sulungs; now for 2½.
Land for 7 ploughs. In lordship 3 ploughs.
   15 villagers with 9 smallholders have 6 ploughs.
    A church; 2 slaves; meadow, 30 acres; woodland, 5 pigs.
Value before 1066 and later £7; now £16. Value of what Richard
holds in his territory 7s.

13   FRINDSBURY. Before 1066 it answered for 10 sulungs; now 7.
Land for 15 ploughs. In lordship 5 ploughs.
   40 villagers with 28 smallholders have 11 ploughs.
    A church; 9 slaves; a mill at 12s; meadow, 40 acres;
      woodland, 5 pigs.
Value before 1066 and later £8; now £25. Value of what Richard
holds in his territory 10s.

in the Hundred of ROCHESTER

14   BORSTALL. Before 1066 it answered for 2 sulungs; now for 1½
sulungs. Land for 4 ploughs. In lordship 2 ploughs;
   6 villagers with 3 ploughs.
   Meadow, 50 acres; 2 mills at 20s.
Value before 1066 and later £6; now £10.

In Rovecestre habuit eps 7 ht̃ adhuc q̃t xx . mãnſuras
trae quae p̃tin ad Frandeſberie 7 Borcſtele p̃pa ej̃ maneria.
T.R.E. 7 poſt: ualebãɴ . III . lib̃ . m̃ ualeɴ . VIII . lib̃ . 7 tam̃
p̃ annũ reddunt . XI . lib̃ 7 XIII . ſot 7 IIII . denar̃.

Iſdẽ eps ten *Estoches* . T.R.E. ſe defð *In How Hvnd*.
p̃ v . ſolins . 7 m̃ p̃ trib̃ . Tra . ẽ . v . car̃ . In dñio ſunt . II . car̃.
7 x . uilti cũ . v . borð hñt . IIII . car̃ . Ibi aeccła 7 IIII . ſerui.
7 IIII . ãc p̃ti . T.R.E. 7 poſt 7 modo uał . VIII . lib̃ 7 xx . den̄.
7 tam̃ reddit qui tenet . XIII . lib̃ 7 xx . denar̃.

Hoc m̃ fuit 7 eſt de epiſcopatu rofenſi . ſed Goduin̄
comes T.R.E. emit illud de duob̃ hõib₂ qui eũ teneð
de epo . 7 eo ignorante facta . ẽ haec uenditio.

Poſtmodũ ũ regnante W . rege . diratiocinauit
illud Lanfranc̃ archiep̃s c̃tra baiocenſẽ ep̃m . et
inde eſt m̃ ſaiſita rofenſis aeccła.

Terra Ep̃i Baiocensis.

In Lest De Svdtone.   *In Achestan Hvnð.*

.v. **D**e epo Baiocenſi ten̄ Hugo de porth *Hagelei*.
p̃ dimidio ſolin ſe defð . Tra . ẽ .   In dñio ſunt . III .
car̃ . 7 XIIII . uilti cũ . III . borð hñt . IIII . car̃ . Ibi . III . ſerui . 7 XII .
ãc p̃ti . 7 uñ mold de . xx . ſot . 7 una dena ſiluae de . v . porc̃.
Tot̃ m̃ uał m̃ . xv . lib̃ . de . xx . in ora.
In hoc m̃ ten̄ un hõ . xx . ãcs trae . ualentes p̃ annũ . v . ſot . Vluret
uocat̃ . nec p̃tin ad illud m̃ . neq₂ potuit habe dñm p̃t regẽ.

Helto ten̄ *Svinescamp* de epo . p̃ x . ſolins ſe defð.
Tra . ẽ . XIIII . car̃ . In dñio ſunt . III . 7 XXXIII . uilti cũ . III . borð
hñt XIII . car̃ . Ibi uñ miles 7 x . ſerui . 7 XL . ãc p̃ti . Silua
III . porc̃ . 7 v . piſcariae de . xxx . den̄ . 7 vI . que ſeruit ad hallã.
7 una heda de . v . ſolið . 7 IIII . den̄ . De Silua huj̃ m̃ tenet
Ricard̃ in ſua leuua qð . uał . IIII . ſolið.
Totũ m̃ ualeb̃ xx . lib̃ .   7 m̃ uał XXXII . lib̃.

5 d, 6 a

15   In ROCHESTER the Bishop had and still has 80 dwellings of the land which belongs to Frindsbury and Borstall, his own manors. Value before 1066 and later £3; value now £8; however, they pay £11 13s 4d a year.

In HOO Hundred

16   The Bishop also holds STOKE. Before 1066 it answered for 5 sulungs; now for 3. Land for 5 ploughs. In lordship 2 ploughs.

      10 villagers with 5 smallholders have 4 ploughs.

      A church; 4 slaves; meadow, 4 acres.

Value before 1066, later and now £8 0s 20d; however, it's holder pays £13 0s 20d.

    This manor was and is the Bishopric of Rochester's, but Earl Godwin bought it before 1066 from two men who held it from the Bishop. This sale was made without his knowledge, but afterwards, in the reign of King William, Archbishop Lanfranc proved (his claim to) it against the Bishop of Bayeux; and so the Church of Rochester is in possession.

5   **LAND OF THE BISHOP OF BAYEUX**   6 a

In the [Half-] lathe of SUTTON
In AXTON Hundred

1   Hugh of Port holds HAWLEY from the Bishop of Bayeux. It answers for ½ sulung. Land for ... In lordship 2 ploughs.

      14 villagers with 3 smallholders have 4 ploughs.

      3 slaves; meadow, 12 acres; a mill at 20s; 1 pig pasture of woodland at 5 pigs.

Value of the whole manor now £15 at 20 (pence) to the *ora*.

    In this manor one man holds 20 acres of land which are valued at 5s a year. He is called Wilfred and he does not belong to that manor nor could he have any lord except the King.

From the Bishop

2   Helto holds SWANSCOMBE. It answers for 10 sulungs.

Land for 14 ploughs. In lordship 3.

      33 villagers with 3 smallholders have 13 ploughs. 1 man-at-arms; 10 slaves.

      Meadow, 40 acres; woodland, 3 pigs; 5 fisheries at 30d; a sixth which serves the hall; 1 landing place at 5s 4d.

    Of the woodland of this manor Richard holds in his territory what is valued at 4s.

Value of the whole manor £20; value now £32.

Radulf fili Turaldi ten de epo ERCLEI . p uno solin se

defd . Tra . e̅   In d̅nio sunt . ii . car̅ . 7 ix . uilti cu̅ . vi .

cot h̅nt . iii . car̅ . Ibi . iii . serui . 7 silua . x . porc̅ .

Tot̅ m̅ uale̅b . iii . li̅b .   7 m̅ . c . sol . Quæda̅ mulier tenuit .

Radulf ten de epo EDDINTONE . p dimid solin .

Tra . e̅ . i . car̅ . 7 ibi . e̅ cu̅ . iiii . bord 7 ii . seruis . 7 ibi . i . molin

de . xxiii . sol . Totu̅ m̅ appciat . iiii . li̅b . T . R . E . paru̅ uale̅b .

Lestan tenuit de rege E . 7 post morte̅ ej uertit se ad

Alnod . 7 m̅ est in calu̅pnia .

Ansgot de Roueceftre ten de epo MAPLEDESCAM . p di

midio solin . Tra . e̅   In d̅nio . e̅ . i . car̅ . cu̅ uno uilto 7 iiii .

bord . 7 iiii . seruis . Ibi una ac̅ p̅ti . 7 silua viii . porc̅ . 7 xvi .

denar plus . Valuit . iiii . li̅b .   7 m̅ . c x . sol .

Euftan tenuit de rege . E .

Ada̅ filius Hu̅bti ten de epo REDLEGE . p uno solin se

defd . Tra . e̅   In d̅nio sunt . ii . car̅ . 7 vi . uilti cu̅ . v . bord .

h̅nt . ii . car̅ . Ibi . v . serui . 7 dim ac̅ p̅ti . 7 una dena siluæ

qua̅ ten Ricard de Tonebrige . Valuit | iii . li̅b . 7 m̅ . iiii . li̅b .

7 x . sol . Siuuard tenuit de rege . E .

Hugo de port ten de epo EISSE . p trib͡z solins se defd .

Tra . e̅   In d̅nio . e̅ una car̅ . 7 xii . uilti cu̅ . viii . bord

h̅nt . iii . car̅ . Ibi q̅da̅ miles h̅ns . viii . int̅ seruos 7 ancillas .

7 tra̅ ad una̅ car̅ . Præter hoc h̅ Hugo . ii . hōes tenentes

dimid solin . qui potera̅ . T . R . E . ire quolibet sine licentia .

Vna tra uocat Didele . 7 alia Soninges . Tra . e̅ ibi . ad una̅ car̅ .

7 appciat . xx . sol . Tot̅ m̅ appciabat . vii . li̅b . 7 m̅ similit̅ .

Q̅d Ricard ten de Tonebrige . xl . sol . appciat . Rex h̅

inde . ii . denas . quæ appciant . vii . sol . Godric tenuit

de rege . E .

3   Ralph son of Thorold holds HARTLEY.   It answers for 1 sulung.
Land for ...   In lordship 2 ploughs.
   9 villagers with 6 cottagers have 3 ploughs.
   3 slaves; woodland, 10 pigs.
Value of the whole manor £3; now 100s.
   A woman held it.

4   Ralph holds EDDINTONE. It answers for ½ sulung.
Land for 1 plough; it is there, with
   4 smallholders and 2 slaves.
   1 mill at 23s.
The whole manor is assessed at £4; value before 1066 a little more.
   Leofstan held it from King Edward; after his death it went to
Young Alnoth; now it is in dispute.

5   Ansgot of Rochester holds MAPLESCOMBE for ½ sulung.
Land for ...   In lordship 1 plough, with
   1 villager, 4 smallholders and 4 slaves.
   Meadow, 1 acre; woodland, 8 pigs and 16d too.
The value was £4; now 110s.
   Alstan held it from King Edward.

6   Adam son of Hubert holds RIDLEY.   It answers for 1 sulung.
Land for ...   In lordship 2 ploughs.
   6 villagers with 5 smallholders have 2 ploughs.
   5 slaves; meadow, ½ acre; 1 pig pasture of woodland which
      Richard of Tonbridge holds.
The value of the manor was £3; now £4 10s.
   Siward held it from King Edward.

7   Hugh of Port holds ASH.   It answers for 3 sulungs.
Land for ...   In lordship 1 plough.
   12 villagers with 8 smallholders have 3 ploughs. A man-at-arms
      who has 8 male and female slaves; land for 1 plough.
   In addition to this Hugh has 2 men who hold ½ sulung, who
could go where ever they would before 1066 without permission.
   One piece of land is called Idleigh, another 'Sonnings'.
Land for 1 plough. It is assessed at 20s.
The whole manor was assessed at £7; now the same; what
Richard of Tonbridge holds is assessed at 40s.
   From it the King has 2 pig pastures which are assessed
at 7s. Godric held it from King Edward.

Goisfrid de Ros ten *LOLINGESTONE* . p uno folin fe defd.

Tra . ē   In dñio . ē una car . 7 iiii . uilli cū uno cot hñt

ii . car . Ibi . vii . ferui . 7 vi . ac pafturæ . Silua . xx . porc.

Qdo recep. ualeb . lx . fot . 7 m . c . fot . Rex ht in manu fua

qd uat . x . folid . Brixe cilt tenuit de rege . E.

6 b

De epo ten Malgeri *LOLINGESTONE* . p dim folin.

fe defd . Tra . ē.   In dñio . ē una car . 7 iii . uilli

cū . vi . bord hñt . i . car . Ibi . v . ac pti:

Totū m̄ ualeb . lx . fot . modo . lxx . fot . De ifto m̄ ht

Rex qd uat . x . folid . Bruning tenuit de rege . E.

Ifdē Malgeri ten in *FERLINGEHA* . dimid jugū træ.

Tra . ē . iii . bou . Ibi funt . ii . boues . cū uno bord . 7 ii . ac pti.

Valuit 7 uat . xv . fot . Brunefune tenuit . 7 potuit

cū tra fua uertere fe quo uoluit : De hoc m̄ ten rex

qd uat . viii . fot.

Ifdē Malgeri ten in Pinnedene . dimid folin de epo.

Tra . ē . vii . bou . Ibi . ē una car cū . vi . uiltis . 7 vi . ac pti:

Valuit 7 uat . xvi . fot : Aluret tenuit T . R . E . 7 potuit

fe uertere quo uoluit.

Osbnus paftforeire ten in Lolingefton dimid folin

de epo . Tra . ē   In dñio . ē . i . car . 7 iii . uilli cū . i . bord

7 . i . feruo hñt . i . car . Ibi . v . ac pti . Silua . v . porc . 7 uñ

moliñ de . xv . folid . 7 cl . anguill . Rex ht filuā p nouo

dono epi . 7 uat . iii . fot . Totū m̄ ualeb . lx . fot . Modo

lxxvii . fot . Seuuart fot tenuit . T . R . E . 7 potuit fe

uertere cū tra fua quo uoluit.

Wadard ten de epo dimid folin in Ferningeha:

Tra . ē . iii . car . In dñio funt . ii . car . cū uno uilto 7 ii . cot.

7 v . feruis . Ibi dimid mold de . v . folins . 7 iiii . ac pti . Silua

v . porc . Excepto i̇ fto dim folin . ten Wadard dimid jugū

in ead uilla . qd nunq̇ fe quietauit apud regē . Int

8 Geoffrey of Rots holds LULLINGSTONE. It answers for 1 sulung.
Land for ... In lordship 1 plough.
    4 villagers with 1 cottager have 2 ploughs.
    7 slaves; pasture, 6 acres; woodland, 20 pigs.
Value when acquired 60s; now 100s; the King has in his hand
what is valued at 10s.
    Young Brictsi held it from King Edward.

9 Mauger holds LULLINGSTONE from the Bishop. It answers for ½   6 b
sulung. Land for ... In lordship 1 plough.
    3 villagers with 6 smallholders have 1 plough.
    Meadow, 5 acres.
The value of the whole manor was 60s; now 70s; of that manor
the King has what is valued at 10s.
    Browning held it from King Edward.

10 Mauger also holds ½ yoke of land in FARNINGHAM. Land
for 3 oxen. 2 oxen, with
    1 smallholder.
    Meadow, 2 acres.
The value was and is 15s.
    Brown's son held it and could go where he would with his land.
Of this manor the King holds what is valued at 8s.

11 Mauger also holds ½ sulung in PINDEN from the Bishop.
Land for 7 oxen. 1 plough, with
    6 villagers.
    Meadow, 6 acres.
The value was and is 16s.
    Alfred held it before 1066 and could go where he would.

12 Osbern Paisforiere holds ½ sulung in LULLINGSTONE from the Bishop.
Land for ... In lordship 1 plough.
    3 villagers with 1 smallholder and 1 slave have 1 plough.
    Meadow, 5 acres; woodland, 5 pigs; a mill at 15s and 150 eels.
    The King has a wood as a new gift of the Bishop; value 3s.
The value of the whole manor was 60s; now 77s.
    Siward Sot held it before 1066 and could go where he would
with his land.

13 Wadard holds ½ sulung in FARNINGHAM from the Bishop.
Land for 3 ploughs. In lordship 2 ploughs, with
    1 villager, 2 cottagers and 5 slaves.
    ½ mill at 5s; meadow, 4 acres; woodland, 5 pigs.
    Apart from that ½ sulung Wadard holds ½ yoke in the same
village which never was exempt (from tax) to the King.

totū ualuit iiii . liɓ . 7 m̃ . vi . liɓ . Eſtan tenuit . T . R . E .

7 potuit ſe uertere quo uoluit.

Iſđ Wadard teñ de epō *MALPLESCAP* . ꝓ dim̃ ſolin ſe
defđ . Tra . e̅ . ii . car̄ . Ibi ſunt cū . i . uillo 7 iiii . borđ 7 v.
ſeruis . 7 una ac̄ · 7 dim p̃ti . Silua . viii . porc̄ 7 xvi . denar̄.
Valuit . iii . liɓ . 7 m̃ . vi . liɓ . Vltan tenuit ſub Heraldo.

Ernulf de Heſding teñ *FERNINGEHĀ* . ꝓ . iii . jugis
ſe defđ . Tra . e̅ . ii . car̄ . Ibi ſunt m̃ . vi . boues cū . ii . uillis
7 iii . borđ . Ibi uñ molđ de . x . ſoł . 7 viii . ac̄ p̃ti . Paſtura
c . ouib̄ . Silua . x . porc̄ 7 xiiii . den . Rex h̄t de ſilua
huj m̃ . qđ uat . viii . ſoł . Totū m̃ ualuit . iii . liɓ . 7 m̃
xl . ſoliđ . Dering tenuit . 7 potuit ſe uertere quo uoluit.

Anſchitillus de ros teñ *TARENT* de epō . ꝓ dim̃ ſolin
ſe defđ . Tra . e̅ . i . car̄ 7 dim̃ . In dño . e̅ una . 7 iiii . uilli
cū . iiii . borđ h̃nt . i . car̄ . Ibi . iii . ac̄ p̃ti . 7 ii . molini de . xviii.
ſoł . Silua . iii . porc̄ . Rex h̄t de iſto m̃ ꝓ nouo dono epi
qđ uat . x . denar̄ . Totū m̃ ualuit 7 uat . c . ſoł . Aluric
tenuit de rege . E.

In eađ uilla h̄t iſđe . A . i . manerium de epō . ꝓ dim̃
ſolin ſe defđ . Tra . e̅ . i . car̄ 7 dimiđ . Ibi . v . uilti 7 v . borđ
7 uñ molđ de . xx . ſoliđ . Ibi . iii . ac̄ p̃ti . 7 i . ſeru .
Totū m̃ ualuit . lx . ſoł . 7 modo . lxx . ſoliđ . Oſiert
tenuit de rege . E.

Iſđe Anſchitill teñ de epō *HORTVNE* . ꝓ uno ſolin ſe

6 c   ꝟ defđ.

Tra . e̅ . iii . car̄ . 7 ibi ſunt . iiii . borđ 7 uñ molđ de . v . ſoł.
7 vi . ac̄ p̃ti . Ibi æccła . e̅ . 7 ſilua . iii . porc̄ . Rex h̄t ꝓ nouo
dono epi tant̄ ſiluæ de iſto m̃ . qđ uat . v . ſoł . Totū m̃
ualuit . iiii . liɓ . 7 m̃ . vi . liɓ . Godel de Brixi tenuit.
7 potuit ſe uertere cū hac tra quo uoluit.

Iſđe Anſchitill teñ de epō in eođ m̃ dimiđ ſolin . Tra . e̅
uñ car̄ . 7 ibi . e̅ in dño . 7 viii . uilti cū . vi . borđ h̃nt . i . car̄.

In total the value was £4, now £6.
Alstan held it before 1066 and could go where he would.

14 Wadard also holds MAPLESCOMBE from the Bishop. It answers
for ½ sulung. Land for 2 ploughs. They are there, with
1 villager, 4 smallholders and 5 slaves.
Meadow, 1½ acres; woodland, 8 pigs and 16d.
The value was £3; now £6.
Wulfstan held it under Harold.

15 Arnulf of Hesdin holds FARNINGHAM. It answers for 3 yokes.
Land for 2 ploughs. Now 6 oxen, with
2 villagers and 3 smallholders.
A mill at 10s; meadow, 8 acres; pasture, 100 sheep; woodland
10 pigs and 14d.
Of the woodland of this manor the King has what is valued at 8s.
The value of the whole manor was £3; now 40s.
Dering held it and could go where he would.

16 Ansketel of Rots holds DARENTH from the Bishop. It answers for
½ sulung. Land for 1½ ploughs. In lordship 1.
4 villagers with 4 smallholders have 1 plough.
Meadow, 3 acres; 2 mills at 18s; woodland, 3 pigs.
Of that manor the King has what is valued at 10d as a new
gift of the Bishop.
The value of the whole manor was and is 100s.
Aelfric held it from King Edward.

17 In the same village Ansketel also has 1 manor from the Bishop. It
answers for ½ sulung. Land for 1½ ploughs.
5 villagers and 5 smallholders.
A mill at 20s; meadow, 3 acres; 1 slave.
The value of the whole manor was 60s; now 70s.
Osgeard held it from King Edward.

18 Ansketel also holds HORTON (Kirby) from the bishop. It answers
for 1 sulung. Land for 3 ploughs.   6 c
4 smallholders.
A mill at 5s; meadow, 6 acres. A church; woodland, 3 pigs.
The King has as a new gift of the Bishop as much woodland
of that manor as is valued at 5s.
The value of the whole manor was £4; now £6.
Godel held it from Brictsi and could go where he would
with this land.
Ansketel also holds ½ sulung in the same manor from the Bishop.
Land for 1 plough. It is there in lordship.
8 villagers with 6 smallholders have 1 plough.

Ibi . I . moliñ de xv . ſot . 7 IX . ãc p̃ti . Silua . v . porc̃.

Totū m̃ ualuit . xL . ſot . 7 m̃ . Lx . Ording tenuit de rege.

Iſdē Anſchitill ten de ep̃o in eod̃ m̃ unū ſolin . T̃ra . ẽ

III . car̃ . In dñio eſt una car̃ . 7 VIII . uiłłi cū . II . car̃ . Ibi

uñ ſeruus . 7 VIII . ãc p̃ti . dim mold de . v . ſolid . Silua

xv . porc̃ . Totū m̃ ualuit . IIII . lib̃ . 7 m̃ . c . ſolid.

Aluuard tenuit de Heraldo . H̃ . IIII . Maneria.

ſunt m̃ p̃ uno m̃   *IN LITELAI HVND.*

Rob̃t Latiñ ten de ep̃o *LOISNES* . T̃ra . ẽ . xvII.

car̃ . In dñio . ẽ una . 7 Lx . uiłłi cū . III . bord h̃nt . xv.

car̃ . Ibi . II . ſerui . 7 III . cot . 7 III . piſcariæ de . IIII . ſot.

7 xxx . ãc p̃ti . Silua . xx . porc̃ . T . R . E . ual . xx . lib̃.

Q̃do ep̃s recep̃ . xvIII . lib̃ . 7 m̃ xxII . lib̃ . 7 tam

qui ten redd̃ . xxx . lib̃ . Hoc m̃ ſe defd̃ T . R . E.

p̃ . x . ſolins . 7 m̃ p̃ . IIII . ſolins . Azor tenuit.

Anſgot ten de ep̃o *HOV* . qd̃ ſe defd̃ p̃ uno ſolin.

T̃ra . ẽ   In dñio . ẽ una car̃ . 7 v . uiłłi cū . I . car̃

7 dimid . 7 uñ mold de . x . ſot . Ibi . II . cot 7 uñ ſeruus.

7 xII . ãc p̃ti . Silua . III . porc̃ . T . R . E . ualeb̃ Lx . ſot . Q̃do

recep̃ . tntd̃ . 7 m̃ . IIII . lib̃ . Anſchil de rege E . tenuit.

Abb̃ S̃ Auguſtini ten de ep̃o baioceñſi *PLVMESTEDE.*

p̃ . II . ſolins 7 uno jugo ſe defd̃ . T̃ra . v . car̃ . In dñio . ẽ

una car̃ . 7 xvII . uiłłi cū . III . bord h̃nt . IIII . car̃ . Ibi

ſilua . v . porc̃ . T . R . E . ualeb̃ . x . lib̃ . Q̃do recep̃ . vIII . lib̃.

7 m̃ tntd̃ . 7 tam qui ten redd̃ . xII . lib̃ . Brixi cilt

tenuit de rege . E .   *IN HELMESTREI HVND.*

Malgeri ten de ep̃o *ROCHELEI* . p̃ uno ſolin ſe defd̃.

T̃ra . ẽ   In dñio . ẽ una car̃ 7 dimid . 7 x . uiłłi

cū . x . bord h̃nt . II . car̃ 7 dim . Ibi . I . moliñ de . xII.

ſolid . Silua . III . porc̃ . T . R . E . ualeb̃ . IIII . lib̃ Q̃do recep̃.

III . lib̃ . 7 m̃ . c . ſolid . Aluuard tenuit de rege . E.

1 mill at 15s; meadow, 9 acres; woodland, 5 pigs.
The value of the whole manor was 40s; now 60s.
Ording held it from the King.
Ansketel also holds 1 sulung in the same manor from the Bishop.
Land for 3 ploughs. In lordship 1 plough;
8 villagers with 2 ploughs. 1 slave.
Meadow, 8 acres; ½ mill at 5s; woodland, 15 pigs.
The value of the whole manor was £4; now 100s.
Alfward held it from Harold.
Now there are 4 manors in place of 1 manor.

In LITTLE Hundred

19 Robert Latimer holds LESSNESS from the Bishop. Land for 17
ploughs. In lordship 1.
60 villagers with 3 smallholders have 15 ploughs. 2 slaves.
3 cottagers.
3 fisheries at 4s; meadow, 30 acres; woodland, 20 pigs.
Value before 1066 £20; when the Bishop acquired it £18; now
£22; however, its holder pays £30.
This manor answered for 10 sulungs before 1066; now 4 sulungs.
Azor held it.

20 Ansgot holds HOWBURY from the Bishop which answers for 1 sulung.
Land for ... In lordship 1 plough,
5 villagers with 1½ ploughs.
A mill at 10s.
2 cottagers and 1 slave.
Meadow, 12 acres; woodland, 3 pigs.
Value before 1066, 60s; when acquired as much; now £4.
Askell held it from King Edward.

21 The Abbot of St. Augustine's holds PLUMSTEAD from the Bishop of
Bayeux. It answers for 2 sulungs and 1 yoke. Land for 5 ploughs.
In lordship 1 plough.
17 villagers with 3 smallholders have 4 ploughs.
Woodland, 5 pigs.
Value before 1066 £10; when acquired £8; now as much;
however, its holder pays £12.
Young Brictsi held it from King Edward.

In RUXLEY Hundred
From the Bishop

22 Mauger holds RUXLEY. It answers for 1 sulung. Land for ...
In lordship 1½ ploughs.
10 villagers with 10 smallholders have 2½ ploughs.
1 mill at 12s; woodland, 3 pigs.
Value before 1066 £4; when acquired £3; now 100s.
Alfward held it from King Edward.

Ernulf de hesding ten de epo CIRESFEL.

.p. ii. solins se defd. Tra. e̅   In dn̅io sunt. ii. car̅.

7 xx. uitti cu̅. iiii. bord hn̅t. viii. car̅. Ibi. iiii. serui.

7 un̅ molin de. x. sol. 7 x. ac̅ p̅ti. 7 silua. x. porc.

T.R.E. uale b̅ xvi. lib̅. 7 post. xii. lib̅. 7 m̅ xxv. lib̅.

7 tam qui ten redd. xxx.v. lib̅. Tochi tenuit de rege. E.

Ada̅ fili Hubti ten de epo SVDCRAI .p uno solin se

defd. Tra. e̅.   In dn̅io sunt. ii. car̅. 7 xiiii. uitti

cu̅. i. bord hn̅t. iiii. car̅. Ibi. vi : serui. 7 x. ac̅ p̅ti.

Silua. x. porc. T.R.E. uale b̅. vi. lib̅. 7 post. iiii. lib̅.

7 modo. x. lib̅. Toli tenuit de rege. E.

Isde̅ Ada̅ ten de epo WICHEHA .p uno solin se defd.

6 d

Tra. e̅   In dn̅io sunt. ii. car̅. 7 xxiiii. uitti hn̅t. iiii. car̅.

Ibi. xiii. serui. 7 una æccta. 7 un̅ molin de. xx. den̅. 7 una silua

de. x. porc. T.R.E. uale b̅. viii. lib̅. 7 post. vi. lib̅. 7 m̅. xiii. lib̅.

fit carle
Godric tenuit de rege. E.

Goisfrid de ros ten de epo LASELA .p. vii. solins se defd.

Tra. e̅   In dn̅io sunt. iii. car̅. 7 xxxi. uitts cu̅. xiiii. bord

hn̅t xvi. car̅. Ibi. x. serui. 7 una piscar̅ de q̅t xx. anguitt. 7 x.

Silua. lxxv. porc. Totu̅ M̅ uale b̅. T.R.E. xxx. lib̅. Qdo recep:

xvi. lib̅. 7 m̅. xxiiii. lib̅ qd Goisfrid ten. Ricard de Tone

brige qd ten in Leuua sua. appciat. vi. lib̅. Qd rex tenet

de hoc manerio: xxii. sol. Brixi cilt tenuit de rege. E.

Anschitil de ros ten de epo CRAIE .p dim̅ solin se defd.

Tra. e̅.   In dn̅io. e̅. i. car̅. 7 vii. uitti cu̅. vi. bord hn̅t

una̅ car̅. Ibi æccta. 7 una ac̅ p̅ti. 7 iii. ac̅ pasturæ.

T.R.E. 7 post. uale b̅. iiii. lib̅. 7 m̅. iii. lib̅. Leuric tenuit de rege. E.

Isde̅ Anschitill ten de epo alia CRAIE .p dim̅ solin se defd.

Tra. e̅   In dn̅io. e̅ una car̅. 7 vii. uitti cu̅. v. bord

hn̅t. i. car̅. Ibi. i. molin de. xlii. den̅. 7 v. serui. Silua. vii. porc.

T.R.E. 7 post. ualuit. iiii. lib̅. 7 m̅: iii. lib̅.   de Alnod cilt.

Hæ duæ træ fuer̅. ii. M̅ T.R.E. 7 m̅ sunt in uno. M̅. Aluuin tenuit

23   Arnulf of Hesdin holds CHELSFIELD. It answers for 2 sulungs.
Land for ... In lordship 2 ploughs.
   20 villagers with 4 smallholders have 8 ploughs.
   4 slaves; a mill at 10s; meadow, 10 acres; woodland, 10 pigs.
Value before 1066 £16; later £12; now £25; however, its holder
pays £35.
   Toki held it from King Edward.

24   Adam son of Hubert holds (St Mary) CRAY. It answers for 1 sulung.
Land for ... In lordship 2 ploughs.
   14 villagers with 1 smallholder have 4 ploughs.
   6 slaves; meadow, 10 acres; woodland, 10 pigs.
Value before 1066 £6; later £4; now £10.
   Toli held it from King Edward.

25   Adam also holds (West) WICKHAM. It answers for 1 sulung.   6 d
Land for ... In lordship 2 ploughs.
   24 villagers have 4 ploughs.
   13 slaves; a church; a mill at 20d; a wood at 10 pigs.
Value before 1066 £8; later £6; now £13.
   Godric son of Karl held it from King Edward.

26   Geoffrey of Rots holds SEAL. It answers for 7 sulungs.
Land for ... In lordship 3 ploughs.
   31 villagers with 14 smallholders have 16 ploughs.
   10 slaves; a fishery at 90 eels; woodland, 75 pigs.
Value of the whole manor before 1066 £30; when acquired £16;
now what Geoffrey holds £24. What Richard of Tonbridge holds
in his territory is assessed at £6; what the King holds from this
manor 22s.
   Young Brictsi held it from King Edward.

27   Ansketel of Rots holds (NORTH) CRAY. It answers for ½ sulung.
Land for ... In lordship 1 plough.
   7 villagers with 6 smallholders have 1 plough.
   A church; meadow, 1 acre; pasture, 3 acres.
Value before 1066 and later £4; now £3.
   Leofric held it from King Edward.

28   Ansketel also holds another (St Paul's) CRAY. It answers for ½ sulung.
Land for ... In lordship 1 plough.
   7 villagers with 5 smallholders have 1 plough.
   1 mill at 42d; 5 slaves; woodland, 7 pigs.
Value before 1066 and later £4; now £3.
   These two lands were 2 manors before 1066; now they are in
1 manor.
   Alwin held them from Young Alnoth.

Eps Lisiacensis teñ de epo baioc̄si GRENVIZ . p̄ . II . solins
se deſd . T̄ra . ē   In dn̄io sunt . II . car̄ . 7 XXIIII . uitti hn̄t
IIII . car̄ . 7 IIII . bord 7 I . cot̄ . 7 v . serui . Ibi . IIII . mold de . LXX . sot.
7 XXI . ac̄ p̄ti . 7 XL . ac̄ pasturæ . 7 Silua . x . porc.
Hi . II . solins T.R.E. fuer̄ . II . M̄. Vn̄u tenuit Herold . 7 aliū
Brixi . 7 m̄ sunt in uno . T.R.E 7 post. ǀualeba‷ . VIII . liħ.
7 modo ap̄pciant . XII . liħ.

H̄aimo ten de epo ALTEHĀ . p̄ uno solin 7 dim̄ se deſd . T̄ra
ē XII . car̄ . In dn̄io sunt . II . car̄ . 7 XL.II . uitti cū . XII . bord
hn̄t . XI . car̄ . Ibi . IX . serui . 7 XXII . ac̄ p̄ti . Silua . L . porc
T.R.E. ualeħ . XVI . liħ . Q̄do recep̄: XII . liħ . 7 m̄ . XX . liħ.
Aluuold tenuit de rege.

Filius Turaldi de Rouecest teñ de epo WITENEMERS . p̄ uno
solin se deſd . T̄ra . ē . IIII . car̄ . In dn̄io sunt . II . car̄ . 7 XI . uitti
cū . II . cot hn̄t . II . car̄ . Ibi . IIII . ac̄ p̄ti . Silua . XV . porc.
T.R.E. ualeħ . C . sot . Q̄do recep̄: IIII . liħ . 7 m̄ . C . sot . Anschil
tenuit de rege . E.

Walteri de douuai teñ de epo LEE . p̄ dim̄ solin se deſd.
T̄ra . ē . IIII . car̄ . In dn̄io sunt . II . car̄ . 7 XI . uitti cū . II . cot
hn̄t . II . car̄ . Ibi . II . serui . 7 v . ac̄ p̄ti . Silua . x . porc. ⌒ de rege.
T.R.E. 7 q̄do eps recep̄: uat . III . liħ . Modo: c . sot . Aluuin tenuit

Witts filius Ogerii teñ de epo CERLETONE . p̄ uno solin
se deſd . T̄ra . ē . v . car̄ . In dn̄io ē . I . car̄ . 7 XIII . uitti hn̄t . IIII.
car̄ . Ibi . II . serui . 7 VIII . ac̄ p̄ti . Silua . v . porc.
T.R.E. 7 post . 7 modo: uat . VII . liħ . Hanc tr̄a tenuer̄
de rege . II . fr̄s p̄ . II . maneriis . Goduin 7 Aluuard.

Ist Witts teñ de epo CRAI . **IN HELMESTREI HVND.**
p̄ dimid solin se deſd . T̄ra . ē   In dn̄io . ē una car̄.
7 VIII . uitti cū . I . car̄ 7 dimid . 7 IIII . cot . 7 I . moliñ de . x . solid.

6 d

In the Half-Lathe of SUTTON
In GREENWICH Hundred

29 The Bishop of Lisieux holds GREENWICH from the Bishop
of Bayeux. It answers for 2 sulungs. Land for ... In lordship 2
ploughs.
    24 villagers have 4 ploughs; 4 smallholders, 1 cottager
        and 5 slaves.
    4 mills at 70s; meadow, 22 acres; pasture, 40 acres;
        woodland, 10 pigs.
    These 2 sulungs were two manors before 1066. Earl Harold
held one, Brictsi the other; now they are in one.
Value together before 1066 and later £8; now they are
assessed at £12.

30 Hamo the Sheriff holds ELTHAM from the Bishop. It answers
for 1½ sulungs. Land for 12 ploughs. In lordship 2 ploughs.
    42 villagers with 12 smallholders have 11 ploughs.
    9 slaves; meadow, 22 acres; woodland, 50 pigs.
Value before 1066 £16; when acquired £12; now £20.
    Alfwold held it from the King.

31 Thorold of Rochester's son holds WRICKLESMARSH from the Bishop.
It answers for 1 sulung. Land for 4 ploughs. In lordship 2 ploughs.
    11 villagers with 2 cottagers have 2 ploughs.
    Meadow, 4 acres; woodland, 15 pigs.
Value before 1066, 100s; when acquired £4; now 100s.
    Askell held it from King Edward.

32 Walter of Douai holds LEE from the Bishop. It answers for
½ sulung. Land for 4 ploughs. In lordship 2 ploughs.
    11 villagers with 2 cottagers have 2 ploughs.
    2 slaves; meadow, 5 acres; woodland, 10 pigs.
Value before 1066 and when the Bishop acquired it £3; now 100s.
    Alwin held it from the King.

33 William son of Odger holds CHARLTON from the Bishop.
It answers for 1 sulung. Land for 5 ploughs. In lordship 1 plough.
    13 villagers have 3 ploughs.
    2 slaves; meadow, 8 acres; woodland, 5 pigs.
Value before 1066, later and now £7.
    Two brothers, Godwin and Alfward, held this land as two
manors from the King.

In RUXLEY Hundred
34 William also holds (Foots) CRAY from the Bishop. It answers
for ½ sulung. Land for ... In lordship 1 plough;
    8 villagers with 1½ ploughs and 4 cottagers.

Ibi . uñ ſeru . 7 ſilua . vi . porc̄ . T.R.E. ualeb̄ . iiii . lib̄ . 7 poſt.'
iii . lib̄ . Modo.' iiii . lib̄ . Goduin tenuit de rege . E.

Anſchitill ten de ep̄o CROCTVNE . p uno ſolin 7 uno jugo
ſe defd̄ . T̄ra . ē   In dñio nichil . ē . ſed . iii . uiłłi 7 iiii . bord̄
ibi ſunt.

T.R.E. 7 poſt ualebat . c . ſolid̄ 7 m̄ . vi . lib̄ . Aluuin tenuit
hanc t̄ra de rege . E . p duob̄z M̄.

Giſlebt maminot ten de ep̄o CODEHĀ . p . iiii . ſolins ſe defd̄.
T̄ra . ē . x . car̄ . In dñio ſunt . iiii . 7 xv . uiłłi cū . vi . bord̄ h̄nt
vi . car̄ . Ibi æccła . 7 xi . ſerui . 7 ii . molini de . xiiii . ſolid̄ . 7 ii .
denar̄ . Silua . xl . porc̄ . T.R.E. ualeb̄ . xx . lib̄ . 7 poſt.' xvi .
lib̄ . Modo.' xxiiii . lib̄.

Iſdē Giſlebt ten de ep̄o CHESTAN . p dimid̄ ſolin ſe defd̄.
T̄ra . ē   In dñio . ē . i . car̄ . 7 iiii . uiłłi cū . i . car̄ . Ibi ſilua
. v . porc̄ . T.R.E. 7 poſt.' ualeb̄ . lx . ſoł . Modo.' xl . ſolid̄.
Sberne biga tenuit de rege . E.

Hugo nepos herbti ten de ep̄o SENTLINGE . p uno ſolin
7 dim ſe defd̄ . T̄ra . ē   In dñio ſunt . ii . car̄ . 7 xx . uiłłi
cū . ii . car̄ . Ibi æccła 7 ix . ſerui . 7 vi . ac̄ p̄ti . 7 xx . ac̄ paſturæ.
Silua . viii . porc̄ . T.R.E. ualeb̄ . viii . lib̄ . 7 poſt.' vi . lib̄.
Modo.' viii . lib̄ . Bonde tenuit de Archiep̄o.

Anſgot de Rouec ten de ep̄o BACHEHĀ . IN BRVNLEI HD̄.
p . ii . ſolins ſe defd̄ . T̄ra . ē . viii . car̄ . In dñio ſunt . ii . 7 xxii .
uiłłi cū . viii . bord̄ h̄nt . viii . car̄ 7 dimid̄ . Ibi . xii . ac̄ p̄ti.
7 iiii . ſerui . 7 uñ mold̄ . 7 ſilua . lx . porc̄ .   ſ de rege . E.
T.R.E. 7 poſt.' ualeb̄ . ix . lib̄ . Modo.' xiii . lib̄ . Anſchil tenuit

1 mill at 10s. 1 slave; woodland, 6 pigs.
Value before 1066 £4; later £3; now £4.
  Godwin Foot held it from King Edward.

35 Ansketel holds CROFTON from the Bishop. It answers for 1
sulung and 1 yoke. Land for ... In lordship nothing but
  3 villagers and 4 smallholders are there.
Value before 1066 and later 100s; now £6.
  Alwin held this land from King Edward as two manors.

36 Gilbert Maminot holds CUDHAM from the Bishop. It answers
for 4 sulungs. Land for 10 ploughs. In lordship 4.
  15 villagers with 6 smallholders have 6 ploughs.
  A church; 11 slaves; 2 mills at 14s 2d; woodland, 40 pigs.
Value before 1066 £20; later £16; now £24.

37 Gilbert also holds KESTON from the Bishop. It answers
for ½ sulung. Land for ... In lordship 1 plough;
  4 villagers with 1 plough.
  Woodland, 5 pigs.
Value before 1066 and later 60s; now 40s.
  Esbern Big held it from King Edward.

38 Hugh nephew of Herbert holds SANDLINGS from the Bishop.
It answers for 1½ sulungs. Land for ... In lordship 2 ploughs;
  20 villagers with 2 ploughs.
  A church; 9 slaves; meadow, 6 acres; pasture, 20 acres;
    woodland, 8 pigs.
Value before 1066 £8; later £6; now £8.
  Bondi held it from the Archbishop.

In BROMLEY Hundred
39 Ansgot of Rochester holds BECKENHAM from the Bishop.
It answers for 2 sulungs. Land for 8 ploughs. In lordship 2.
  22 villagers with 8 smallholders have 8½ ploughs
  Meadow, 12 acres; 4 slaves; a mill; woodland, 60 pigs.
Value before 1066 and later £9; now £13.
  Askell held it from King Edward.

Adā teñ de epo *Leleburne*. ꝑ. 11. ſolins ſe defđ. Tra. ē

　　　　In dñio ſunt. 111. car. 7 xvi. uilli cū. 11. borđ

hñt. vii. car. Ibi æccła 7 x. ſerui. 7 uñ moliñ de. vii. ſolid.

7 xii. ac ꝑti. Silua. l. porc. T.R.E. ualeƀ. viii. liƀ.

Qđo recep. vii. liƀ. Modo. viii. liƀ. Ricard de Tonebrige

teñ in ſua Leuua. qđ uał. xxiiii. ſoł. Rex teñ ꝑ ñouo

dono epi qđ uał. xxiiii. ſolid 7 11. deñ. Hoc ꟽ tenuit

Turgis de Goduino comite.

Anſchitil teñ de epo *Elentun*. ꝑ uno ſolin ſe defđ.

Tra. ē. 111. car. In dñio ſunt. 11. 7 xv. uilli cū'. 11. borđ hñt

. 1. car 7 dimiđ. Ibi æccła 7 11. ſerui. 7 dimiđ moliñ 7 una

dena de. xv. ſoł. Silua. viii. porc. 7 una ac ꝑti.

T.R.E. ualeƀ. c. ſoł. Qđo recep. lx. ſoł. Modo. c. ſolid.

Vluric tenuit de Alnod cilt.

Haimo teñ de epo *Dictune*. ꝑ uno ſolin ſe defđ. Tra. ē

1111. car. In dñio ſunt. 11. 7 xx. uilli cū. v. borđ hñt. 111. car.

Ibi æccła 7 vi. ſerui. 7 uñ moliñ de. x. ſolid. 7 viii. ac ꝑti.

7 xxx.v. ac paſturæ. Silua. vi. porc. T.R.E. ualeƀ. viii.

liƀ. Qđo recep. c. ſoł. Modo. viii. liƀ. Sbern tenuit

de rege. E.

Uttalis teñ de epo *Sifletone*. ꝑ. 111. jugis ſe defđ.

Tra. ē. 1. car. In dñio. 1. car 7 dimiđ. 7 vi. uilli cū uno

borđ hñt đim car.　　　Ibi. vi. ſerui. 7 1. moliñ de. x.

　　　　　　　　　　　　　　　　　　ſolid.

7 b

Ibi. x. ac ꝑti. 7 xxx. ac paſturæ.

T.R.E. ualeƀ. xl. ſoł. Qđo recep. 1111. liƀ. Modo.

c. ſolid. Hanc tenueꝛ T.R.E. duo hoēs in para

gio. Leuuiñ 7 Vluuiñ. 7 potueꝛ cū tra ſua

ſe uerteꝛe quo uolueꝛ.

In the Lathe of AYLESFORD
In LARKFIELD HUNDRED

40 Adam holds LEYBOURNE from the Bishop. It answers for 2
sulungs. Land for ... In lordship 3 ploughs.
16 villagers with 2 smallholders have 7 ploughs.
A church; 10 slaves; a mill at 7s; meadow, 12 acres;
woodland, 50 pigs.
Value before 1066 £8; when acquired £7; now £8. Richard
of Tonbridge holds in his territory what is valued at 24s.
The King holds as a new gift from the Bishop what is valued
at 24s 2d.
Thorgils held this manor from Earl Godwin.

41 Ansketel holds ALLINGTON from the Bishop. It answers for 1
sulung. Land for 3 ploughs. In lordship 2.
15 villagers with 2 smallholders have 1½ ploughs.
A church; 2 slaves; ½ mill; 1 pig pasture at 15s;
woodland, 8 pigs; meadow, 1 acre.
Value before 1066, 100s; when acquired 60s; now 100s.
Wulfric held it from Young Alnoth.

42 Hamo the Sheriff holds DITTON from the Bishop. It answers
for 1 sulung. Land for 4 ploughs. In lordship 2.
20 villagers with 5 smallholders have 3 ploughs.
A church; 6 slaves; a mill at 10s; meadow, 8 acres;
pasture, 35 acres; woodland, 6 pigs.
Value before 1066 £8; when acquired 100s; now £8.
Esbern held it from King Edward.

43 Vitalis holds SIFFLETON from the Bishop. It answers for 3
yokes. Land for 1 plough. In lordship 1½ ploughs.
6 villagers with 1 smallholder have ½ plough.
6 slaves; 1 mill at 10s. Meadow, 10 acres; pasture, 30 acres.   7 b
Value before 1066, 40s; when acquired £4; now 100s.
Before 1066 two men, Leofwin and Wulfwin, held this land
jointly and could go where they would with their land.

Radulf fili Turoldi ten de epo *AIGLESSA* . p . III . jugis
se defd . Tra . e   In dnio . e . I car . 7 VII . uitti cu . XIIII .
bord hnt . I . car . Ibi . I . feru . 7 XI . ac pti . Silua . x . porc .
T.R.E. 7 poft. ualeb . III . lib . Modo . IIII . lib .
Ricard qd ten in fua Leuua . xv . den . Rex . VI . folid
7 v . den p nouo dono epi . 7 in Roueceft habuit eps
III . domos de xxxi . denar . qs cepit de ifto M in | fua manu .
Hoc M tenuit Alnod cilt.

Hugo de port ten de epo *PELLESORDE* . p dimid
folin se defd . Tra . e   In dnio . e . I . car . 7 un uitts
cu . IIII . bord hnt . III . boues . Ibi æccta 7 II . ferui .
7 v . ac pti . 7 una ac pafturæ . T.R.E . ualeb . xx . fot .
Qdo recep . xxx . fot . Modo . XL . fot .
Godric tenuit de rege . E.

Ifde Hugo ten de epo *RIESCE* . p . II . folins 7 dim
se defd . Tra . e . v . car . In dnio funt . II . 7 x . uitti cu
II . bord hnt . III . car . Ibi æccta 7 x . ferui . 7 I . molin
de . x . fot . 7 IX . ac pti . Silua . v . porc . T.R.E . ualeb
VIII . lib . Qdo recep . c . fot . Modo . VI . lib . Aluric
tenuit de rege . E.

Ifde Hugo ten de epo *OFEHA* . p uno folin se defd .
Tra . e . III . car . In dnio nichil . Ibi . VI . uitti cu . I . bord
hnt . II . car . Ibi . I . molin de . L . den . 7 III . ferui . 7 IIII .
ac pti . Silua . x . porc . T.R.E . ualeb . XL . fot . Qdo
recep . xx . fot . Modo . xxx . fot . Godric tenuit de rege . E

Rannulf de Colubels ten de epo *ESSEDENE* .
p uno folin se defd . Tra . e .   In dnio . e una car .
7 XIX . uitti cu . III . bord hnt . III . car . Ibi . III . ferui .
7 VIII . ac pti . T.R.E . ual . III . lib . Qdo recep . IIII . lib .
Modo . v . lib . Leuuin tenuit .

44   Ralph son of Thorold holds ECCLES from the Bishop. It answers
for 3 yokes. Land for ... In lordship 1 plough.
     7 villagers with 14 smallholders have 1 plough.
     1 slave; meadow, 11 acres; woodland, 10 pigs.
Value before 1066 and later £3; now £4; what Richard holds
in his territory 15d; (what) the King (holds) 8s 5d as a new
gift from the Bishop.
     In Rochester the Bishop had 3 houses at 31d which he took
into his own hand from that manor.
     Young Alnoth held this manor.

45   Hugh of Port holds PADDLESWORTH from the Bishop. It answers
for ½ sulung. Land for ... In lordship 1 plough.
     1 villager with 4 smallholders have 3 oxen.
     A church; 2 slaves; meadow, 5 acres; pasture, 1 acre.
Value before 1066, 20s; when acquired, 30s; now 40s.
     Godric held it from King Edward.

46   Hugh also holds RYARSH from the Bishop. It answers for 2½
sulungs.Land for 5 ploughs. In lordship 2.
     10 villagers with 2 smallholders have 3 ploughs.
     A church; 10 slaves; 1 mill at 10s; meadow, 9 acres;
       woodland, 5 pigs.
Value before 1066 £8; when acquired, 100s; now £6.
     Aelfric held it from King Edward.

47   Hugh also holds OFFHAM from the Bishop. It answers for 1
sulung. Land for 3 ploughs. Nothing in lordship.
     6 villagers with 1 smallholder have 2 ploughs.
     1 mill at 50d; 3 slaves; meadow, 4 acres; woodland, 10 pigs.
Value before 1066, 40s; when acquired, 20s; now 30s.
     Godric held it from King Edward.

48   Ranulf of Colombières holds   NASHENDEN from the Bishop.
It answers for 1 sulung. Land for ... In lordship 1 plough.
     19 villagers with 3 smallholders have 3 ploughs.
     3 slaves; meadow, 8 acres.
Value before 1066 £3; when acquired, £4; now £5.
     Earl Leofwin held it.

Rotbt Latin ten ad firmã de Rege TOTINTVNE.

de nouo dono epi baioc . ꝑ dim̃ ſolin ſe defđ . Tra . ē

uni car 7 dim̃ . In dñio . ē una . 7 iii . uitti cũ . ix . borđ

hñt dim̃ car̃ . Ibi . iiii . ſerui . 7 v . ac ꝑti . Silua . ii . porc̃.

T.R.E . ualeb . xxx . ſot . Q̃do recep̃ . xx . ſot . Modo . xl . ſot.

Vlnod tenuit de rege . E.

Iſdẽ Rotbt ten In Totintune ad firmã de rege . i . jugũ.

7 iſtud . ē de nouo dono epi baioc̃ . 7 ibi nil . ē niſi . ii . ac

ꝑti . Vat 7 ualuit ſep . x . ſot . Goduin tenuit de rege . E.

Radulf fili Turaldi ten de epo EDDINTVNE . ꝑ . ii . ſolins

ſe defđ | Tra . ē . v . car̃ . In dñio ſunt . ii . 7 vi . uitti cũ

. ix . borđ hñt . i . car̃ . Ibi æccta 7 x . ſerui . 7 ii . molini

de . xi . ſolid 7 ii . den̄ . 7 xii . ac ꝑti . Silua . x . porc̃.

T.R.E . ualeb . viii . lib . Q̃do recep̃ . c . ſot . Modo . vi . lib.

Agelred tenuit de rege . E.

Radulf fili Turoldi . ten de epo IN TOLLENTREV HĐ.

MELETVNE . ꝑ uno ſolin 7 iii . jugis ſe defđ . Tra . ē . iiii.

car̃ . In dñio . ē una . 7 xxi . uitts cũ . ii . borđ hñt . ii . car̃.

Ibi æccta . 7 i . molin̄ de xlix . den̄ . 7 Heda de xx . ſolid.

7 iii . ſerui . T.R.E . ualeb . iiii . lib . 7 poſt . iii . lib . Modo.

vi . lib . Ricard qđ ten in ſua Leuua . v . ſot in una ſilua.

Iſdẽ Radulf ten de epo   ∠ Leuuin com̃ tenuit.

LEDESDVNE . ꝑ ii . ſolins 7 dimidio . 7 dim̃ jugo ſe defđ.

Tra . ē . vi . car̃ . In dñio ſunt . ii . 7 xvii . uitti cũ . iiii . borđ

hñt . v . car̃ . Ibi æccta 7 i . ſeruus . 7 iii . ac ꝑti 7 dimiđ.

Silua . xx . porc̃ . T.R.E . ualeb . vi . lib . 7 poſt . c . ſolid.

Modo . viii . lib . Ricard qđ h̄t in ſua Leuua . xx . den̄.

Eps ten in ſua manu jnt ciuitatẽ Rouceſt . iiii.

dom̄ ad hoc Ɔ ꝑtin̄ . de quibᴢ h̄t . ix . ſot 7 x . den̄.

49   Robert Latimer holds TOTTINGTON at a revenue from the King
by a new gift of the Bishop of Bayeux. It answers for ½
sulung. Land for 1½ ploughs. In lordship 1.
     3 villagers with 9 smallholders have ½ plough.
     4 slaves; meadow, 5 acres; woodland, 2 pigs.
   Value before 1066, 30s; when acquired, 20s; now 40s.
     Wulfnoth held it from King Edward.

50   Robert also holds 1 yoke in TOTTINGTON at a revenue from the
King, that is by a new gift from the Bishop of Bayeux. There is
nothing there except
     meadow, 2 acres.
   The value is and always was 10s.
     Godwin held it from King Edward.

51   Ralph son of Thorold holds ADDINGTON from the Bishop.
It answers for 2½ sulungs. Land for 5 ploughs. In lordship 2.
     6 villagers with 9 smallholders have 1 plough.
     A church; 10 slaves; 2 mills at 11s 2d; meadow, 12 acres;
       woodland, 10 pigs.
   Value before 1066 £8; when acquired, 100s; now £6.
     Aethelred held it from King Edward.

In TOLTINGTROUGH Hundred   7 c
52   Ralph son of Thorold holds MILTON from the Bishop. It answers
for 1 sulung and 3 yokes. Land for 4 ploughs. In lordship 1.
     21 villagers with 2 smallholders have 2 ploughs.
     A church; 1 mill at 49d; an enclosure at 20s; 3 slaves.
   Value before 1066 £4; later £3; now £6; what Richard holds in
his territory in a wood, 5s.
     Earl Leofwin held it.

53   Ralph also holds LUDDESDOWN from the Bishop. It answers for
2½ sulungs and ½ yoke. Land for 6 ploughs. In lordship 2.
     17 villagers with 4 smallholders have 5 ploughs.
     A church; 1 slave; meadow, 3½ acres; woodland, 20 pigs.
   Value before 1066 £6; later 100s; now £8; what Richard has
in his territory 20d.
     The Bishop holds 4 houses in his hand in the City of
Rochester which belong to this manor, from which he has
9s 10d.
     Earl Leofwin held it.

Herbt fili Iuonis ten de epo GRAVESHĀ. L̄ Leuuin ten
p̄ II . solins 7 uno jugo se defd . Tra . ē . IIII . car̄ . In dnīo
est una . 7 IIII . uilti cū VIII . seruis hn̄t . II . boues . Ibi æcc̄ta
7 I . heda . T.R.E. ualeb . x . lib̄ . Q̄do recep̄: tn̄td . Modo.
XI . lib̄ . Hoc M̄ fuer III . M̄ T.R.E. Leuric 7 Vluuin
7 Goduin tenuer . Nc̄ est in unū.

Wadard ten de epo NOTESTEDE . p̄ . II . solins se
defd . Tra . ē . II . car̄ . In dnīo . ē una . 7 ibi . IIII . bord . 7 æcc̄ta.
7 IIII . serui . Silua . III . porc̄ . T.R.E. ualeb . IIII . lib̄.
Q̄do recep̄: III . lib̄ . Modo . v . lib̄ . Vlstan tenuit de rege . E.

Anschitil ten de epo OFEHĀ IN LAVROCHESFEL HD̄.
p̄ uno solin se defd Tra . ē   In dnīo . ē . I . car̄ . 7 VI.
uilti cū . II . bord hn̄t . I . car̄ . Ibi . IIII . serui . 7 I . molin̄
de . x . sol̄ . 7 VII . ac̄ p̄ti . Silua . x . porc̄ . 7 in ciuitate
Rouec̄ . I . dom reddens . xxx . den̄ . T.R.E. ualeb M̄
c . sol̄ . Q̄do recep̄: IIII . lib̄ . Modo . IIII . lib̄ 7 IX . solid̄.
Ricard de Tonebrige q̄d ten̄: XI . sol̄ ual̄ . Vluric
tenuit de Alnod cilt.

Radulf de Curbespine ten̄ de epo BERLINGE.
p̄ . VI . solins se defd . Tra . ē .   In dnīo . ē una car̄.
7 x . uilti cū XIIII . bord hn̄t . VI . car̄ . Ibi æcc̄ta . 7 VI.
serui . 7 I . molin̄ de . x . sol̄ . 7 ccc . 7 xxx . anguill̄ . 7 piscaria
de . LX . anguill̄ . Ibi . XII . ac̄ p̄ti . 7 pastura . L . animalib̄.
Silua . XL . porc̄ . T.R.E. ualeb . XII . lib̄ . Q̄do recep̄:
VI . lib̄ . Modo: XII . lib̄ . Sbern biga tenuit de rege . E.

Isdē Radulf ten̄ de epo BORHAM . p̄ . VI . solins se
defd . Tra . ē . VIII . car̄ . In dnīo sunt . II . 7 xv . uilti cū
xx . bord hn̄t . VI . car̄ . Ibi æcc̄ta 7 VII . serui . 7 I . molin̄
de . VI . sol̄ . 7 x . ac̄ p̄ti . Silua . xx . porc̄.
T.R.E. ualeb . x . lib̄ . 7 q̄do recep̄: tn̄td . Modo: XII . lib̄.

54   Herbert son of Ivo holds GRAVESEND from the Bishop. It answers
for 2 sulungs and 1 yoke. Land for 4 ploughs. In lordship 1.
    4 villagers with 8 slaves have 2 oxen.
    A church; 1 enclosure.
Value before 1066 £10; when acquired as much; now £11.
    Before 1066 this manor was three manors. Leofric, Wulfwin
and Godwin held them. Now it is in one.

55   Wadard holds NURSTEAD from the Bishop. It answers for 2
sulungs. Land for 2 ploughs. In lordship 1.
    4 smallholders.
    A church; 4 slaves; woodland, 3 pigs.
Value before 1066 £4; when acquired £3; now £5.
    Wulfstan held it from King Edward.

In LARKFIELD Hundred
56   Ansketel holds OFFHAM from the Bishop; It answers for 1
sulung. Land for ... In lordship 1 plough.
    6 villagers with 2 smallholders have 1 plough.
    4 slaves; 1 mill at 10s; meadow, 7 acres; woodland, 10 pigs.
    In the City of Rochester 1 house which pays 30d.
Value of the manor before 1066, 100s; when acquired £4;
now £4 9s. Value of what Richard of Tonbridge holds 11s.
    Wulfric held it from Young Alnoth.

57   Ralph of Courbépine holds BIRLING from the Bishop. It
answers for 6 sulungs. Land for ... In lordship 1 plough.
    10 villagers with 14 smallholders have 6 ploughs.
    A church; 6 slaves; 1 mill at 10s and 330 eels; a fishery
     at 60 eels. Meadow, 12 acres; pasture for 50 cattle;
     woodland, 40 pigs.
Value before 1066 £12; when acquired £6; now £12.
    Esbern Big held it from King Edward.

58   Ralph also holds BURHAM from the Bishop. It answers
for 6 sulungs. Land for 8 ploughs. In lordship 2.
    15 villagers with 20 smallholders have 6 ploughs.
    A church; 7 slaves; 1 mill at 6s; meadow, 10 acres;
     woodland, 20 pigs.
Value before 1066 £10; when acquired as much; now £12.

Ep̄s de Rouecest h̄t domos de h· Ꝏ. 7 ual̄. vii. solid.

Hoc Ꝏ tenuit Leuuin⁹ᶜᵒⁱⁿ   IN LITEFELLE HVND.

Corbin⁹ ten̄ de ep̄o PECHEHĀ. ꝑ. ii. solins se defd̄.

Tra. ē. vi. car̄. In dn̄io. ē una. 7 xii. uilli hn̄t. v. car̄.

7 viii. bord 7 v. serui. 7 iii. ac̄ p̄ti. Silua. x. porc̄. T.R.E.

7 post. ual̄eb xii. lib̄. Modo: viii. lib̄. Rex h̄t de h· Ꝏ

⌐ 7 tam̄ redd̄. xii. lib̄. ⌐

tres denas. ubi maneꝫ. iiii. uilli. 7 ual̄. xl. sol̄. Leuuin⁹ᶜᵒⁱⁿ tenuit.

Ricard⁹ de Tonebrige ten̄ de ep̄o HASLOW. ꝑ. vi. solins se defd̄.

Tra. e. xii. car̄. In dn̄io sunt. iii. 7 xlvii. uilli cū. xv. bord

hn̄t. xv. car̄. Ibi æccla 7. x. serui. 7 ii. molini de. xi. solid.

7 xii. piscariæ de. vii. solid 7 vi. den̄. 7 xii. ac̄ p̄ti. Silua. lx.

porc̄. T.R.E. 7 post. 7 modo. ual̄. xxx. lib̄. Eddeuā tenuit de rege. ·E·

Radulf⁹ fili⁹ Turoldi ten̄ de ep̄o dimid̄ solin In ESTOCHINGE

BERGE. T.R.E. tenuer̄. ii. libi hōes 7 m̄ similit̄. 7 ual̄. xx. sol̄.

IN LEST DE ELESFORD.   IN WACHELESTAN HVND.

Ricard⁹ de Tonebrige ten̄ de ep̄o TIVEDELE. ꝑ uno jugo se.

defd̄. Tra. ē. i. car̄. 7 ibi. ē in dn̄io. 7 æccla. 7 Silua. ii. porc̄.

Val̄ 7 ualuit sēp. xv. sol̄. Eddeua tenuit de rege.

Hugo nepos Herb̄ti ten̄ de ep̄o   IN AIHORDE HVND.

HARIARDESHAM. ꝑ. ii. solins se defd̄. Tra. ē. vi. car̄. In dn̄io

xviii. uilli cū. x. bord hn̄t. iiii. car̄. Ibi æccla

7 xi. serui. 7 ii. molini de xi. solid 7 vi. den̄. 7 vii. ac̄ p̄ti.

Silua. xv. porc̄. T.R.E. ualeb. x. lib̄. Qdo recep̄: viii. lib̄.

Modo: x. lib̄. Osuuard⁹ tenuit de rege. E.

Isdē Hugo ten̄ de ep̄o FEREBVRNE. ꝑ uno solin se defd̄.

Tra. ē. ii. car̄. In dn̄io   iiii. uilli cū. i. car̄ 7 dimid̄.

7 ii. molini de. xl. den̄. T.R.E. ualeb. iiii. lib̄. Post 7 m̄: iii. lib̄.

Aluuin⁹ tenuit de Goduino.ᶜᵒⁱⁿ

The Bishop of Rochester has houses from this manor; value 7s.
Earl Leofwin held this manor.

In LITTLEFIELD Hundred

59 Corbin holds (West) PECKHAM from the Bishop. It answers for 2
sulungs. Land for 6 ploughs. In lordship 1.
12 villagers have 5 ploughs; 8 smallholders and 5 slaves.
Meadow, 3 acres; woodland, 10 pigs.
Value before 1066 and later £12; now £8; however, it pays £12.
From this manor the King has 3 pig pastures where 4 villagers
live; value 40s. Earl Leofwin held this manor.   7 d

60 Richard of Tonbridge holds HADLOW from the Bishop. It answers
for 6 sulungs. Land for 12 ploughs. In lordship 3.
47 villagers with 15 smallholders have 15 ploughs.
A church; 10 slaves; 2 mills at 11s; 12 fisheries at 7s 6d;
    meadow, 12 acres; woodland, 60 pigs.
Value before 1066, later and now £30.
Edeva held it from King Edward.

61 Ralph son of Thorold holds ½ sulung in 'STOKENBURY' from the
Bishop. Before 1066 2 free men held it; now likewise.
Value 20s.

In the Lathe of AYLESFORD
In WASHLINGSTONE Hundred

62 Richard of Tonbridge holds TUDELEY from the Bishop. It answers
for 1 yoke. Land for 1 plough. It is there, in lordship.
A church; woodland, 2 pigs.
The value is and always was 15s.
Edeva held it from the King.

In EYEHORNE Hundred

63 Hugh nephew of Herbert holds HARRIETSHAM from the Bishop.
It answers for 2 sulungs. Land for 6 ploughs. In lordship ...
18 villagers with 10 smallholders have 4 ploughs.
A church; 11 slaves; 2 mills at 11s 6d; meadow, 7 acres;
    woodland, 15 pigs.
Value before 1066 £10; when acquired £8; now £10.
Osward held it from King Edward.

64 Hugh also holds FAIRBOURNE from the Bishop. It answers for
1 sulung. Land for 2 ploughs. In lordship ...;
4 villagers with 1½ ploughs.
2 mills at 40d.
Value before 1066 £4; later and now £3.
Alwin held it from Earl Godwin.

Iſdē Hugo ten de epo . i . jugū liberæ træ in SELESBVRNE.

7 ibi hr̄ dimid̄ car̄ cū . i . bord 7 v . ſeruis . 7 una ac̄ p̄ti 7 dim̄.

Val 7 ualuit ſēp . xx . ſol . Aluuin tenuit de Goduino comite.

Iſdē Hugo 7 Adelold camerari ten de epo FREDENESTEDE.

.p uno ſolin ſe defd̄ . Tra . ē . iii . car̄ . In dr̄io   iii . uiłłi

hr̄t . vii . boues . Ibi æccła 7 ii . ac̄ p̄ti 7 dimid̄ . 7 ſilua . ii . porc̄.

Val 7 ualuit ſēp . xx . ſol . Leuuin tenuit de rege . E.

Adelold ten epo ESLEDES . .p . iii . ſolins ſe defd̄ . Tra . ē

xii . car̄ . In dr̄io ſunt . ii . car̄ . 7 xxviii . uiłłi cū . viii . bord

hr̄t . vii . car̄ . Ibi æccła 7 xviii . ſerui . Ibi . ii . Arpendi uineæ

7 viii . ac̄ p̄ti . Silua . xx . porc̄ . 7 v . molini uillanoᵴ.

T . R . E . ualeb̄ . xvi . lib̄ . Similit̄ q̄do recep̄ . Modo . xx . lib̄.

7 tam̄ reddit . xxv . lib̄ .   Leuuin com̄ tenuit.

De hoc m̄ hr̄ abb̄ S̄ Avguſtini dimid̄ ſolin . qd̄ ual . x . ſol.

.p excābio parchi epi baioc̄ . Comes de Ow hr̄ . iiii . denas.

de iſto m̄ . quæ ual . xx . ſolid̄.

Anſgot de Roueceſt ten de epo AVDINTONE . .p . ii . ſolins

ſe defd̄ . Tra . ē . iii . car̄ 7 dimid̄ . In dr̄io ſunt . ii . 7 vii . uiłłi cū . v.

bord hr̄t . i . car̄ 7 dim̄ . Ibi æccła 7 iiii . ſerui . 7 vi . ac̄ p̄ti . 7 i . molin̄

de . iiii . ſol 7 ii . den . Silua . x . porc̄ . T . R . E . 7 poſt̄ ualuit . iiii . lib̄.

Modo . vii . lib̄ . Goduin 7 Aluuin tenuer̄ de rege E . .p . ii . m̄.

Iſdē Anſgot ten de epo STOCHINGEBERGE . .p . ii . ſolins ſe defd̄.

Tra . ē   In dr̄io . ē . i . car̄ . 7 v . uiłłi cū ix . bord hr̄t . ii.

car̄ . Ibi æccła 7 ii . ſerui . 7 i . molin̄ de . lxiiii . den . Silua . xv . porc̄.

T . R . E . 7 poſt . ualuit . iiii . lib̄ . Modo . vi . lib̄ . Elueua tenuit de rege . E.

Hugo de Port ten de ALNOITONE . .p . iii . ſolins ſe defd̄ . Tra . ē

viii . car̄ . In dr̄io ſunt . ii . car̄ . 7 xviii . uiłłi cū . vi . bord hr̄t

vi . car̄ . Ibi æccła . 7 viii . ſerui .   7 ii . molini 7 dim̄ de . xvii.

                                       ſolid̄.

Ibi . v . ac̄ p̄ti . Silua . xl . porc̄ . T . R . E . ualeb̄ . ix . lib̄ . 7 tntd̄

q̄do recep̄ . Modo . x . lib̄ . 7 tam̄ reddit . xii . lib̄.

65 Hugh also holds 1 yoke of free land in SHELBOROUGH from the
Bishop. He has ½ plough, with
    1 smallholder and 5 slaves.
    Meadow, 1½ acres.
The value is and always was 20s.
    Alwin held it from Earl Godwin.

66 Hugh and Aethelwold the Chamberlain also hold FRINSTED from
the Bishop. It answers for 1 sulung. Land for 3 ploughs.
In lordship ...
    3 villagers have 7 oxen.
    A church; meadow, 2½ acres; woodland, 2 pigs.
The value is and always was 20s.
    Leofwin held it from King Edward.

67 Aethelwold holds LEEDS from the Bishop. It answers for 3
sulungs. Land for 12 ploughs. In lordship 2 ploughs.
    28 villagers with 8 smallholders have 7 ploughs.
    A church; 18 slaves. 2 arpents of vines; meadow, 8 acres;
        woodland, 20 pigs; 5 villagers' mills.
Value before 1066 £16; the same when acquired; now £20;
however, it pays £25.
    Earl Leofwin held it.
From this manor the Abbot of St. Augustine's has ½ sulung,
in exchange for the Bishop of Bayeux's park, value 10s. The
Count of Eu has 4 pig pastures of this manor, value 20s.

68 Ansgot of Rochester holds ALDINGTON from the Bishop. It
answers for 2 sulungs. Land for 3½ ploughs. In lordship 2.
    7 villagers with 5 smallholders have 1½ ploughs.
    A church; 4 slaves; meadow, 6 acres; 1 mill at 4s 2d;
        woodland, 10 pigs.
Value before 1066 and later £4; now £7.
    Godwin and Alwin held it from King Edward as two manors.

69 Ansgot also holds STOCKBURY from the Bishop. It answers
for 2 sulungs. Land for ... In lordship 1 plough.
    5 villagers with 9 smallholders have 2 ploughs.
    A church; 2 slaves; 1 mill at 64d; woodland, 15 pigs.
Value before 1066 and later £4; now £6.
    Aelfeva held it from King Edward.

70 Hugh of Port holds ALLINGTON. It answers for 3 sulungs. Land
for 3 sulungs. Land for 8 ploughs. In lordship 2 ploughs.
    18 villagers with 6 smallholders have 6 ploughs.
    A church; 8 slaves; 2½ mills at 17s. Meadow, 5 acres;
        woodland, 40 pigs.
Value before 1066 £9; as much when acquired; now £10;
however, it pays £12.

8 a

Huic M̃ adjaceɴᵗ . iii . manfiones trǣ in Rouecestre.

7 reddt̃ . v . fol p annū . Ofuuard tenuit de rege . E.

Adã fili Hubti ten de epo *SVDTONE* . p . iiii . folins fe defd.

Tra . ē . vii . car̃ . In dñio funt . ii . 7 xviii . uitti cū v . bord

hñt . iiii . car̃ . Ibi æccła 7 iiii . ac p̃ti . 7 i . molin

Silua . l . porc̃ . T . R . E . ualeɓ . xii . liɓ . Q̃do recep̃ . x . liɓ.

Modo . xiiii . liɓ . 7 tam̃ reddit . xviii . liɓ . Leuuin tenuit.

Ifdē Adã ten de epo *CERTH* . p . iii . folins fe defd . Tra . ē

viii . car̃ . In dñio . ē una . 7 xx . uitti cū . v . bord hñt

. vi car̃ . Ibi æccła 7 viii . ferui . 7 vi . ac p̃ti . Silua . l . porc̃.

Ibi . iii . arpend uineæ . 7 parc filuatic beftiarū.

T . R . E . 7 poft . 7 modo . ual . xii . liɓ . Alnod tenuit.

Ifdē Adã ten de epo *SVDTONE* . p uno folin 7 dimid

fe defd . Tra . ē . viii . car̃ . In dñio funt . ii . 7 xv . uitti

cū . ix . bord . hñt . iiii . car̃ . Ibi æccła 7 x . ferui . 7 viii . ac

p̃ti . Silua . l . porc̃ . T . R . E . 7 poft . ualeɓ . x . liɓ.

Modo . xii . liɓ . 7 tam̃ redd xviii . liɓ . Leuenot tenuit de rege . E.

Ifdē Adã ten de epo *BOGELEI* . p . ii . folins fe defd.

Tra . ē . ii . car̃ 7 dim . In dñio . ē una car̃ . 7 ii . uitti cū

ii . bord hñt dimid car̃ . Ibi æccła 7 iiii . ferui . 7 i . molin

de . v . folid . 7 vi . ac p̃ti . Silua . xx . porc̃.

De ifto M̃ ht̃ un hõ Adã uñ folin 7 uocat Merlea.

7 ibi ht̃ . i . car̃ . 7 iiii . uittos cū . i . car̃ . 7 ecclam . 7 ii.

feruos . 7 filua . iiii . porc̃ . ⫝ Turgis tenuit de rege . E.

Totū M̃ T . R . E . ualeɓ . vi . liɓ . 7 poft . tñtd . Modo vii . liɓ.

Ifdē Adã ten de epo *LANGVELEI* . p uno folin 7 dim

fe defd . Tra . ē . iiii . car̃ . In dñio funt . ii . 7 vii . uitti cū

v . bord hñt . iii . car̃ . Ibi æccła 7 vii . ferui . 7 iii . ac p̃ti.

Silua . xx . v . porc̃ . T . R . E . ualeɓ . lx . fol . Q̃do recep̃.

l . fol . Modo . lx . folid . Turgis tenuit de rege . E.

To this manor are attached 3 measures of land in Rochester; they pay 5s a year.

    Osward held it from King Edward.

71   Adam son of Hubert holds SUTTON (Valence) from the Bishop. It answers for 4 sulungs. Land for 7 ploughs. In lordship 2.

    18 villagers with 5 smallholders have 4 ploughs.

    A church; meadow, 4 acres; 1 mill; woodland, 50 pigs.

Value before 1066 £12; when acquired, £10; now £14; however, it pays £18.

    Earl Leofwin held it.

Adam also holds from the Bishop

72   CHART (Sutton). It answers for 3 sulungs. Land for 8 ploughs. In lordship 1.

    20 villagers with 5 smallholders have 6 ploughs.

    A church; 8 slaves; meadow, 6 acres; woodland, 50 pigs.

        3 *arpents* of vines; a park of wild beasts.

Value before 1066, later and now £12.

    Young Alnoth held it.

73   (East) SUTTON. It answers for 1½ sulungs. Land for 8 ploughs. In lordship 2.

    15 villagers with 9 smallholders have 4 ploughs.

    A church; 10 slaves; meadow, 8 acres; woodland, 50 pigs.

Value before 1066 and later £10; now £12; however, it pays £18.

    Leofnoth held it from King Edward.

74   BOWLEY. It answers for 2 sulungs. Land for 2½ ploughs. In lordship 1 plough.

    2 villagers with 2 smallholders have ½ plough.

    A church; 4 slaves; 1 mill at 5s; meadow, 6 acres;
        woodland, 20 pigs.

One man, Adam, has 1 sulung of this manor; it is called Marley. He has 1 plough, and

    4 villagers with1 plough.

    A church; 2 slaves; woodland, 4 pigs.

    Thorgils held it from King Edward.

Value of the whole manor before 1066 £6; later as much; now £7.

75   LANGLEY. It answers for 1½ sulungs. Land for 4 ploughs. In lordship 2.

    7 villagers with 5 smallholders have 3 ploughs.

    A church; 7 slaves; meadow, 3 acres; woodland, 25 pigs.

Value before 1066, 60s; when acquired, 50s; now 60s.

    Thorgils held it from King Edward.

Iſdē Adā ten de epo *OTRINGEDENE* . ᵽ dimiđ ſolin

ſe defđ . Tra . ē . ii . cař . In dñio . ē una . 7 ii . uiłłi cū . iiii.

borđ hñt dim cař . Ibi . ii . ſerui . 7 una aĉ ᵽti . Silua.

v . porĉ . T . R . E . 7 poſt . ualuit . x . ſoł . Modo . xxx . ſoł.

Huic ⨕ ᵽtiñ . ii . manſure træ in Cantuaria . de . xii.

denař . Aluuarđ tenuit de rege . E . hoc ⨕.

Iſdē Adā ten de epo *ESSELVE* . ᵽ dimiđ ſolin ſe

defđ . Tra . ē . i . cař . 7 ibi . ē in dñio . cū uno uiłło 7 uno

borđ . 7 v . ſeruis . Ibi . iiii . aĉ ᵽti . Silua . iiii . porĉ.

T . R . E . 7 poſt . 7 modo : ual . xx . ſolid . Godric tenuit

Wiłłs fili Roḃti ten de epo ꝯ de rege . E.

WESTSELVE . ᵽ uno ſolin ſe defđ . Tra . ē . iii . cař

7 dimiđ . In dñio ſunt . ii . 7 qđā francig cū . x . uiłłis

7 i . borđ . hñt . i . cař 7 dim . Ibi . v . ſerui . 7 i . aĉ ᵽti.

7 uñ moliñ de . xv . den . Silua xv . porĉ.

T . R . E . 7 poſt . 7 modo : ual . iiii . liḃ . Eddiđ tenuit

de rege . E . Huic ⨕ ᵽtineḃ in cantuaria . T . R . E.

una dom . reddeś . xxv . denař.

8 b

Hugo nepos Herḃti ten de epo *BOLTONE* . ᵽ uno ſoliñ

ſe defđ . Tra . ē . ii . cař . In dñio nichil . ſed . v . uiłłi

hñt . i . cař . ibi . 7 ii . aĉ ᵽti . Silua . xx . porĉ . Ibi æccła,

T . R . E . 7 poſt : ualeḃ . viii . liḃ . Modo : vi . liḃ,

Aluuiñ tenuit de Goduino.

Iſdē Hugo ten de epo *GODESELLE* . ᵽ uno ſolin ſe

defđ . Tra . ē . ii . cař . In dñio . ē una . 7 v . uiłłi hñt . i . cař

7 dim . Ibi eccła . 7 ii . ſerui . 7 ii . aĉ ᵽti . 7 ſilua . x . porĉ,

T . R . E . 7 poſt . 7 modo : ual . iiii . liḃ . Eduuiñ tenuit

de rege . E . 7 potuit ire cū tra ſua quo uoluit.

Iſdē Hugo ten de epo *WINCHELESMERE.*

ᵽ dimiđ ſolin ſe defđ . Tra . ē . i . cař . 7 ibi . ē in dñio

cū . iii . ſeruis . 7 æccła . 7 ſilua . v . porĉ . 7 T . R . E . in can

tuaria . iii . dom ᵽtineḃ huic ⨕ reddđes . xl . den.

76 OTTERDEN. It answers for ½ sulung. Land for 2 ploughs. In lordship 1.
2 villagers with 4 smallholders have ½ plough.
2 slaves; meadow, 1 acre; woodland, 5 pigs.
Value before 2066 and later 10s; now 30s.
To this manor belong 2 measures of land in Canterbury at 12d.
Alfward held this manor from King Edward.

77 (Old) SHELVE. It answers for ½ sulung. Land for 1 plough. It is
there in lordship, with
1 villager, 1 smallholder and 5 slaves.
Meadow, 4 acres; woodland, 4 pigs.
Value before 1066, later and now 20s.
Godric held it from King Edward.

78 William son of Robert holds (New) SHELVE from the Bishop.
It answers for 1 sulung. Land for 3½ ploughs. In lordship 2.
A Frenchman with 10 villagers and 1 smallholder have 1½ ploughs.
5 slaves; meadow, 1 acre; a mill at 15d; woodland, 15 pigs.
Value before 1066, later and now £4.
Edith held it from King Edward.
Before 1066 one house in Canterbury which pays 25d belonged
to this manor.

79 Hugh nephew of Herbert holds BOUGHTON (Malherbe) from the   8 b
Bishop It answers for 1 sulung. Land for 2 ploughs. In lordship
nothing, but
5 villagers have 1 plough there.
Meadow, 2 acres; woodland, 20 pigs. A church.
Value before 1066 and later £8; now £6.
Alwin held it from Earl Godwin.

Hugh also holds from the Bishop
80 WORMSHILL.   It answers for 1 sulung. Land for 2 ploughs.
In lordship 1.
5 villagers have 1½ ploughs.
A church; 2 slaves, meadow, 2 acres; woodland, 10 pigs.
Value before 1066, later and now £4.
Edwin held it from King Edward and could go with his land
where he would.

81 WICHLING. It answers for ½ sulung. Land for 1 plough. It is there,
in lordship, with
3 slaves.
A church; woodland, 5 pigs.
Before 1066 3 houses in Canterbury which pay 40d belonged
to this manor.

Tot̃ T.R.E. ualeb̃ . c . fot̃ . 7 poſt . 7 modo: xl . fot̃.

Vluiet tenuit de rege . E . 7 potuit ire quo libuit.

Iſdẽ Hugo ten̄ de ep̃o ESTSELVE . p̃ dimid̃ folin

ſe defd̃ . Tra . ē . i . car̃ . 7 ibi . ē in dñio . cũ . i . uitto 7 uno

bord̃ . 7 ii . feruis . Ibi . iiii . ac̃ p̃ti . 7 filua . iiii . porc̃.

T.R.E . 7 poſt . 7 m̃: ual̃ xl . fot̃ . Vluiet tenuit de rege . E.

Goisfrid de Ros ten̄ de ep̃o OTEHÃ . p̃ uno folin 7 uno jugo ſe

defd̃ . Tra . ē . ii . car̃ 7 dimid̃ . In dñio . ē una . 7 ix . uitti cũ . iii .

bord̃ hñt . i . car̃ . Ibi eccta . 7 ii . ferui . 7 i . molin̄ de . v . folid̃.

7 iii . ac̃ p̃ti . Silua . viii . porc̃ . T.R.E . ualeb̃ . iiii . lib̃ . Q̃do

recep̃: iii . lib̃ . Modo: iiii . lib̃ . Aluuin̄ tenuit de rege . E.

Rotb̃t Latin̄ ten̄ ad firma HERBRETITOV . Adeloldus

tenuit de ep̃o . p̃ uno folin ſe defd̃ . Tra . ē   In dñio

ē una car̃ . 7 ii . uitti cũ . i . bord̃ hñt . ii . Aalia . 7 ibi . iiii . ac̃

p̃ti . T.R.E . 7 poſt. | modo: ual̃ . lx . fot̃ . 7 tam eſt ad firma . p̃ . iiii . lib̃.

Aluric tenuit de Goduino. com̃

Iſdẽ Rotb̃t ten̄ ad firma BRVNFELLE . Adelold tenuit de ep̃o.

p̃ uno folin ſe defd̃ . Tra . ē   In dñio funt . ii . car̃ . 7 v . uitti

cũ . x . bord̃ hñt . i . car̃ 7 dim̃ . Ibi . i . molin̄ de . vi . folid̃

7 viii . den̄ . 7 paſtura de xv . fot̃ . Ibi . xii . ferui . 7 viii . ac̃

p̃ti . Silua . xx . porc̃ . T.R.E . 7 poſt . ual̃ . iiii . lib̃ . M . c . folid̃.

Aluuin̄ tenuit de Goduino . Huic com̃ Ꝑ ptin̄ quædã libera

tra ad . iii . boues . 7 ual̃ . v . fot̃.

Radulf curbeſpine ten̄ de ep̃o TVRNEHÃ . p̃ iii . folins

ſe defd̃ . Tra . ē . viii . car̃ . In dñio . ē una . 7 xvi . uitti cũ xviii .

bord̃ hñt . iiii . car̃ . Ibi æccta 7 vi . ferui . 7 i . molin̄ de . vi .

folid̃ . 7 iiii . ac̃ p̃ti . Silua . xl . porc̃.

T.R.E . 7 poſt . ualeb̃ . x . lib̃ . Modo xii . lib̃ . 7 tam redd̃ . xiiii.

Sbern biga tenuit de rege . E.

Value of the whole before 1066, 100s; later and now 40s.
   Wulfgeat held it from King Edward and could go where
he would.

82   (Old) SHELVE.   It answers for ½ sulung. Land for 1 plough.
It is there, in lordship, with
   1 villager, 1 smallholder and 2 slaves.
   Meadow, 4 acres; woodland, 4 pigs.
Value before 1066, later and now 40s.
   Wulfgeat held it from King Edward.

83   Geoffrey of Rots holds OTHAM from the Bishop. It answers for
1 sulung and 1 yoke. Land for 2½ ploughs. In lordship 1.
   9 villagers with 3 smallholders have 1 plough.
   A church; 2 slaves; 1 mill at 5s; meadow, 3 acres;
      woodland, 8 pigs.
Value before 1066 £4; when acquired, £3; now £4.
   Alwin held it from King Edward.

84   Robert Latimer holds HARBILTON at a revenue. Aethelwold
held it from the Bishop. It answers for 1 sulung. Land for ...
In lordship 1 plough.
   2 villagers with 1 smallholder have 2 cattle.
   Meadow, 4 acres.
Value before 1066, later and now 60s; however, it is at a
revenue for £4.
   Aelfric held it from Earl Godwin.

85   Robert also holds BROOMFIELD at a revenue. Aethelwold held it
from the Bishop. It answers for 1 sulung. Land for ...
In lordship 2 ploughs.
   5 villagers with 10 smallholders have 1½ ploughs.
   1 mill at 6s 8d; pasture at 15s. 12 slaves; meadow, 8 acres;
      woodland, 20 pigs.
Value before 1066 and later £4; now 100s.
   Alwin held it from Earl Godwin.
To this manor belongs free land for 3 oxen, value 5s.

86   Ralph (of) Courbépine holds THURNHAM from the Bishop.
It answers for 3 sulungs. Land for 8 ploughs. In lordship 1.
   16 villagers with 18 smallholders have 4 ploughs.
   A church; 6 slaves; 1 mill at 6s; meadow, 4 acres;
      woodland, 40 pigs.
Value before 1066 and later £10; now £12; however, it pays [£] 14.
   Esbern Big held it from King Edward.

Iſđ Radulf⁹ ten de eṕo *FEREBVRNE* . ꝓ uno ſolin ſe defđ.

Tra . e̅ In dn̅io . e̅ una car . 7 ii . uiłłi cu̅ . i . borđ . 7 ii.

ſerui . 7 una a̅c p̅ti 7 dimiđ . Silua . vi . porc̅ . T . R . E . 7 poſt.

7 modo : ual . xxx . ſoliđ . Sbern biga tenuit de rege . E.

Odo teń de eṕo *GELINGEHA̅* . ꝓ dimiđ ſolin ſe defđ.

Tra . e̅ . i . car . In dn̅io ſunt . ii . 7 vi . borđ hn̅t dim car.

Ibi . i . molin̅ de . xvi . ſol 7 vii . den̅ . 7 xiii . a̅c p̅ti . 7 viii . a̅c

ᚠ paſturæ.

T . R . E . ualeɓ . xl . ſol . Q̇do receṗ : xxx . ſol . Modo . lx . ſol.

Rotɓt Latin⁹ ten ad firma̅ de eṕo *IN CETEHA̅ HVND*.

CETEHAM . ꝓ vi . ſolins ſe defđ . Tra . e̅ . xvi . car̅ . In dn̅io

ſunt . iii . 7 xxx.iii . uiłłi cu̅ . iiii . borđ hn̅t . x . car̅ , Ibi

æccła 7 xv . ſerui . 7 i . molin̅ de . xxx.ii . den̅ . 7 xx . a̅c p̅ti.

7 piſcariæ vi . de . xii . den̅ . Silua . i . porc̅.

T . R . E . 7 poſt : ualuit . xii . liɓ . Modo . xv . liɓ . 7 tam redđ

xxxv . liɓ . Goduin tenuit.

IN LEST DE EILESFORD . *IN ROVECESTRE HVND*.

Filius Wiłłi tahu̅ ten de eṕo *DELGE* . ꝓ uno ſolin

7 uno jugo ſe defđ . Tra . e̅ In dn̅io . e̅ . una car̅.

7 v . uiłłi hn̅t . ii . car̅ . Ibi . xii . a̅c p̅ti . Silua . i . porc̅.

T . R . E . 7 poſt . ualuit . iii . liɓ . 7 m̅ lxx . ſol.

Godric⁹ tenuit de rege . E.

Anſgot⁹ de Rouecestre ten de eṕo *DELGE* . ꝓ uno ſolin

ſe defđ . Tra . e̅ . ii . car̅ . 7 ibi ſunt in dn̅io . 7 cu̅ uno uiłło

7 v . borđ . 7 vi . ſeruis . Ibi . xii . a̅c p̅ti . 7 lx . a̅c paſturæ.

T . R . E . 7 poſt . 7 modo : ual . c . ſoliđ . Oſuuard⁹ tenuit de rege . E.

Iſdem Anſgot⁹ ten de eṕo *STOCHES* . *IN HOV HVND*.

ꝓ . ii . ſolins ſe defđ . Tra . e̅ . ii . car̅ . 7 ibi ſunt in dn̅io cu̅

vii . borđ . Ibi una piſcaria de . ii . ſoliđ . T . R . E . 7 poſt :

ualuit . c . ſoliđ . Modo . cx . ſoliđ . Anſchil tenuit de rege . E.

87 Ralph also holds FAIRBOURNE from the Bishop. It answers for 1
sulung. Land for ... In lordship 1 plough;
    2 villagers with 1 smallholder and 2 slaves.
    Meadow, 1½ acres; woodland, 6 pigs.
Value before 1066, later and now 30s.
    Esbern Big held it from King Edward.

88 Odo holds GILLINGHAM from the Bishop. It answers for ½ sulung.
Land for 1 plough. In lordship 2.
    6 smallholders have ½ plough.
    1 mill at 16s 7d; meadow, 13 acres; pasture, 8 acres.
Value before 1066, 40s; when acquired, 30s; now 60s.   8 c

In CHATHAM Hundred
89 Robert Latimer holds CHATHAM from the Bishop at a revenue.
It answers for 6 sulungs. Land for 16 ploughs. In lordship 3.
    33 villagers with 4 smallholders have 10 ploughs.
    A church; 15 slaves; 1 mill at 32d; meadow, 20 acres;
        6 fisheries at 12d; woodland, 1 pig.
Value before 1066 and later £12; now £15; however, it pays £35.
    Earl Godwin held it.

In the Lathe of AYLESFORD
In ROCHESTER Hundred
90 The son of William Thaon holds (Little) DELCE from the Bishop.
It answers for 1 sulung and 1 yoke. Land for ... In lordship
1 plough.
    5 villagers have 2 ploughs.
    Meadow, 12 acres; woodland, 1 pig.
Value before 1066 and later £3; now 70s.
    Godric held it from King Edward.

91 Ansgot of Rochester holds (Great) DELCE from the Bishop.
It answers for 1 sulung. Land for 2 ploughs. They are there,
in lordship, with
    1 villager, 5 smallholders and 6 slaves.
    Meadow, 12 acres; pasture, 60 acres.
Value before 1066, later and now 100s.
    Osward held it from King Edward.

In HOO Hundred
92 Ansgot also holds STOKE from the Bishop. It answers for 2
sulungs. Land for 2 ploughs. They are there, in lordship, with
    7 smallholders,
    A fishery at 2s.
Value before 1066 and later 100s; now 110s.
    Askell held it from King Edward.

Ipſe eps Baiocſis ten in dnio *Hov.*

p . L . ſolins ſe defd T.R.E. 7 m̄ p xxx.iií. Tra . ē . L . car̄.

In dnio ſunt . iiii . 7 c . uitti . iiii . min cū . Lxi . cot hn̄t

xL.iii . car̄ . Ibi . vi . æcctæ . 7 xii . ſerui . 7 xxx.ii . ac̄ pti.

Silua . xxx . porc̄.

Totū m̄ T.R.E. . ualeb . Lx . lib . Q̇do eps recep̄ . ſimilit.

7 modo tntd . 7 tam qui eū ten reddit . c 7 xiii . lib.

Huic m̄ ptineb . ix . dom in Roueceſt ciuitate . 7 vi . ſolid

reddeb . nc̄ ablatæ ſunt . Hoc m̄ tenuit Goduin comes.

De hoc m̄ ten Ricard de Tonebrige dimid ſolin.

7 ſiluā . xx . porc̄ . T.R.E. 7 poſt . 7 modo . ual . xL . ſolid.

Adā filius Hubti ten de eod m̄ un ſolin . 7 un jugū de epo.

7 ibi ht̄ un hō ej in dnio dimid car̄ . 7 iiii . uittos cū dim car.

7 uno cot̄ . Val 7 ualuit . xxx . ſolid.

Anſchitil de Ros ten de ipſo m̄ . iii . ſolins . 7 ibi ht̄ in dnio

. i . car̄ . 7 v . uitti cū . xii . cot hn̄t . i . car̄ 7 dim . Ibi . v . ſerui.

7 un molin de . x . ſolid . 7 xii . ac̄ pti . 7 ii . piſcar̄ . de . v . ſol.

T.R.E. 7 poſt . ualeb . vi . lib . Modo . vi . lib . 7 v . ſolid.

Adā ten de epo . i . jugū in *PINPA.*   *IN TVIFERDE HVND.*

Tra . ē   Ibi ht̄ dim car̄ cū . ii . ſeruis . 7 iiii . ac̄s pti.

7 dimid piſcariā ſine cenſu . Silua . vi . porc̄ .   ⌠ xv . ſol.

T.R.E. ualeb . vi . ſol . 7 poſt . v . ſol . Modo . x . ſol . 7 tam redd

Godric tenuit de rege . E.

Rannulf de Colūbels ten de epo *FERLAGA* . p uno ſolin

ſe defd . Tra . ē . iiii . car̄ . Rann n̄ ten niſi . iii . juga . 7 ibi

ht̄ in dnio . i . car̄ . 7 x . uittos cū . iiii . cot hn̄t . iii . car̄.

Ibi æccta . 7 vii . ſerui . 7 i . molin de . v . ſol . 7 x . ac̄ pti . Silua.

xv . porc̄ . T.R.E. 7 poſt . 7 modo . ual . vii . lib . Alnod de rege tenuit

De iſto ſolin ten Raȳner . i . jugū de epo in m̄ *PINPE.*

7 ibi ht̄ . i . car̄ cū . ix . ſeruis . 7 iii . ac̄s pti . Silua . iiii . porc̄.

T.R.E. ualeb . xx . ſol . Modo . xL . ſolid . Alnod tenuit de rege . E.

93 The Bishop of Bayeux himself holds HOO in lordship.
Before 1066 it answered for 50 sulungs; now for 33.
Land for 50 ploughs. In lordship 4.
    100 villagers less 3 with 61 cottagers have 43 ploughs.
    6 churches; 12 slaves; meadow, 32 acres; woodland, 30 pigs.
Value of the whole manor before 1066 £60; when the Bishop
acquired it, the same; now as much; however, its holder pays
£113.
    9 houses in the City of Rochester belonged to this manor;
they paid 6s; now they have been taken away.
    Earl Godwin held this manor.
    Richard of Tonbridge holds ½ sulung of this manor.
        Woodland, 20 pigs.
Value before 1066, later and now, 40s.
    Adam son of Hubert holds 1 sulung and 1 yoke of the same
manor from the Bishop. One of his men has ½ plough in
lordship, and
    4 villagers with ½ plough and 1 cottager.
The value is and was 30s.
    Ansketel of Rots holds 3 sulungs of this manor. He has 1
plough in lordship.
    5 villagers with 12 cottagers have 1½ ploughs.
    5 slaves; a mill at 10s; meadow, 12 acres; 2 fisheries at 5s.
Value before 1066 and later £6; now £6 5s.

In TWYFORD Hundred
94 Adam holds 1 yoke in PIMP'S (Court) from the Bishop. Land for ...
He has ½ plough, with
    2 slaves.
    Meadow, 4 acres; ½ fishery without dues; woodland, 6 pigs.
Value before 1066, 6s; later 5s; now 10s; however, it pays 15s.
    Godric held it from King Edward.

95 Ranulf of Colombières holds (West) FARLEIGH from the Bishop.
It answers for 1 sulung. Land for 4 ploughs. Ranulf holds only
3 yokes. He has 1 plough in lordship.
    10 villagers with 4 cottagers have 3 ploughs.
    A church; 7 slaves; 1 mill at 5s; meadow, 10 acres;
        woodland, 15 pigs.
Value before 1066, later and now £7.
    Alnoth held it from the King.
    Rainer holds 1 yoke of this sulung in the manor of Pimp's (Court)
from the Bishop. He has 1 plough, with   8 d
    9 slaves.
    Meadow, 3 acres; woodland, 4 pigs.
Value before 1066 and later 20s; now 40s.
    Young Alnoth held it from King Edward

Haimo teñ de epo *NEDESTEDE* . ꝑ . iii . ſolins ſe defđ . Tra . ē
vi . car . In dñio . ē una . 7 xiiii . uiłłi hñt . v . car . Ibi æccła .
7 xiiii . ſerui . 7 ii . molini de xiiii . ſoliđ . 7 piſcaria de . ii . ſoł .
7 vii . ac̄ p̄ti . Silua . xxx.v . porc̄ . T.R.E. ualeɓ . viii . liɓ .
7 poſt : vi . liɓ . Modo : viii . liɓ 7 v . ſoł . Norman tenuit de rege . E .
De iſto m̄ hī eps̄ . xxx . ſoł . ꝑ . ii . hagas .

Radulf⁹ fili⁹ Turaldi teñ de epo *OTRINGEBERGE* . ꝑ . ii .
ſolins ſe defđ . Tra . ē . v . car . In dñio ſunt . ii . 7 vi . uiłłi
cū . viii . borđ hñt . iii . car . Ibi æccła . 7 ii . molini de . iii . ſoliđ .
7 ii . ac̄ p̄ti . 7 piſcaria de . xxx . anguiłł . Silua . ii . porc̄ .
T.R.E. 7 poſt ualuit . xl . ſoliđ . Modo : vi . liɓ . Leueua tenuit
de rege . E . Huic m̄ adjaceꝃ . iiii . hagæ in ciuitate . redđ . iii . ſcł .

Hugo de braiboue teñ de epo *OTRINBERGE* . ꝑ . ii . ſolins
ſe defđ . Tra . ē . iiii . car . In dñio . ē una . 7 ix . uiłłi cū . iiii .
borđ hñt . ii . car . Ibi . iii . ſerui . 7 i . moliñ de . xvi . denar .
7 iii . ac̄ p̄ti . Silua . ii . porc̄ . T.R.E. 7 poſt : ualuit . iiii . liɓ .
Modo : c . ſoliđ . Godil tenuit de rege . E .

Adelold tenuit de epo *TESTAN* . 7 Roƀt⁹ m̄ teñ ad firmā .
ꝑ uno ſolin ſe defđ . Tra ē   In dñio ſunt . ii . car 7 dimiđ .
7 vii . uiłłi cū . iii . ƀorđ hñt . i . car . Ibi . xii . ſerui . 7 i . moliñ
de . iii . ſoł . 7 viii . ac̄ p̄ti . Silua . xx . porc̄ .
T.R.E. ualeɓ . c . ſoł . 7 poſt : lx . ſoł . Modo : c . ſoliđ . Eduuard⁹ teñ *de rege . E.*
Hanc trā tenuer̄ . iii . frs T.R.E. ꝑ triƀƺ Manerijs . Nc̄ . ē in unū .

Iſdē Adelold tenuit de epo *BENEDESTEDE* . 7 Roƀt⁹ teñ ad firmā .
ꝑ uno jugo ſe defđ . Tra . ē   In dñio . ē . i . car . cū . v . ſeruis .
7 una ac̄ p̄ti . Silua . vi . porc̄ . T.R.E. 7 poſt : ualuit . xx . ſoliđ .
Modo : xl . ſoł . Godric tenuit de Alnodo . *IN MEDESTAN HD* .

Rannulf⁹ de Colūbels teñ de epo *BERMELIE* . ꝑ uno jugo
ſe defđ . Tra . ē   In dñio . ē una car . cū . v . ſeruis . 7 iiii . ac̄
p̄ti . Silua . iii . porc̄ . T.R.E. ualeɓ . xv . ſoł . Q̄do recep : xx . ſoł .
Modo : xl . ſoł .

8 d

96   Hamo holds NETTLESTEAD from the Bishop. It answers for 3
sulungs. Land for 6 ploughs. In lordship 1.
    14 villagers have 5 ploughs.
    A church; 14 slaves; 2 mills at 14s; a fishery at 2s;
      meadow, 7 acres; woodland, 35 pigs.
    Value before 1066 £8; later £6; now £8 5s.
    Norman held it from King Edward.
Of this manor the Bishop has 30s for 2 sites.

97   Ralph son of Thorold holds WATERINGBURY from the Bishop.
It answers for 2 sulungs. Land for 5 ploughs. In lordship 2.
    6 villagers with 8 smallholders have 3 ploughs.
    A church; 2 mills at 3s; meadow, 2 acres; a fishery at 30 eels;
      woodland, 2 pigs.
    Value before 1066 and later 40s; now £6.
    Leofeva held it from King Edward.
3 sites in the city are attached to this manor; they pay 3s.

98   Hugh of Brêboeuf holds WATERINGBURY from the Bishop.
It answers for 2 sulungs. Land for 4 ploughs. In lordship 1.
    9 villagers with 4 smallholders have 2 ploughs.
    3 slaves; 1 mill at 16d; meadow, 3 acres; woodland, 2 pigs.
    Value before 1066 and later £4; now 100s.
    Godil held it from King Edward.

99   Aethelwold held TESTON from the Bishop; now Robert holds
it at a revenue. It answers for 1 sulung. Land for ...
In lordship 2½ ploughs.
    7 villagers with 3 smallholders have 1 plough.
    12 slaves; 1 mill at 3s; meadow, 8 acres; woodland, 20 pigs.
    Value before 1066, 100s; later 60s; now 100s.
    Edward held it from King Edward.
Before 1066, 3 brothers held this land as three manors, now
it is in one.

100   Aethelwold also held BENSTED from the Bishop; Robert holds
it at a revenue. It answers for 1 yoke. Land for ... In lordship
1 plough, with 5 slaves.
    Meadow, 1 acre; woodland, 6 pigs.
    Value before 1066 and later 20s; now 40s.
    Godric held it from Young Alnoth.

In MAIDSTONE Hundred

101   Ranulf of Colombières holds (West) BARMING from the Bishop.
It answers for 1 yoke. Land for ... In lordship 1 plough,
with 5 slaves.
    Meadow, 4 acres; woodland, 3 pigs.
    Value before 1066, 15s; when acquired, 20s; now 40s.

Rotbt Latin ten ad firmā *BOSELEV* . Tra . ē . xx . car . in

dñio funt . III . car . ⁊ xlvii . uiłłi cū . xi . bord hñt . xvi . car.

Ibi . III . molini de xxxvi . fot ⁊ viii . den . ⁊ xvi . ferui . ⁊ xx.

ac p̃ti . Silua . L . porc . T.R.E . ⁊ poft . ualuit . xxv . lib.

Modo . xxx . lib . ⁊ tam Robt reddit . lv . lib . Alnod tenuit.

De hoc m̄ ten Helto dim̄ folin . ⁊ ibi hȳ . I . car . cū uno

bord . ⁊ I . franc ⁊ II . acs p̃ti . ⁊ filuā: vi . porc . ⁊ Vał . xl . fot.

Radulf fili Turaldi ten de ep̄o

LITELBROTEHA . p uno folin ⁊ dim̄ fe defd . Tra . ē

In dñio . ē . I . car . ⁊ IIII . uiłłi cū . IIII . bord hñt . II . car . Ibi

II . ferui . ⁊ II . molini de . IIII . folid . ⁊ II . ac p̃ti . Silua . v . porc.

T.R.E . ⁊ poft . ualuit . xl . fot . Modo . Lx . fot ⁊ LIIII . den.

Ricard de Tonebrige hȳ in fua Leuua qd̄ uał . xiii . fot.

⁊ Siluā . L . porc . ⁊ Rex hȳ de eod m̄ qd̄ uał . xvi . den.

Hanc trā T.R.E . tenuer Goduin ⁊ Eduun p . II . Maner.

Adā ten de ep̄o *CELCA* p . III . folins fe defd . Tra . ē

VII . car . In dñio funt . II . ⁊ XIIII . uiłłi cū . vi . bord hñt

v . car . Ibi æccła . ⁊ IIII . ferui . ⁊ uñ molin de . v . folid.

⁊ xvi . ac p̃ti .   T.R.E . ualeb . vii . lib . ⁊ poft:

                                              ⌐c . folid.

9 a

Modo . x . lib . ⁊ tam qui|redd . xiiii . lib.

De hoc m̄ eft in manu regis qd̄ uał . vii . fot . de nouo

dono epi.

In manu fua retinuit ep̃s in Ciuitate Roueceftre . I.I.

hagas . quæ ualent . L . deñar.

In Exeffe . ē una hida que jufte ad hoc m̄ p̃tinet.

Goduin fili dudeman tenuit . Modo ten Rannulf peurel.

Ifdē Adā ten de ep̄o *HEᴴAM* . p . v . folins fe defd.

Tra . ē . xii . car . In dñio funt . III . car . ⁊ XXIIII . uiłłi cū

xii . bord . hñt . vi . car ⁊ dimid . Ibi . xx . ferui . ⁊ xxx . ac

p̃ti . Ibi æccła ⁊ I . molin de . x . fot . ⁊ pifcaria de . III . folid.

102 Robert Latimer holds BOXLEY at a revenue. Before 1066 it
answered for 7 sulungs; now for 5 sulungs. Land for 20 ploughs.
In lordship 3 ploughs.
    47 villagers with 11 smallholders have 16 ploughs.
    3 mills at 36s 8d; 16 slaves; meadow, 20 acres; woodland,
      50 pigs.
Value before 1066 and later £25; now £30; however, Robert
pays £55.
    Young Alnoth held it.
Helto holds ½ sulung of this manor. He has 1 plough, with
    1 smallholder and 1 Frenchman.
    Meadow, 2 acres; woodland, 6 pigs.
Value 40s.

103 Ralph son of Thorold holds WROTHAM (Heath) from the Bishop.
It answers for 1½ sulungs. Land for ... In lordship 1 plough.
    4 villagers with 4 smallholders have 2 ploughs.
    2 slaves; 2 mills at 4s; meadow, 2 acres; woodland, 5 pigs.
Value before 1066 and later 40s; now 60s 54d.
    Richard of Tonbridge has in his territory what is valued at 13s.
      Woodland, 50 pigs.
    The King has what is valued at 16d from this manor.
    Before 1066 Godwin and Edwin held this land as two manors.

104 Adam holds CHALK from the Bishop. It answers for 3 sulungs.
Land for 7 ploughs. In lordship 2.
    14 villagers with 6 smallholders have 5 ploughs.
    A church; 4 slaves; a mill at 5s; meadow, 16 acres.
Value before 1066 £7; later 100s; now £10; however, its   9 a
holder pays £14.
    Of this manor there is in the King's hands what is valued at
7s from a new gift of the Bishop. The Bishop kept in his hands
3 sites in the City of Rochester, value 50d.
    In Essex there is 1 hide which rightly belongs to this manor.
Godwin son of Dudeman held it; now Ranulf Peverel holds it.

105 Adam also holds HIGHAM from the Bishop. It answers for 5
sulungs. Land for 12 ploughs. In lordship 3 ploughs.
    24 villagers with 12 smallholders have 6½ ploughs.
    20 slaves; meadow, 30 acres. A church; 1 mill at 10s;
      a fishery at 3s;

7 in Exeſſe paſtura . cc . ouibȝ . T . R . E . ualeƀ . xii . liƀ.

7 poſt . vi . liƀ . Modo . xv . liƀ.

Hanc trā tenueꝛ . T . R . E . Goduin fili carli . 7 Toli . ꝑ . ii . Man.

Iſdē Adā ten de epo COLINGE . i . ſolin 7 dimiđ . Tra . ē

. i . car 7 dim . In dñio ſunt . ii . car . 7 v . uiłłi hñt

dimiđ car . Ibi . iiii . ſerui . 7 vii . ac̃ p̃ti . Silua . x . porc.

T . R . E . 7 poſt . ualuit . xl . ſoł . Modo . iiii . liƀ.

Ricarđ de Tonebrige qđ hƀ in ſua Leuua . uał . vii . ſoł.

Vluuin tenuit de Leuuino comite.

Iſdē Adā ten de epo BICHELEI . ꝑ dimiđ ſolin ſe deſđ.

Tra . ē dim car . In dñio . ē dim car . 7 un uiłłs cū dim car.

7 ii . borđ . Ibi . i . molin de . v . ſoł. Vluuin⁹ tenuit de [Leuuino coiñ.]

T . R . E . 7 poſt . ualuit . x . ſoł . Modo . xv . ſoliđ . *IN ESSĀLE HÐ.*

Radulf⁹ fili Turaldi ten de epo ARCLEI . ꝑ uno ſolin ſe

deſđ . Tra . ē dim car . 7 ibiđ ſuꝶ adhuc . xxx . ac̃ træ

In dñio . ē una car . 7 vi . uiłłi hñt dimiđ car . Ibi . xii.

ac̃ p̃ti . T . R . E . 7 poſt . ualuit . xl . ſoł . Modo . iiii . liƀ.

Hvnef tenuit de Heraldo. [coiñ]

Anſgot de Rouecest ten HANEHEST . ꝑ dim ſolin

ſe deſđ . Tra . ē . i . car . In dñio . ē una car . 7 ii . uiłłi cū . iiii.

ſeruis . T . R . E . ualeƀ . xx . ſoł . Qdo recep . xxx . ſoł . Modo.

xł . ſoliđ . Goduin tenuit de Goduino. [com']

Ernulf⁹ de Heſding ten de epo CLIVE . ꝑ dim ſolin

ſe deſđ . Tra . ē   In dñio dimiđ car . 7 ii . uiłłi . 7 x.

ac̃ p̃ti . 7 Paſtura . c . ouiũ . T . R . E . 7 poſt . uał xxx . ſoł.

Duo frs tenueꝛ de rege . E . Aluric 7 Ordric.

Iſdē Ernulf ten de epo HADONE . ꝑ iii . jugis ſe

deſđ . Tra . ē . i . car . 7 ibi . ē in dñio . 7 vi . uiłłi cū . i . borđ

hñt . i . car . Ibi . vi . ac̃ p̃ti . T . R . E . 7 poſt . uał . l . ſoliđ.

Modo . lx . ſoł . Oſuuarđ tenuit de rege . E.

in Essex pasture for 200 sheep.
Value before 1066 £12; later £6; now £15.
Before 1066 Godwin son of Karl and Toli held this land
as two manors.

106   Adam also holds 1½ sulungs in COOLING from the Bishop.
Land for 1½ ploughs. In lordship 2 ploughs.
    5 villagers have ½ plough.
    4 slaves; meadow, 7 acres; woodland, 10 pigs.
Value before 1066 and later 40s; now £4; value of what
Richard of Tonbridge has in his territory, 7s.
    Wulfwin held it from Earl Leofwin.

107   Adam also holds BECKLEY from the Bishop. It answers for ½
sulung. Land for ½ plough. In lordship ½ plough;
    1 villager with ½ plough and 2 smallholders.
    1 mill at 5s.
Value before 1066 and later 10s; now 15s.
    Wulfwin held it from Earl Leofwin.

In SHAMWELL Hundred
108   Ralph son of Thorold holds OAKLEIGH from the Bishop. It
answers for 1 sulung. Land for ½ plough. There are a further
30 acres of land. In lordship 1 plough.
    6 villagers have ½ plough.
    Meadow, 12 acres.
Value before 1066 and later 40s; now £4.
    Hunef held it from Earl Harold.

109   Ansgot of Rochester holds HENHURST. It answers for ½
sulung. Land for 1 plough. In lordship 1 plough.
    2 villagers with 4 slaves.
Value before 1066, 20s; when acquired, 30s; now 40s.
    Godwin held it from Earl Godwin.

110   Arnulf of Hesdin holds CLIFFE from the Bishop. It answers
for ½ sulung. Land for ... In lordship ½ plough.
    2 villagers.
    Meadow, 10 acres; pasture, 100 sheep.
Value before 1066 and later 30s.
    Two brothers, Aelfric and Ordric, held it from King Edward.

111   Arnulf also holds HAVEN from the Bishop. It answers for 3 yokes.
Land for 1 plough. It is there, in lordship.
    6 villagers with 1 smallholder have 1 plough.
    Meadow, 6 acres.
Value before 1066 and later 50s; now 60s.
    Osward held it from King Edward.

Odo ten de ep̄o in ead Hadone . I . jugū . Tra . ē dim
car̄ . In dn̄io nichil . ē . T . R . E . 7 poſt . 7 m̄ uaℓ . xx . ſoliđ.

Iſđe Odo ten de ep̄o COLINGES . ꝑ dim ſolin ſe defđ.
Tra . ē dimiđ car̄ . Ibi . ē cū uno borđ . 7 IIII . ac̄ p̄ti.
T . R . E . 7 poſt . ualuit . xx . ſoliđ . Modo. xxx . ſoliđ . God

Helto ten de ep̄o MELESTVN . ꝑ dimiđ ſolin ſ tenuit de rege.
ſe defđ . Tra . ē . I . car̄ . 7 ibi . ē cū . v . uiℓℓis . 7 I . ac̄ p̄ti.
T . R . E . 7 poſt. ualuit . x . ſoliđ . Modo. xxx . ſoliđ.

Vluuard tenuit de rege . E.

IN DIMIDIO LEST DE MIDDELTONE . IN MILDETONE . HVND.

9 b

Hugo de port ten de ep̄o TVNESTELLE . ꝑ . III . ſolins
. . . . . . 7 dim ſe defđ . Tra . ē . IIII . car̄ . In dn̄io ſunt . II . car̄.
7 IX . uiℓℓi cū . I . car̄ . 7 IX . ſerui . Silua . x . porc . 7 ſalina de . XII.
denar̄ . T . R . E . 7 poſt . ualeƀ . VII . liƀ . Modo. VIII . liƀ.
Oſuuard tenuit de rege . E.

Iſđe Hugo ten de ep̄o CERCE . ꝑ . II . ſolins ſe defđ . Tra . ē . II.
car̄ . In dn̄io . ē una . 7 cū . v . borđ 7 uno ſeruo . 7 uñ molin de
VI . ſoliđ 7 VIII . deñ . Vaℓ xxx . ſoliđ . Oſuuard tenuit.

Iſđe Hugo ten de ep̄o TANGAS . ꝑ . II . ſolins ſe defđ . Tra . ē
III . car̄ . In dn̄io ſunt . II . 7 v . uiℓℓi cū . I . car̄ . Ibi æccla 7 IIII . ſerui.
7 uñ molin de . VIII . ſoliđ . Silua . IIII . porc.
T . R . E . 7 poſt . ualuit . VII . liƀ . Modo. x . liƀ 7 x . ſoliđ . Oſuuard

De iſtis ſolins quos hugo de port h̄ . tenuit Oſuuard . v.
ad gablū . 7 III . ſolins 7 uñ jugū 7 dimiđ . quos abſtulit
uillanis regis .

Iđ . H . ten' de ep̄o
STEPEDONE . Oſuuard
teneƀ T . R . E . 7 t̄ ſe defđƀ
ꝑ . I . ſolin dimidio jugo m̄
Tra . ē . II . car̄ . In dn̄io . cū
cū . I . ſeruo 7 v . borđ.
Vaℓ . xxx . ſoliđ.

112   Odo holds 1 yoke from the Bishop, also in HAVEN. Land for
½ plough. In lordship nothing.
Value before 1066, later and now 20s.

113   Odo also holds COOLING from the Bishop. It answers for ½
sulung. Land for ½ plough. It is there, with
    1 smallholder.
    Meadow, 4 acres.
Value before 1066 and later 20s; now 30s.
    Godwin held it from King Edward.

114   Helto holds MERSTON from the Bishop. It answers for ½
sulung. Land for 1 plough. It is there, with
    5 villagers.
    Meadow, 1 acre.
Value before 1066 and later 10s; now 30s.
    Wulfward White held it from King Edward.

In the Half-Lathe of MILTON

In MILTON Hundred

115   Hugh of Port holds TUNSTALL from the Bishop. It answers   9 b
for 3 sulungs .... and ½. Land for 4 ploughs. In lordship 2 ploughs;
    9 villagers with 1 plough and 9 slaves.
    Woodland, 10 pigs; a salt-house at 12d.
Value before 1066 and later £7; now £8.
    Osward held it from King Edward.

116   Hugh also holds UPCHURCH from the Bishop. It answers for 2
sulungs. Land for 2 ploughs. In lordship 1, with
    5 smallholders and 1 slave.
    A mill at 6s 8d.
Value £6.
    Osward held it.

117   Hugh also holds STUPPINGTON from the Bishop. Osward held it before
1066. Then it answered for 1 sulung less ½ yoke. Land for 2 ploughs.
In lordship ... with 1 slave and 5 smallholders.
Value 30s.

118   Hugh also holds TONGE from the Bishop. It answers for 2 sulungs.
Land for 3 ploughs. In lordship 2;
    5 villagers with 1 plough.
    A church; 4 slaves; a mill at 8s; woodland, 4 pigs.
Value before 1066 and later £7; now £10 10s.
    Osward held it.
    Of these sulungs which Hugh of Port has, Osward held 5 for
tribute, and 3 sulungs and 1½ yokes which he took from the
King's villagers.

Ricard fili' Witti ten de epo *Borne* . p̄ . vi . ſolins ſe
defđ . Tra . ē . viii . car . In dn̄io ſunt . iii . ear . 7 xliiii . uitti
cū . iii . borđ hn̄t . x . car . Ibi æccła . 7 un̄ ſeru . 7 iiii . mo
lini de . xvi . ſoliđ 7 viii . den̄ . Piſcaria de . vi . den̄ . Paſtura
unde arauer extnei hōes . vi . ac̄s terræ . Silua . iiii . porc̄ .

T . R . E . ualeb . xviii . lib̄ . Q̄do recep̄ . x . lib̄ . Modo . xix . lib̄ .
Ipſe eps̄ Baioc̄ ten in dn̄io *Hardes* . p̄ ii . ſolins ſe defđ .
Tra . ē . iiii . car . In dn̄io . ē una . 7 ix . uitti cū . ii . car . Ibi
æccła 7 v . ſerui . Silua . xx . porc̄ . T . R . E . ualeb . vii . lib̄ .
7 poſt . c . ſoł . Modo . vii . lib̄ . 7 tam̄ reddit . x . lib̄ . Eduin̄ tenuit
Iſđe eps̄ ten in dn̄io *Stellinges* . p̄ uno jugo   ꝭ de rege . E .
ſe defđ . Tra . i . car 7 dimiđ . In dn̄io nichil . ē niſi . i . borđ
Ibi æccła . Silua . ii . porc̄ .

T . R . E . ualeb . lx . ſoł . 7 poſt 7 modo . xl . ſoliđ . Alret tenuit de rege . E .
Iſđe eps̄ ten | dn̄io *Bvrnes* . p̄ . ii . ſolins ſe defđ . Tra . ē . vi . car .
In dn̄io ſunt . ii . 7 xxv . uitti cū . iiii . borđ hn̄t . vii . car .
Ibi æccła . 7 vi . ſerui . 7 un̄ molin̄ de . xxxviii . denar . 7 una
ſalina de . xxx . den̄ . 7 dimiđ piſcaria . iiii . den̄ . De paſtura
xl . den̄ . Silua . vi . porc̄ 7 dimiđ .   ꝭ Leuinc tenuit de rege . E .
T . R . E . ualeb . xii . lib̄ . 7 poſt . vii . lib̄ . Modo . xii . lib̄ . 7 tam̄
redđ xviii . lib̄ . Q̄đ Hugo de monfort ten . uał . v . ſoł .
H̄ iii . Maneria epi Baioc̄ . tenet Rannulf ad firmā .

Rannulf de colūbels ten de epo *Hardes* . p̄ uno ſolin̄
ſe defđ . Tra . ē . iiii . car . In dn̄io . ē dimiđ car . 7 ix . uitti
hn̄t . ii . car . Ibi æccła 7 viii . ſerui . 7 xiii . ac̄ pti . Silua
iiii . porc̄ . T . R . E . ualeb . vi . lib̄ . 7 poſt . iiii . lib̄ . Modo .
c . ſoliđ . Azor tenuit de rege . E . *In Donamesford hvnd.*
Ipſe eps̄ ten in dn̄io *Wicheha* . p̄ iiii . ſolins ſe defđ .
Tra . ē . xi . car . In dn̄io ſunt . ii . car . 7 xxxvi . uitti cū xxx.ii .
cot hn̄t . ix . car . Ibi æccła 7 un̄ pbr qui dat . xl . ſoł p̄ ann̄ .

In BOROUGH Lathe
In BRIDGE Hundred

119 Richard son of William holds PATRIXBOURNE from the Bishop.
It answers for 6 sulungs. Land for 8 ploughs. In lordship 3 ploughs.
44 villagers with 3 smallholders have 10 ploughs.
A church; 1 slave; 4 mills at 16s 8d; a fishery at 6d; pasture,
from which outsiders have ploughed 6 acres of land;
woodland, 4 pigs.
Value before 1066 £18; when acquired, £10; now £19.

120 The Bishop of Bayeux himself holds (Upper) HARDRES in lordship.
It answers for 2 sulungs. Land for 4 ploughs. In lordship 1;
9 villagers with 2 ploughs.
A church; 5 slaves; woodland, 20 pigs.
Value before 1066 £7; later 100s; now £7; however, it pays £10.
Edwin held it from King Edward.

121 The Bishop also holds STELLING in lordship. It answers for 1 yoke.
Land for 1½ ploughs. In lordship nothing except
1 smallholder.
A church; woodland, 2 pigs.
Value before 1066, 60s; later and now 40s.
Aelred held it from King Edward.

122 The Bishop also holds BEKESBOURNE in lordship. It answers
for 2 sulungs. Land for 6 ploughs. In lordship 2.
25 villagers with 4 smallholders have 7 ploughs.
A church; 6 slaves; a mill at 38d; assalt-house at 30d;
½ fishery at 4d; from pasture 40d; woodland, 6½ pigs.
Leofwin held it from King Edward.
Value before 1066 £12; later £7; now £12; however, it pays £18.
Value of what Hugh de Montfort holds 5s.

Ranulf holds these three manors from the Bishop of Bayeux
at a revenue.

123 Ranulf of Colombières holds (Lower) HARDRES from the Bishop.
It answers for 1 sulung. Land for 4 ploughs. In lordship ½ plough.
9 villagers have 2 ploughs.
A church; 8 slaves; meadow, 13 acres; woodland, 4 pigs.
Value before 1066 £6; later £4; now 100s.
Azor held it from King Edward.

In DOWNHAMFORD Hundred
124 The Bishop himself holds WICKHAMBREUX in lordship. It answers
for 4 sulungs. Land for 11 ploughs. In lordship 2 ploughs.
36 villagers with 32 cottagers have 9 ploughs.
A church; a priest who gives 40s a year.

Ibi uñ parcus . 7 11 . molini de . L . folið . 7 ïï . falinæ de
xxxii . denař . 7 iii . pifcariæ de . iiii . folið . 7 xxx.ii . aĉ
p̃ti . Paftura . ad . ccc . oues . 7 ad xxxi . anim . Silua . q̃t xx.
porĉ . T.R.E. ualeɓ xx.v . liɓ . Q̃do recep: xx . liɓ . Modo:
xxx . liɓ . Huic m̃ p̃tin in cantuaria . iii . mafuræ . reddt̃es
vi . folið 7 viii . denař . Hoc m̃ tenuit Alured de rege . E.
Adhuc jacet ad hunc m̃ dimidiū folin liberæ terræ

9 c

quā Sired tenuit de Alured biga . 7 m̃ teñ Goisfrid
fili malæ træ de epo baioĉ . 7 ual 7 f̃ep ualuit . Lx . folið.
IN HVNDRET 7 in Ciuitate cantuarienfi h̃ Adã
filius Huɓti de epo . iiii . domos . 7 ii . foris ciuitatẽ.
quæ reddunt . viii . folið .   *IN EOÐ HVNÐ.*
Haimo uicecom̃ teñ de epo *LATINTONE* . p̃ dim̃ folin
fe defð . Tra . ẽ . i . cař 7 dim . In dñio . ẽ una . cũ . ii . borð.
Ibi paruū nem de . xii . acris pafturæ . T.R.E. 7 poft . 7 m̃
ual . iii . liɓ.
Ifdẽ Haimo teñ de epo dimidiū folin . 7 ẽ tra . iiii . cař.
In dñio funt . ii . cař . 7 xi . borð cũ . iii . cař . 7 xvi . aĉ filuæ
minutæ . T.R.E. ualeɓ . c . fol . 7 poft . vi . liɓ . 7 m̃ . ix . liɓ.
Has tras . T.R.E. tenueř burgenfes cantuariæ . 7 ufq̨ ad epm
baioĉ qui ab eis cepit.
IN LIMOWART LEST .   *IN FVLCHESTAN HVNÐ.*
Willelm̃ de arcis teñ *FVLCHESTAN.*
T.R.E. fe defð p̨ . xl . folins . 7 m̃ p̨ xxxix.
Tra . ẽ . c 7 xx . cař . In dñio funt . xiiii . cař . 7 cc . 7 ix.
uiłłi 7 q̃ter xx 7 iii . borð . Int om̃s h̃nt . xl.v . cař.
Ibi . v . æcclæ . de qɓ꠵ h̃ Archieps . Lv . folið . Ibi . iii.
ferui . 7 vii . molini de . ix . liɓ . 7 xii . fol . Ibi . c . aĉ
p̃ti . Silua . xl . porĉ . Hoc m̃ tenuit Goduin comes.

De hoc m̃ teñ Hugo fili Wiłłi . ix . folins de tra
uillano꠵ . 7 ibi h̃ in dñio . iiii . cař 7 dim . 7 xxx
viii . uiłłos cũ . xvii . borð qui h̃nt . xvi . cař . Ibi

9 b, c

A park; 2 mills at 50s; 2 salt-houses at 32d; 3 fisheries at 4s; meadow, 32 acres; pasture for 300 sheep and for 31 cattle; woodland, 80 pigs.
Value before 1066 £25; when acquired £20; now £30.

To this manor belong 3 dwellings in Canterbury which pay 6s 8d. Alfred Big held this manor from King Edward. Further, in (the lands of) this manor lies ½ sulung of free land which Sired held from Alfred Big, and which Geoffrey son of Malleterre now holds from the Bishop of Bayeux.
The value is and always was 60s.

125 In the Hundred and in the City of CANTERBURY Adam son of Hubert has 4 houses, and 2 outside the City, from the Bishop which pay 8s.

In the same Hundred
126 Hamo the Sheriff holds NACKINGTON from the Bishop. It answers for ½ sulung. Land for 1½ ploughs. In lordship 1, with
  2 smallholders.
  A small wood of 12 acres of pasture.
Value before 1066, later and now £3.

127 Hamo also holds ½ sulung from the Bishop. Land for 4 ploughs. In lordship 2 ploughs;
  11 smallholders with 3 ploughs.
  Underwood, 16 acres.
Value before 1066, 100s; later £6; now £9.

The burgesses of Canterbury held these lands before 1066 and until [the time of] the Bishop of Bayeux, who took them from them.

In LYMPNE Lathe
In FOLKESTONE Hundred
128 William of Arques holds FOLKESTONE. Before 1066 it answered for 40 sulungs; now for 39. Land for 120 ploughs. In lordship 14 ploughs;
  209 villagers and 83 smallholders; between them all they have 45 ploughs.
  5 churches, from which the Archbishop has 55s. 3 slaves.
  7 mills at £9 12s. Meadow, 100 acres; woodland, 40 pigs.
Earl Godwin held this manor.
Of this manor Hugh son of William holds 9 sulungs of the villagers' land. He has 4½ ploughs there in lordship, and
  8 villagers with 17 smallholders who have 16 ploughs.

III . æcclæ 7 uñ moliñ 7 dimid de . XVI . solid 7 v . den.

7 una salina de . XXX . den . Silua . VI . porc . Val . XX . lib.

Walter de Appeuile ten de hoc M̄ . III . juga 7 XII . acs træ.

7 ibi hɫ . I . car in dñio . 7 III . uiɫɫos cū . I . bord . Val . XXX . solid.

Alured ten . I . soliñ . 7 XL . acs træ . 7 ibi hɫ in dñio . II . car.

cū . VI . bord . 7 XII . acs p̄ti.   Val . IIII . lib.

Walter fili Engelbti ten dimid solin 7 XL . acs . 7 ibi hɫ

in dñio . I . car . cū . VII . bord . 7 v . ac p̄ti.   Val . XXX . solid.

Wesman ten . I . solin . 7 ibi hɫ in dñio . I . car . 7 II . uiɫɫos cū

VII . bord hñtes . I . car 7 dim.   Val . IIII . lib.

Alured dapifer ten . I . solin 7 uñ jugū . 7 VI . acs træ . 7 ibi hɫ

in dñio . I . car . cū . XI . bord.   Val . L . solid.

Eudo ten dimid solin . 7 ibi hɫ in dñio . I . car cū . IIII.

bord . 7 III . ac p̄ti.   Val . XX . solid.

Bernard de S̄ Audoeno . IIII . solins . 7 ibi hɫ in dñio . III.

car . 7 VI . uiɫɫi cū . XI . bord hñt . II . car . Ibi . IIII . serui.

7 II . molini de . XXIIII . solid . 7 XX . ac p̄ti . Silua . II . porc.

De una Dena 7 de tra quæ data . ē ab his solins ad firmā

exeuɴ . III . lib.   Int totū Val . IX . lib.

Baldric ten dimid solin . 7 ibi hɫ . I . car . 7 II . uiɫɫos

cū . VI . bord hñt . I . car . 7 uñ moliñ de . XXX . den . Val . XXX . sot.

Ricard ten . LVIII . acs træ . 7 ibi hɫ . I . car cū . v . bord . Val . X . sot.

Totū Fulcheftan T . R . E . ualeb . c 7 x . lib . Q̄do recep̄ . XL.

lib . Modo qd hɫ iā dñio : ual . c . lib . Q̄d milites ten sup̄dicɫi :

                    ⌐ fimul ual . XL . v . lib.

                        7 x . sot.

3 churches; 1½ mills at 16s 5d; a salt-house at 30d;
    woodland, 6 pigs.
Value £20.
    Of this manor Walter of Abbeville holds 3 yokes and 12 acres
of land. He has 1 plough in lordship, and
    3 villagers with 1 smallholder.
Value 30s.
    Alfred holds 1 sulung and 40 acres of land. He has 2 ploughs
in lordship, with
    6 smallholders.
    Meadow, 12 acres.
Value £4.
    Walter son of Engelbert holds ½ sulung and 40 acres. He has
1 plough in lordship, with
    7 smallholders.
    Meadow, 5 acres.
Value 30s.
    Wesman holds 1 sulung. He has 1 plough in lordship, and
    2 villagers with 7 smallholders who have 1½ ploughs.
Value £4.
    Alfred the Steward holds 1 sulung, a yoke and 6 acres of land.
He has 1 plough in lordship, with
    11 smallholders.
Value 50s.
    Eudo holds ½ sulung. He has 1 plough in lordship, with
    4 smallholders.
    Meadow, 3 acres.
Value 20s.
    Bernard of St. Ouen (holds) 4 sulungs. He has 3 ploughs
in lordship.
    6 villagers with 11 smallholders have 2 ploughs.
    4 slaves; 2 mills at 24s; meadow, 20 acres; woodland, 2 pigs.
    From a pig pasture and from the land which has been given
    from these sulungs at a revenue comes £3.
In total, value £9.
    Baldric holds ½ sulung. He has 1 plough.
    2 villagers with 6 smallholders have 1 plough.
    A mill at 30d.
Value 30s.
    Richard holds 58 acres of land. He has 1 plough, with
    5 smallholders.
Value 10s.
Value of the whole of Folkestone before 1066 £110; when
acquired, £40; now value of what he has in lordship £100;
value of what the aforesaid men-at-arms hold together £45 10s.

Eps baiocsis ten in dñio *ALHAM* . p . vi . solins se defd.

Tra . ē . xxiiii . car . In dñio sunt . v . car . 7 xl.i . uilts

cū . viii . bord hñt . xviii . car . Ibi æccta 7 viii . serui.

7 ii . molini de . vi . solid . 7 xxviii . ac pti . Silua . c . porc.

T.R.E. 7 post: ualuit . xxx . lib | 7 tam reddit . l . lib.

Hoc M̄ tenuit Ederic de rege . E.   *IN ROVINDEN HVND.*

Adā fili hubti ten de epo . i . denā de dimid jugo . quæ

remansit ext diuisionē hugon de montfort . 7 jacuit in

Belice . Ibi ht . ii . uiltos cū dim car . Val 7 ualuit h sep . x . sot.

Ansfrid ten de epo jn Bochelande *IN STOTINGES HVND.*

dimid solin . 7 ibi ht in dñio . i . car . cū uno uilto . Tra . ē . ii . car.

T.R.E.ualeb . xx . sot . Qdo recep: xxx . solid . Modo: xl . sot.

IN ESTREA LEST .   *IN ESTRE HVND.*

Radulf de curbespine ten de epo uñ jugū in Berfrestone.

Ibi una paupcula mulier redd . iii . den 7 uñ obolū.

Val 7 ualuit sep . x . sot hoc jugū.

Rannulf de Colūbels ten ibi uñ jugū . qd in hardes esco

tauit . 7 nunc usq, scotū regis ñ scotauit.

Adelold tenuit de epo *ESWALT* . p . iii . solins se defd . Tra . ē

         In dñio . ē una car . 7 vi . uilti cū . ii . bord hñt . iii.

car . Ibi . ii . serui . 7 siluula ad clausurā . T.R.E . ual . ix . lib . m̄ . xv.

Alnod cit tenuit de rege . E.

Osbñ fili Letardi ten de epo . i . solin in *SELINGE* . Ibi ht uñ

uittm reddentē . ii . sot . T.R.E.ualeb . lx . sot . 7 post 7 m̄: xxxx solid.

Aluuin tenuit T.R.E.

Isdē Osbñ ten de epo *POPESELLE* . p uno solin se defd.

Tra . ē .   In dñio sunt . ii . car . 7 uñ uilts cū . iiii . bord . hñt

dimid car . Hanc trā tenuer . ii . libi hōes de rege . E.

Quidā miles ej ten dimid jugū . 7 ibi ht . i . car in dñio.

Totū T.R.E. ualuit . lx . sot . 7 post: xx . sot . Modo . c . solid.

In LONINGBOROUGH Hundred

29   The Bishop of Bayeux holds ELHAM in lordship. It answers
for 6 sulungs. Land for 24 ploughs. In lordship 5 ploughs.
   41 villagers with 8 smallholders have 18 ploughs.
   A church; 8 slaves; 2 mills at 6s; meadow, 28 acres;
     woodland, 100 pigs.
Value before 1066 and later £30; now £40; however, it pays £50.
Edric held this manor from King Edward.

In ROLVENDEN Hundred

30   Adam son of Hubert holds 1 pig pasture of ½ yoke which
remained outside Hugh de Montfort's territory from the
Bishop; it lay in *Belice*. He has
   2 villagers with ½ plough.
The value of this is and always was 10s.

In STOWTING Hundred

31   Ansfrid holds ½ sulung in *BOCHELANDE* from the Bishop.
He has 1 plough in lordship, with
   1 villager.
Land for 2 ploughs.
Value before 1066, 20s; when acquired, 30s; now 40s.

In EASTRY Lathe
In EASTRY Hundred

32   Ralph of Courbépine holds 1 yoke in BARFRESTON from the
Bishop. There a poor woman pays 3½d.
The value of this yoke is and always was 10s.

33   Ranulf of Colombières holds 1 yoke there which paid the levy
in Hardres; it has never yet paid the King's levy.

34   Aethelwold held EASOLE from the Bishop. It answers for 3
sulungs. Land for ... In lordship 1 plough.
   6 villagers with 2 smallholders have 3 ploughs.
   2 slaves; a little wood for fencing.
Value before 1066 £9; now £15.
Young Alnoth held it from King Edward.

35   Osbern son of Ledhard holds 1 sulung in SHELVING from the
Bishop. He has
   1 villager who pays 2s.
Value before 1066, 60s; later and now 40s.
   Alwin held it before 1066.

36   Osbern also holds (North) PONSHALL from the Bishop. It answers
for 1 sulung. Land for ... In lordship 2 ploughs.
   1 villager with 4 smallholders have ½ plough.
   2 free men held this land from King Edward.
   A man-at-arms of his holds ½ yoke; he has 1 plough there
in lordship.
Value of the whole before 1066, 60s; later 20s; now 100s.

Radulf⁹ de Curbeſpine ten̄ ⁊   *IN BEVSBERGE HVND̄.*

dimid̄ jugū in Popeſſale . ⁊ ibi hŧ . III . boues.

T.R.E. ⁊ poſt: ualuit , IIII . ſoŧ. m̄ .VIII. ſolid̄ . Vluric tenuit de rege. E.

Fulbŧ ten de epō *BERHAM* . p̄. VI.   *IN BERHĀ HVND̄.*

ſolins ſe defđ . Tra̅ . e̅ . XXXII . cař . In dn̄io ſunt . III . cař.

⁊ LII . uiŧŧi cū . XX . coŧ hn̄t . XVIII . cař . Ibi æccŧa . ⁊ unū

molin̄ de . XX . ſolid̄ ⁊ IIII . den̄ . Ibi . XXV . piſcariæ de . XXXV.

ſolid̄ . IIII . den̄ min⁹ . De Auera . ideſt ſeruitiū . LX . ſoŧ . De

herbagio . XXVI . ſoŧ . ⁊ . xx̅ . ac̄s p̄ti . De paſnagio . CL . porc̄.

De iſto M̄ dedit ep̄s unā bereuuichā herbŧo filio Iuonis . quæ

uocaŧ *HVHĀ* . ⁊ ibi hŧ . I . cař in dn̄io . ⁊ XII . uiŧŧos cū . IX . cař.

⁊ xx . ac̄s p̄ti.

De eod̄ q̆q̨̄ M̄ dedit ep̄s Osbno paiſforere . I . ſolin . ⁊ II . molin̄.

de L . ſoŧ . ⁊ ibi . e̅ in dn̄io . I . cař . ⁊ IIII . uiŧŧi cū . I . cař.

Totū *BERHĀ* . T.R.E. ualeb . XL . lib . Q̨do ep̄s receꝑ: ſimiliŧ.

⁊ tam̄ reddebat ei . c . lib.

Modo p̄ ſe Berhā . uaŧ . XL . lib . ⁊ Huchā . X . lib . ⁊ Hoc qđ Osbn⁹

hŧ: VI . lib . ⁊ ŧra cujđā Rannulfi militis . uaŧ . XL . ſoŧ.

Hoc M̄ tenuit Stigand̄ Archiep̄s . ſed n̄ erat de archiep̄atu.

      ſ; fuit de dn̄ica firma regis . E.

Uitalis de epō ten̄ *SOANECLIVE* .   *IN WITENESTAPLE HD̄.*

p̄ dimid̄ ſolin ſe defđ . Tra̅ . e̅ . I . cař ⁊ dim̄ . In dn̄io . e̅ . I . cař : cū.

VŊI . coŧ . q̆ reddŧ . IIII . ſoŧ ⁊ VI : den̄ . Silua : XX . porc̄.

T.R.E. ualeb . XXI . ſolid̄ : Q̨do vitaŧ receꝑ: XII . ſoŧ : Modo: XXX . ſoŧ:

Eduuard̄ Snoch⁹ tenuit de rege . E.

Iſđe Vitaŧ ten̄ de epō . I . jugū in eođ Hund̄ : ⁊ ibi hŧ dimid̄ cař

in dn̄io . cū . IIII . borđ . redđ . VI . ſolid̄ . Tra̅ e̅ dimid̄ cař . Silua . X : porc̄.

T.R.E. ⁊ poſt . ualuit . X . ſolid̄ . Modo: XX . ſolid̄ : Vlſi tenuit de rege . E.

In BEWSBOROUGH Hundred

137   Ralph of Courbépine holds ½ yoke in (South) PONSHALL
he has 3 oxen there.
Value before 1066 and later 4s; now 8s.
    Wulfric held it from King Edward.

In BARHAM Hundred

138   Fulbert holds BARHAM from the Bishop. It answers for 6
sulungs. Land for 32 ploughs. In lordship 3 ploughs.
    52 villagers with 20 cottagers have 18 ploughs.
    A church; a mill at 20s 4d. 25 fisheries at 35s less 4d;
        from cartage, that is, a service, 60s; from grazing, 26s;
        meadow, 20 acres; from pasturage, 150 pigs.
The Bishop gave Herbert son of Ivo an outlier of this manor
which is called Hougham. He has 1 plough in lordship, and
    12 villagers with 9 ploughs.
    Meadow, 20 acres.
From the same manor the Bishop also gave 1 sulung to
Osbern Paisforiere.
    2 mills at 50s.
In lordship 1 plough, and
    4 villagers with 1 plough.
Value of the whole of Barham before 1066 £40; when the
Bishop acquired it, the same; however, it paid him £100.
Value of Barham by itself now £40; Hougham £10; what
Osbern has £6; value of the land of Ranulf, a man-at-arms, 40s.
    Archbishop Stigand held this manor, but it was not the
Archbishopric's, but was of King Edward's household revenue.

In WHITSTABLE Hundred   10 a

139   Vitalis holds SWALECLIFFE from the Bishop. It answers for ½
sulung. Land for 1½ ploughs. In lordship 1 plough, with
    8 cottagers who pay 4s 6d.
    Woodland, 20 pigs.
Value before 1066, 21s; when Vitalis acquired it, 12s; now 30s.
    Edward Snook held it from King Edward.

140   Vitalis also holds 1 yoke from the Bishop in this Hundred; he
has ½ plough in lordship, with
    4 smallholders who pay 6s.
Land for ½ plough. Woodland, 10 pigs.
Value before 1066 and later 10s; now 20s.
    Wulfsi held it from King Edward.

A̅d̅a̅ ten de e̅p̅o . O<small>RE</small> . ꝑ . ɪɪ . ſolins ſe defđ . Tra . e̅ . ɪɪɪɪ . car.

In d̅n̅io . e̅ una . 7 x . uiłłi cū . x . borđ h̅n̅t . ɪɪ . car . Ibi dimiđ æccła

7 un̅ molin̅ de . xxɪɪ . ſoł . 7 ɪɪ . piſcariæ ſine cenſu . 7 ɪ . ſalina

de . xxvɪɪɪ . den̅ . Silua . vɪ . porc . T.R.E . ualeƀ . ɪɪɪɪ . liƀ . . 7 poſt . ʟx.

ſoł . Modo . c . ſoliđ .   Turgis tenuit de rege . E.

Iſđe̅ Ad̅a̅ ten de e̅p̅o S<small>TANEFELLE</small> . ꝑ . ɪɪ . ſolins ſe defđ . Tra . e̅

. ɪɪɪɪ . car . In d̅n̅io . e̅ . ɪ . car . 7 x . uiłłi h̅n̅t . ɪɪ . car . Ibi æccła.

7 vɪ . ſerui . 7 ɪɪ . a̅c pti . Silua . ʟx . porc . T.R.E . ualeƀ . ʟx . ſoł.

7 poſt . xʟ . ſoł . Modo . c . ſoliđ . Turgis tenuit de Goduino.

Hugo de porth ten de e̅p̅o N<small>ORTONE</small> . ꝑ . ɪɪɪɪ . ſolins ſe dfđ.

Tra . e̅ . ɪɪɪɪ . car . In d̅n̅io ſunt . ɪɪɪ . car . 7 xvɪɪɪ . uiłłi cū . vɪ . borđ

h̅n̅t . v . car . Ibi . ɪɪɪ . æcclæ . 7 ɪɪɪ . molini ſine cenſu . 7 ɪɪ . piſcar

de . xɪɪ . den̅ . Silua . xʟ . porc.

T.R.E . ualeƀ . vɪɪɪ . liƀ . 7 poſt . vɪ . liƀ . Modo . xɪɪ . liƀ.

Oſuuard tenuit de rege . E.   I<small>N</small> F<small>ELEBERGE</small> H<small>VND</small>.

Fulƀt ten de e̅p̅o C<small>ILLEHAM</small> . ꝑ . v . ſolins ſe defđ . Tra . e̅ . xx.

car . In d̅n̅io ſunt . ɪɪ . car . 7 xxxvɪɪɪ . uiłłi cū . xɪɪ . cot h̅n̅t . xɪɪ.

car . Ibi æccła 7 vɪ . molini de . vɪ . liƀ 7 vɪɪɪ . ſoliđ . 7 ɪɪ . piſca

riæ de xvɪɪ . den̅ . 7 paſtura de . xvɪɪɪ . ſoł 7 vɪɪ . den̅.

In cantuaria ciuitate . xɪɪɪ . maſuræ ptin̅ huic M̅ . redđ . xv.

ſoliđ . 7 ɪx . a̅c pti . Silua . q̅t xx . porc.

T.R.E . ualeƀ . xʟ . liƀ . 7 poſt . xxx . liƀ . Modo . xxx . liƀ ſimiliť.

7 tam reddeƀ e̅p̅o baiocſi q̅t xx . liƀ 7 xʟ . ſoł.

Sired tenuit de rege . E.   I<small>N</small> F<small>AVRESHANT</small> H<small>VND</small>.

Hugo nepos Herƀti ten de e̅p̅o O<small>SPRINGES</small> . ꝑ vɪɪ . ſolins 7 dim̅

ſe defđ . Tra . e̅ . xx . car . In d̅n̅io non ſunt car.

Ibi xxɪx . uiłłi cū . vɪ . borđ . h̅n̅t . xɪ . car . Ibi æccła . 7 ɪ . molin̅

de . xɪ . ſoliđ 7 vɪɪɪ . den̅ . 7 piſcaria de . x . den̅ . 7 ſalina de . ɪɪɪɪ.

den̅ . 7 xɪɪɪ . a̅c pti . Silua de q̅t xx . porc.

De tra huj M̅ ten Herƀt dimiđ ſolin 7 ɪɪɪ . uirg . 7 ibi h̅ in

d̅n̅io . ɪ . car . 7 ɪ . uiłłm cū . x . borđ h̅n̅tes . ɪ . car.

In the Lathe of WYE
In FAVERSHAM Hundred

141   Adam holds OARE from the Bishop. It answers for 2 sulungs.
Land for 4 ploughs. In lordship 1.
> 10 villagers with 10 smallholders have 2 ploughs.
> ½ church; a mill at 22s; 2 fisheries without dues; 1 salt-house
>   at 28d; woodland, 6 pigs.

Value before 1066 £4; later 60s; now 100s.
Thorgils held it from King Edward.

142   Adam also holds STALISFIELD from the Bishop. It answers for 2
sulungs. Land for 4 ploughs. In lordship 1 plough.
> 10 villagers have 2 ploughs.
> A church; 6 slaves; meadow, 2 acres; woodland, 60 pigs.

Value before 1066, 60s; later 40s; now 100s.
Thorgils held it from Earl Godwin.

143   Hugh of Port holds NORTON from the Bishop. It answers for 4
sulungs. Land for 4 ploughs. In lordship 3 ploughs.
> 18 villagers with 6 smallholders have 5 ploughs.
> 3 churches; 3 mills without dues; 2 fisheries at 12d;
>   woodland, 40 pigs.

Value before 1066 £8; later £6; now £12.
Osward held it from King Edward.

In FELBOROUGH Hundred

144   Fulbert holds CHILHAM from the Bishop. It answers for 5 sulungs.
Land for 20 ploughs. In lordship 2 ploughs.
> 38 villagers with 12 cottagers have 12 ploughs.
> A church; 6½ mills at £6 8s; 2 fisheries at 17d; pasture at 18s 7d.

To this manor belong 13 dwellings in the City of Canterbury
which pay 15s.
> Meadow, 9 acres; woodland, 80 pigs.

Value before 1066 £40; later £30; now likewise £30; however, it
paid the Bishop of Bayeux £80 and 40s.
Sired held it from King Edward.

In FAVERSHAM Hundred

145   Hugh nephew of Herbert holds OSPRINGE from the Bishop. It
answers for 7½ sulungs. Land for 20 ploughs. In lordship no
ploughs.
> 29 villagers with 6 smallholders have 11 ploughs.
> A church; 1 mill at 11s 8d; a fishery at 10d; a salt-house at 4d;
>   meadow, 13 acres; woodland at 80 pigs.

Herbert holds ½ sulung and 3 virgates of the land of this manor.
He has 1 plough in lordship, and
> 1 villager with 10 smallholders who have 1 plough.

Ricard de maris ten dimid solin de hoc ōo. 7 ibi hr̄ . vi . uillos

7 i . bord cū . i . car . 7 q̃dā Turſtin ten . i . jugū . qd redd . v . ſolid.

Totū ōo T . R . E . ualeb . xx . lib . Q̃do herbt recep. xv . lib.

Modo. xx . lib . Huic ōo ptin in cantuaria . i . maſura

de . xxx . denar . Hoc ōo tenuit

Ansfrid ten de epo CILDRESHĀ . p uno ſolin ſe defd . Tra . ē

iii . car . In dn̄io . ē una . 7 iiii . uilli cū . ii . bord hn̄t . i . car

7 dimid . Ibi . v . ſerui . 7 ii . ac p̃ti . Silua . ē s; nil redd.

De hoc ōo ten q̃dā miles tra ad . i . car . Int tot T . R . E.

ualeb . lx . ſol . 7 poſt. xl . ſol . Modo. iiii . lib.

Iſdē Ansfrid ten de epo ERNOLTVN . p uno ſolin ſe defd.

Tra . ē . iii . car . In dn̄io . ē una . 7 viii . uilli cū . ii . car

7 dimid . Ibi . ii. ſalinæ.

7 in ciuitate cantuaria . i. maſura de . xxi . den.

T . R . E . ualeb . iiii . lib . 7 poſt. xl . ſol . Modo. c . ſol . hoc ōo

Burnod de rege . E . tenuit . De iſto ōo ten Rannulf

x . acs . quæ jacen juxta ciuitate . 7 reddeb . xl . ii . den . T . R . E.

Iſdē Ansfrid ten de epo MACHEHEVET . p uno jugo ſe

defd . Tra . ē dimid car . Ibi ſunt . ii . uilli redd . l . denar.

T . R . E . ualeb . l . den . in̄ ual . lx . den . Seuuold tenuit . T . R . E.

Iſdē Anfrid ten de epo BADELESMERE . p uno ſolin

ſe defd . Tra . ē . ii . car 7 dim . In dn̄io . ē una . 7 x . uilli

hn̄t . i . car 7 dim . Ibi æccla . 7 ii . ſerui . 7 piſcaria de xii.

den . Silua . iiii . porc . T . R . E . ualeb . lx . ſol . 7 poſt. lx . ſol.

Modo. iiii . lib .   Hoc ōo reclamat abt S Auguſtini.

qa habuit T . R . E . 7 hund atteſtant ei . S; fili hōis dicit

patre ſuū ſe poſſe uertere ubi uoluerit . 7 hoc n̄ annuſ monachi.

Iſdē Ansfrid ten de epo PERIE . p uno jugo ſe defendeb.

Ibi . ē un bord redd . v . den . T . R . E . 7 poſt. 7 m̄. ual . xvi . ſolid.

Wlui tenuit de rege . E.

Richard of Le Marais holds ½ sulung of this manor. He has
6 villagers and 1 smallholder with 1 plough.
Thurstan holds 1 yoke which pays 5s.
Value of the whole manor before 1066 £20; when Herbert
acquired it, £15; now £20.
To this manor belongs 1 dwelling in Canterbury at 30d.
... held this manor.

146   Ansfrid holds *CILDRESHAM* from the Bishop. It answers for 1
sulung. Land for 3 ploughs. In lordship 1.
4 villagers with 2 smallholders have 1½ ploughs.
5 slaves; meadow, 2 acres; woodland, but it pays nothing.
Of this manor a man-at-arms holds land for 1 plough.
In total, value before 1066, 60s; later 40s; now £4.

Ansfrid also holds from the Bishop   10 b

147   ARNOLTON. It answers for 1 sulung. Land for 3 ploughs.
In lordship 1.
8 villagers with 2½ ploughs.
2 salt-houses; in the City of Canterbury 1 dwelling at 21d.
Value before 1066 £4; later 40s; now 100s.
Burgnoth held this manor from King Edward.
Of this manor Ranulf holds 10 acres which lie near the city
and paid 42d before 1066.

148   MACKNADE. It answers for 1 yoke. Land for ½ plough.
2 villagers who pay 50d.
Value before 1066, 50d; value now 60d.
Saewold held it before 1066.

149   BADLESMERE. It answers for 1 sulung. Land for 2½ ploughs.
In lordship 1.
10 villagers have 1½ ploughs.
A church; 2 slaves; a fishery at 12d; woodland, 4 pigs.
Value before 1066, 60s; later 60s; now £4.
The Abbot of St. Augustine's claims this manor because he
had it before 1066; the Hundred bear witness for him; but the
man's son says that his father could turn where he would; the
monks do not agree with this.

150   PERRY (Wood). It answered for 1 yoke.
1 smallholder who pays 5d.
Value before 1066, later and now 16s.
Wulfwy held it from King Edward.

Isdē Ansfrid ten de epo *PERIE* . p dimiđ solin se defđ.

Tra . ē . i . car . Ibi . iii . borđ . 7 una masura in ciuitate de . xvi.

denar . T . R . E . 7 post . 7 m̄ . ual . xxiiii . solid . Vlueua tenuit   *7 de rege . E.*

Osbn ten de epo *BOCHELAND* . p . iii . jugis se defđ.

Tra . ē . i . car . In dn̄io . ē una . 7 iiii uilti cū . ii . berđ hn̄t

dimiđ car . Ibi . viii . serui.   *7* Seuuarđ tenuit de rege . E.

T . R . E . ualeb . iiii . lib . 7 post . iii . lib . 7 m̄ . lxx . solid.

Isdē Osbn ten un̄ jugū de epo in eod m̄ . 7 p . i . jugo

se defđ . T . R . E . ualeb . xx . sol . 7 post 7 m̄ . ual . x . sol.

Leuuard tenuit de rege . E.

Hugo de porth ten de epo *HERSTE* . p . iiii . jugis

se defđ . Tra . ē . i . car . In dn̄io . ē cū . ii . borđ 7 ii . seruis.

T . R . E . 7 post . ualuit . x . solid . Modo . xxx . solid.

Osuuard tenuit de rege . E.

Adā ten de epo . unū jugū in *ORE* . 7 p . i . jugo

se defđ . Tra . ē . i . car . Hanc ten . iii . uilti m̄ ad

firmā . 7 redđ . xx . sol . 7 tantđ sep ualuit . Ibi æccła . ē.

Leuuold tenuit de rege . E.

Herfriđ ten *TREVELAI* . p . iii . solins se defnđ.

Tra . ē . viii . car . In dn̄io . ē una . 7 xxiiii . uilti cū . v.

borđ hn̄t . vi . car 7 dim . Ibi æccła . 7 v . serui.

Silua . xx . porc . 7 in ciuitate . iii . hage . de . xxxii.

denar . T . R . E . ualeb . vii . lib . 7 post . vi . lib.

Modo . viii . lib . Vlnod tenuit de rege . E.

Herbt tenuit de epo *NORDESLINGE* . Tra . ē

. i . car . p dim solin se defđ . Ibi . ii . borđ redđ

ii . solid . T . R . E . 7 post . ualuit . xx . sol . Modo . xxv . sol.

Turgod tenuit T . R . E .

Hæc . ii . m̄ tenuit Herbt fili Iuonis de epo Baioc.

151 PERRY (Court). It answers for ½ sulung. Land for 1 plough.
    3 smallholders.
    1 dwelling in the city at 16d.
  Value before 1066, later and now 24s.
    Wulfeva held it from King Edward.

152 Osbern holds BUCKLAND from the Bishop. It answers for 3 yokes.
  Land for 1 plough. In lordship 1.
    3 villagers with 2 smallholders have ½ plough.
    8 slaves.
  Value before 1066 £4; later £3; now 70s.
    Saeward held it from King Edward.
    Osbern also holds 1 yoke in this manor from the Bishop.
  It answers for 1 yoke.
  Value before 1066, 20s; value later and now 10s.
    Leofward held it from King Edward.

153 Hugh of Port holds HURST from the Bishop. It answers for 3 yokes.
  Land for 1 plough. It is in lordship, with
    2 smallholders and 2 slaves.
  Value before 1066 and later 10s; now 30s.
    Osward held it from King Edward.

154 Adam holds 1 yoke in OARE from the Bishop. It answers for 1
  yoke. Land for 1 plough.
    3 villagers now hold it at a revenue.
  It pays 20s; its value was always as much.
    A church.
    Leofwold held it from King Edward.

155 Herfrid holds THROWLEY. It answers for 3 sulungs. Land for 8
  ploughs. In lordship 1.
    24 villagers with 5 smallholders have 6½ ploughs.
    A church; 5 slaves; woodland, 20 pigs; in the city 3 sites at 32d.
  Value before 1066 £7; later £6; now £8.
    Wulfnoth held it from King Edward.

156 Herbert held NORTH EASTLING from the Bishop. Land for 1 plough.
  It answers for ½ sulung.
    2 smallholders pay 2s.
  Value before 1066 and later 20s; now 25s.
    Thorgot held it before 1066.

Herbert son of Ivo held these 2 manors from the Bishop of Bayeux.

Turſtin de girunde ten̄ in Bochelande.1.jugū de eṗo.7 pro
.1.jugo ſe defđ.Ibi.ē un̄ uiłts reddens.vi.ſoliđ.Vał 7 ualuit
ſemp.xii.ſoliđ.Turgot tenuit de rege.E.

Rogeri fili Anſchitil ten̄ de eṗo ESLINGES.ṗ uno ſolin
ſe defđ.Tra.ē.1.car̄.Ibi.ē in dn̄io.7 un̄ borđ hī dimiđ
car̄.Ibi æcćła 7 1.molin̄ de.x.ſoliđ.7 11.āc ṗti.
T.R.E.ualeb lx.ſoł.7 poſt:́ xx.ſoł.Modo:́ xl.ſoliđ.
Vnlot tenuit de rege.E.7 potuit ire quo uoluit cū tra.

Fulbt ten̄ de eṗo ESLINGES.ṗ.v.ſolins ſe defđ.T.R.E.
7 m̄.ṗ.11ᵇ.7 ſic fecit poſtq eṗs dedit ⩝ Hugoni filio fulb̄ti.
Tra.ē.vi.car̄.In dn̄io ſunt.11.car̄.7 xxx.uiłti hn̄t.111.
car̄.Ibi æcćła 7 xxviii.ſerui.7 1.molin̄ de.x.ſoł.Silua
.xxx.porc̄.T.R.E.ualeb.x.lib.7 qdo receṗ:́ vi.lib.
Modo.1111.lib.7 tam̄ eṗs habuit.viii.lib.Sired tenuit de rege.E.

Iſđ Fulbt ten̄ de eṗo DODEHA.ṗ uno ſolin ſe defđ.Tra
.ē   In dn̄io.ē una car̄.7 xvii.uiłti cū.x.borđ
hn̄t.11.car̄.Ibi æcćła 7 vi.ſerui.7 dimiđ piſcar̄ de.ccc.
allecib.7 in cantuaria ciuitate.v.hagæ de.vii.ſoł 7 x.den̄.
T.R.E.ualeb.x.lib.Eṗs miſit ad firmā ẋ.lib.Qdo ful
b̄tus receṗ:́ vi.lib.7 m̄ ſimilit̄.Sired tenuit de rege.E.

Ricarđ ten̄ de eṗo RONGOSTONE.ṗ uno ſolin ſe
defđ.Tra.ē   Ibi.11.uiłti hn̄t.1.car̄.7 reddt̄.vi.ſoł.
T.R.E.7 poſt.7 m̄.uał.xl.ſoliđ.Vluiet tenuit rege.E.

IN FERLEBERGE HĎ.

Anſfrid ten̄ de eṗo HORTONE.ṗ dimiđ ſolin ſe defđ.
Tra.ē.1.car̄.Ibi.ē in dn̄io.7 xiii.uiłti hn̄t dimiđ car̄.
Ibi.1.ſeru.7 11.molini de una marka arg.7 viii.āc ṗti.
7 c.āc ſiluæ minutæ.   T.R.E.ualeb.xl . . . . . .
xxx.ſoł.Modo:́ c.ſoliđ.Godricus ten̄ . . . . ge.E.

157   Thurstan of Gironde holds 1 yoke in BUCKLAND from the Bishop. 10 c
It answers for 1 yoke.
    1 villager who pays 6s.
The value is and always was 12s.
    Thorgot held it from King Edward.

158   Roger son of Ansketel holds EASTLING from the Bishop. It answers
for 1 sulung. Land for 1 plough. It is there, in lordship.
    1 smallholder has ½ plough.
    A church; 1 mill at 10s; meadow, 2 acres.
Value before 1066, 60s; later 20s; now 40s.
    Wulfnoth held it from King Edward; he could go where he would
with his land.

159   Fulbert holds EASTLING from the Bishop. It answered for 5 sulungs
before 1066; now for 2; and did so after the Bishop gave the manor
to Hugh son of Fulbert. Land for 6 ploughs. In lordship 2 ploughs.
    30 villagers have 3 ploughs.
    A church; 28 slaves; 1 mill at 10s; woodland, 30 pigs.
Value before 1066 £10; when acquired £6; now £4; however, the
Bishop had £8.
    Sired held it from King Edward.

160   Fulbert also holds LUDDENHAM from the Bishop. It answers for 1
sulung. Land for ... In lordship 1 plough.
    17 villagers with 10 smallholders have 2 ploughs.
    A church; 6 slaves; ½ fishery at 300 herrings; in the City of
       Canterbury 5 sites at 7s 10d.
Value before 1066 £10; the Bishop put it at a revenue for £10;
when Fulbert acquired it, £6; now the same.
    Sired held it from King Edward.

161   Richard holds RINGLESTONE from the Bishop. It answers for 1
sulung. Land for ...
    2 villagers have 1 plough and pay 6s.
Value before 1066, later and now 40s.
    Wulfgeat held it from King Edward.

    In FELBOROUGH Hundred
162   Ansfrid holds HORTON from the Bishop. It answers for ½ sulung.
Land for 1 plough. It is there, in lordship.
    13 villagers have ½ plough.
    1 slave; 2 mills at 1 silver mark; meadow, 8 acres;
       underwood, 100 acres.
Value before 1066, 40[s; later] 30s; now 100s.
    Godric held it from King Edward.

Adā ten de epo *FANNE* . ꝓ dim̅ ſolin *In* . . . . *HVND*.

ſe defđ . Tra . e̅ . i . car̅ 7 dim . In dn̅io ſunt . ii . car . 7 iii . uiłłi

7 iii . ſerui . 7 æcła . 7 xiii . ać p̅ti . Silua . x . porć.

.T.R.E. ualeƀ . iiii . liƀ . 7 poſt . xx . ſoł . Modo . iiii . liƀ.

Hugo de montfort ten̅ inde qđ ual . xx . ſoliđ.

Wadarđ ten̅ de epo *BERCHVELLE* . ꝓ dim̅ ſolin

ſe defđ . Tra . e̅ . i . car̅ . Ibi . e̅ in dn̅io . 7 iii . uiłłi . 7 iii .

ſerui . 7 un̅ molin̅ de xl . den̅ . 7 x . ać p̅ti . 7 un̅ alnetu̅.

T.R.E. 7 poſt . ualuit . xx . ſoł . Modo . xl . ſoliđ.

Werelm tenuit de rege.

Iſđe̅ Wadarđ ten̅ de epo *CVMBE* . ꝓ uno ſolin ſe defđ.

Tra . e̅ . ii . car̅ . In dn̅io . e̅ una . 7 ix . uiłłi cu̅ . v . borđ

hn̅t . i . car̅ 7 dimiđ . Ibi . xiiii . ać p̅ti . Silua . v . porć.

T.R.E. ualeƀ . lx . ſoł . 7 poſt . l . ſoł . Modo . iiii . liƀ . 7 ſer

uitiu̅ uni militis . Leuret de rochinge tenuit de rege . E.

Radulf de curbeſpine ten̅ de epo *BETMONTESTVN*.

ꝓ uno ſolin ſe defđ . Tra . e̅ . vi . car̅ . In dn̅io ſunt . ii.

7 xiii . uiłłi cu̅ . i . borđ hn̅t . iii . car̅ . Ibi . xxx.iii . ać p̅ti.

7 ſilua . xl . porć . De iſto M̅ ten̅ Hugo de montfort

int ſilua̅ 7 paſtura̅ qđ ualeƀ T.R.E. vi . liƀ . 7 poſt

7 modo . tn̅tđ . Ailric tenuit de rege . E.

10 d

Adelolđ tenuit de epo *DENE* . ꝓ uno ſolin ſe defđ . Tra . e̅ . ii . car̅.

In dn̅io . e̅ una car̅ . 7 iiii . borđ . 7 ii . ſerui . 7 una ać p̅ti . 7 ſilua

vii . porć . De iſto ſolino ten̅ Radulf de curbeſpine . i . jugu̅

7 dimiđ . qđ ual 7 ualuit ſep̅ . x . ſoliđ . ſ Adelolđ habuit dimiđ

ſolin 7 dimiđ jugu̅ . 7 T.R.E. ualeƀ xl . ſoliđ . 7 poſt . xx . ſoliđ.

Modo . xl . ſoł . H̅ tra . e̅ in manu regis . Hanc tra̅ tenuer̅

Vlnod 7 Wana 7 Aluuard 7 Vlueron de rege . E . 7 erat dis

ꝑtita in tribȝ locis.

In [WYE] Hundred

163   Adam holds FANSCOMBE from the Bishop. It answers for ½ sulung.
Land for 1½ ploughs. In lordship 2 ploughs, and
   3 villagers and 3 slaves.
   A church; meadow, 13 acres; woodland, 10 pigs.
Value before 1066 £4; later 20s; now £4.
Of this Hugh de Montfort holds what is valued at 20s.

164   Wadard holds BUCKWELL from the Bishop. It answers for ½
sulung. Land for 1 plough. It is there, in lordship.
   3 villagers and 3 slaves.
   A mill at 40d; meadow, 10 acres; an alder wood.
Value before 1066 and later 20s; now 40s.
   Warhelm held it from the King.

165   Wadard also holds COOMBE (Grove) from the Bishop. It answers
for 1 sulung. Land for 2 ploughs. In lordship 1.
   9 villagers with 5 smallholders have 1½ ploughs.
   Meadow, 14 acres; woodland, 5 pigs.
Value before 1066, 60s; later 50s; now £4 and the service of
1 man-at-arms.
   Leofred of Ruckinge held it from King Edward.

166   Ralph of Courbépine holds BEAMONSTON from the Bishop.
It answers for 1 sulung. Land for 6 ploughs. In lordship 2.
   13 villagers with 1 smallholder have 3 ploughs.
   Meadow, 33 acres; woodland, 40 pigs.
   Of this manor Hugh de Montfort holds both woodland
      and pasture, whose value before 1066 was £6; later and
      now as much.
   Aelfric held it from King Edward.

167   Aethelwold held DEAN (Court) from the Bishop. It answers   10 d
for 1 sulung. Land for 2 ploughs. In lordship 1 plough;
   4 smallholders and 2 slaves.
   Meadow, 1 acre; woodland, 7 pigs.
   Of this sulung Ralph of Courbépine holds 1½ yokes,
whose value is and always was 10s.
   Aethelwold had ½ sulung and ½ yoke; value before 1066,
40s; later 20s; now 40s.
   This land is in the King's hands.
   Wulfnoth, Waua, Alfward and Wulfrun held this land from
King Edward; it was divided out in three places.

Radulf⁹ de curbeſpine ten̄ *PIVENTONE* de feudo epī . ⁊ Hugo
de eo . ꝑ uno ſolin ſe defđ . Tra . ē . v . car̄ . In dn̄io . ē una ⁊ dimiđ .
⁊ VII . uiłłi cū . VII . borđ hn̄t . III . car̄ ⁊ dim . Ibi æccła . ⁊ IX . ſerui .
⁊ un̄ molin̄ de LV . den̄ . ⁊ XX . ãc p̄ti . Silua . LX . porc̄ .
T.R.E. ualeb̄ . VIII . lib̄ . ⁊ poſt:´ c . ſoł . Modo:´ VI . lib̄ . Sbern̄ tenuit de rege . E.
Iſđ Radulf⁹ ten̄ . III . denas quæ remanſer̄ ext̄ diuiſion̄ē Hugon̄
de montfort . de piſtinges m̄ . ⁊ ibi . ē un̄ jugū træ . ⁊ una uirga .
⁊ ibi ſunt . II . uiłłi . Vał ⁊ ualuit ſēp . XV . ſoł . *IN FERLIBERG HĐ.*
Herfrid⁹ ten̄ de feudo epī *ESSAMELESFORD* . ꝑ dim̄ ſolin
ſe defđ . Tra . ē . I . car̄ . In dn̄io . ē . I . car̄ . ⁊ III . uiłłi cū . I . borđ hn̄t
I . car̄ . Ibi . III . ſerui . ⁊ VIII . ãc p̄ti . T.R.E . uał . LX . ſoł . ⁊ poſt:´
XL . ſoł . Modo:´ LX . ſoliđ . Alret tenuit de rege . E.
Osb̄t ten̄ de Wiłło filio taū *ALDELOSE* .   *IN BILISSOLD HĐ.*
Ibi jacet dimiđ ſolin . Tra . ē . II . car̄ . In dn̄io . ē una car̄ . ⁊ III .
uiłłi hn̄t dimiđ car̄ . T.R.E . ualeb̄ xxx . ſoł . ⁊ poſt:´ xx , ſoliđ .
Modo . XL . ſoł . H̄ tra . ē de feudo epī baioc̄ . ⁊ remanſit foris
diuiſion̄ē ſuā . Godric tenuit de rege . E . cū *BRADEBVRNE* m̄ .
IN LIMOWART LEST .   *IN OXENAI HVND.*
Osb̄n paisfor ten̄ de epo *PALESTREI* . ꝑ . III . jugis ſe defđ .
Tra . ē . II . car̄ . In dn̄io . ē una . ⁊ IX . borđ hn̄t dim̄ car̄ . Ibi æccła
⁊ II . ſerui . ⁊ X . ãc p̄ti . ⁊ V . piſcar̄ de . XII . den̄ . Silua . X . porc̄ .
T.R.E . ⁊ poſt:´ ualuit . XL . ſoł . Modo . LX . ſoliđ . Eduui . tenuit de rege . E.
IN LEST DE ESTREI.   *IN BEVSBERGE HVND.*
Iſđē Osb̄n ten̄ de epo XII . ac̄s træ . quæ uał ꝑ annū . IIII . ſoliđ .
Hugo de porth ten̄ de epo *PESINGES* ⁊ *PIHA* . ꝑ . II . ſolins
ſe defđ . Tra . ē   In dn̄io . II . car̄ ⁊ dimiđ . ⁊ VI . uiłłi cū . XIIII .
borđ hn̄t . I . car̄ .   T.R.E . ualeb̄ . c . ſoł . ⁊ poſt:´ nichil . M:´ VI . lib̄ .
Lefſtan ⁊ Leuuin ⁊ Eluret ⁊ Sired ⁊ alii . II . tenuer̄ . T.R.E .
⁊ poterant ire q̄libet cū tris ſuis .

In CALEHILL Hundred

168   Ralph of Courbépine holds PIVINGTON from the Bishop's Holding and Hugh from him. It answers for 1 sulung. Land for 5 ploughs. In lordship 1½.
> 7 villagers with 7 smallholders have 3½ ploughs.
> A church; 9 slaves; a mill at 55d; meadow, 20 acres; woodland, 60 pigs.
> Value before 1066 £8; later 100s; now £6.
> Esbern Big held it from King Edward.

169   Ralph also holds 3 pig pastures of POSTLING manor, which remained outside Hugh de Montfort's territory. 1 yoke of land and 1 virgate.
> 2 villagers.
> The value is and always was 15s.

In FELBOROUGH Hundred

170   Herfrid holds SHALMSFORD (Street) from the Bishop's Holding. It answers for ½ sulung. Land for 1 plough. In lordship 1 plough.
> 3 villagers with 1 smallholder have 1 plough.
> 3 slaves; meadow, 8 acres.
> Value before 1066, 60s; later 40s; now 60s.
> Aelred held it from King Edward.

171   Osbert holds ALDGLOSE from William of Thaon's son. ½ sulung lies there. Land for 2 ploughs. In lordship 1 plough.
> 3 villagers have ½ plough.
> Value before 1066, 30s; later 20s; now 40s.
> This land is from the Bishop of Bayeux' Holding and remained outside his territory.
> Godric held it from King Edward; it is with Brabourne manor.

In LYMPNE Lathe
In OXNEY Hundred

172   Osbern Paisforiere holds PALSTRE (Court) from the Bishop. It answers for 3 yokes. Land for 2 ploughs. In lordship 1.
> 9 smallholders have ½ plough.
> A church; 2 slaves; meadow, 10 acres; 5 fisheries at 12d; woodland, 10 pigs.
> Value before 1066 and later 40s; now 60s.
> Edwy the priest held it from King Edward.

In the Lathe of EASTRY
In BEWSBOROUGH Hundred

173   Osbern also holds 12 acres of land from the Bishop, value 4s a year.

174   Hugh of Port holds PISING and PINEHAM from the Bishop. They answer for 2 sulungs. Land for ... In lordship 2½ ploughs.
> 6 villagers with 14 smallholders have 1 plough.
> Value before 1066, 100s; later nothing; now £6.
> Leofstan, Leofwin, Alfred, Sired and two others held them before 1066; they could go wherever they would with their lands.

Eps Baioc̄sis ten in dn̄io *Bilsvitone* . p̄ iiii . solins

se defd̄ . Tra . ē xv . car̄ . In dn̄io sunt . v . 7 xlvii . uilti cū

xxvii . bord̄ hn̄t . xiiii . car̄ . Ibi æcc̄ta 7 x . salinæ de . c . denar̄ .

7 x . ac̄ p̄ti . Silua . l . porc̄ . 7 ii . piscar̄ de . v . den̄ .

T . R . E . ualeb̄ . x . lib̄ . 7 post . xxx . lib̄ . Modo . l . lib̄ . 7 tam̄ reddit

de firma . lxx . lib̄ . Alnod tenuit . In hoc ꝏ misit ep̄s . iii .

denas . quæ remanser̄ ext̄ diuisionē comitis de Ow .

Rotb̄t de Romenel ten de epo *In Lantport Hvnd* .

Afettvne . p̄ uno solin se defd̄ . Tra . ē . iii . car̄ . In dn̄io . ē una .

7 ix . uilti cū . iii . bord̄ hn̄t . iii . car̄ 7 dimid̄ . Ibi . ii . serui .

T . R . E . ualeb̄ . c . sol . 7 post . l . solid̄ . m̄ . iiii . lib̄ .

Isdē Rotb̄t ten de epo in Maresc dim̄ solin . 7 p̄ tanto se defd̄ .

Tra . ē . ii . car̄ . Ibi . xi . uilti . cū . ii . bord̄ hn̄t . iii . car̄ . 7 piscariā

Isd̄ Rotb̄t hr̄ . l . burḡses in burgo de *Romenel* . 7 de eis ſ de . ii . solid̄ .

hr̄ rex om̄e seruitiū . 7 st q̄eti p̄ seruitio maris ab om̄i c̄suetudine p̄t

tribȝ . Latrocin̄ . pace infracta . 7 forstel .

T . R . E . 7 post ualuit . xl . sol . Modo . l . sol . Alſi tenuit com̄ . de Goduino

Isdē Rob̄tus ten de epo dimid̄ solin in Maresc . 7 p̄ tanto se

defd̄ . Tra . ē . ii . car̄ . In dn̄io . ē dimid̄ car̄ . 7 xv . uilti cū . ii . bord̄

hn̄t . iii . car̄ 7 dimid̄ . T . R . E . 7 post . ualeb̄ . xxx . sol . m̄ . xl . sol .

Sex sochi tenuer̄ T . R . E . *In Rovindene Hvnd* .

Isdē Rotb̄t ten de epo *Benindene* . p̄ dimid̄ solin se defd̄ .

Tra . ē . ii . car̄ . In dn̄io . ē una car̄ . 7 iiii . uilti cū . ix . bord̄ hn̄t . ii . car̄ .

Ibi silua . v . porc̄ . 7 una æcc̄ta . T . R . E . 7 post . ualuit . xl . sol .

Modo . l . solid̄ . Oſier tenuit de rege . E . *In Adilovtesbrige*

Isdē Rotb̄t ten de epo dimid̄ jugū . 7 p̄ tanto se defd̄ . *Hvnd* .

In LYMPNE Lathe
In NEWCHURCH (Hundred)

175   The Bishop of Bayeux holds BILSINGTON in lordship. It answers for 4 sulungs. Land for 15 ploughs. In lordship 5.
>47 villagers with 27 smallholders have 14 ploughs.
>A church; 10 salt-houses at 100d; meadow, 10 acres; woodland, 50 pigs; 2 fisheries at 5d.

Value before 1066 £10; later £30; now £50; however, it pays £70 in revenue.
>Young Alnoth held it.

The Bishop put 3 pig pastures into this manor which remained outside the Count of Eu's territory.

In LANGPORT Hundred

176   Robert of Romney holds *AFETTUNE* from the Bishop. It answers for 1 sulung. Land for 3 ploughs. In lordship 1.
>9 villagers with 3 smallholders have 3½ ploughs. 2 slaves.

Value before 1066, 100s; later 50s; now £4.

177   Robert also holds ½ sulung in (Denge) MARSH from the Bishop. It answers for as much. Land for 2 ploughs.
>11 villagers with 2 smallholders have 3 ploughs.
>A fishery at 2s.

178   Robert also has 50 burgesses in the Borough of ROMNEY. The King has all the service from them; they are exempt because of service at sea from all customary dues except three: theft, breach of the peace and highway robbery.
Value before 1066 and later 40s; now 50s.   11 a
>Alfsi held it from Earl Godwin.

179   Robert also holds ½ sulung in (Denge) MARSH from the Bishop. It answers for as much. Land for 2 ploughs. In lordship ½ plough.
>15 villagers with 2 smallholders have 3½ ploughs.

Value before 1066 and later 30s; now 40s.
>6 Freemen held it before 1066.

In ROLVENDEN Hundred

180   Robert also holds BENENDEN from the Bishop. It answers for ½ sulung. Land for 2 ploughs. In lordship 1 plough.
>4 villagers with 9 smallholders have 2 ploughs.
>Woodland, 5 pigs; a church.

Value before 1066 and later 40s; now 50s.
>Osgeard held it from King Edward.

In ALOESBRIDGE Hundred

181   Robert also holds ½ yoke from the Bishop. It answers for as much.

Ibi unā uidua manet reddes̄ xiii . denar p̄ annū . Val̄ 7 ua

luit sep̄ . x . solid . Duo sochi tenuer̄ T.R.E . sine aulis 7 dn̄iis.

Isdē Rotb̄t ten de epo dimidiā denā de M̄ . *TITENTONE* .

qd̄ ten Hugo de montfort . 7 ibi h̄t trā ad dimid̄ car̄ .

7 uñ uillm cū . iii . bord 7 dimid̄ car̄ . 7 ii . piscar̄ de . v . solid̄ .

Val̄ h̄ totū 7 ualuit . xv . solid̄ . H̄ tra . ē ext̄ diuisionē hugon.

IN LEST DE ESTREI.   *IN ESTREI HVND.*

Herb̄t ten ad firmā de rege *RINGETONE* . De feudo . ē epi .

Tra . ē   In dn̄io sunt . ii . car̄ . 7 iiii . uilti cū . vii . bord

hñt . ii . car̄ 7 dimid̄ . Ibi uñ moliñ de . xl . solid̄ .

T.R.E . ualeb̄ . viii . lib̄ . Q̄do recep̄: c . sol̄ . Modo . viii . lib̄ . 7 tam̄

reddit . xiir . lib̄ . Eduuard tenuit de rege . E.

Adā ten de feudo epi in *HAMOLDE* dimid̄ jugū . Riculf

ten de adā . 7 aliud dimid̄ jugū de *AIMOLDE* ten Herb̄t de

hugone nepote Herb̄ti . Hoc utrunq̄ ual . xx . sol̄.

Hugo ten *EWELLE* de epo . p̄ . iii . solins *IN BEVSBERG HVND.*

se defd̄ . Tra . ē   In dn̄io . ē . i . car̄ . 7 xv . uilti cū . xii . bord

hñt . ii . car̄ . Ibi . ii . molini de . xl.vi . solid̄ . 7 iiii . ac̄ p̄ti . Silua

iiii . porc̄ . T.R.E . ualeb̄ xii . lib̄ . 7 post̄: c . sol̄ . Modo: x . lib̄ .

7 tam̄ redd xii . lib̄ 7 xii . solid̄ . Edric de Alhā tenuit de rege . E.

De isto M̄ ten Hugo de Montfort . xvii . ac̄s tre . 7 unā denā.

7 dimid̄ . qd̄ app̄ciat̄ . vii . solid̄.

Isdē Hugo ten de epo *WESCLIVE* . p̄ ii . solins se defd̄ . Tra . ē

            In dn̄io . ē . i . car̄ . 7 xvii . uilti hñt . ii . car̄.

T.R.E . ualeb̄ . viii . lib̄ . Q̄do recep̄: vi . lib̄ . Modo: viii . lib̄.

De hoc M̄ ten Hugo de montfort . ii . moliñ . de . xxviii . solid̄.

Edricus tenuit . de rege . E.

Isdē Hugo ten *SOLTONE* . de epo . p̄ uno solin se defd̄ . Tra . ē

            In dn̄io . ē una car̄ . 7 iii . uilti cū uno bord

reddt̄ . iiii . solid̄ 7 vii . den.

T.R.E . ualeb̄ . xv . lib̄ . 7 post . 7 modo: xxx . solid̄ . In hoc M̄

mansit Godric 7 ten . xx . ac̄s de alodio suo.

A widow who pays 22d a year lives there.
The value is and always was 10s.
    Before 1066, 2 Freemen held it without halls and lordships.

182   Robert also holds ½ pig pasture from TINTON manor from the
Bishop, which Hugh de Montfort holds. He has land for ½ plough;
    1 villager with 3 smallholders and ½ plough.
    2 fisheries at 5s.
The value of the whole of this is and was 15s.
    This land is outside Hugh's territory.

In the Lathe of EASTRY
In EASTRY Hundred
183   Herbert holds RINGLETON at a revenue from the King. It is of
the Bishop's Holding. Land for ... In lordship 2 ploughs.
    4 villagers with 7 smallholders have 2½ ploughs.
    A mill at 40s.
Value before 1066 £8; when acquired 100s; now £8; however,
it pays £13.
    Edward held it from King Edward.

184   Adam holds ½ yoke in HAMMIL from the Bishop's Holding. Riculf
holds from Adam. Herbert holds another ½ yoke of Hammil from
Hugh nephew of Herbert.
Value of both of these 20s.

In BEWSBOROUGH Hundred
185   Hugh holds (Temple) EWELL from the Bishop. It answers for 3 sulungs.
Land for ... In lordship 1 plough.
    15 villagers with 12 smallholders have 2 ploughs.
    2 mills at 46s; meadow, 4 acres; woodland, 4 pigs.
Value before 1066 £12; later 100s; now £10; however, it pays
£12 12s.
    Edric of Elham held it from King Edward.
    Of this manor Hugh de Montfort holds 17 acres of land and
1½ pig pastures which are assessed at 7s.

186   Hugh also holds WEST CLIFFE from the Bishop. It answers for 2
sulungs. Land for ... In lordship 1 plough.
    17 villagers have 2 ploughs.
Value before 1066 £8; when acquired £6; now £8.
    Of this manor Hugh de Montfort holds 2 mills at 28s.
    Edric held it from King Edward.

187   Hugh also holds SOLTON from the Bishop. It answers for 1
sulung. Land for ... In lordship 1 plough.
    3 villagers with 1 smallholder pay 4s 7d.
Value before 1066 £15; later and now 30s.
    Godric lived in this manor; he held 20 acres as his freehold.

Idē Hugo ten̄ in *DOVERE* uñ molin̄ . qui reddit . XLVIII .
ferlingels de frum̄to . 7 ñ p̄tiñ ulli Manerio.

Ansfrid ten̄ de feuᵈo ep̄i in Leucberge dimiđ jugū . 7 ibi
ht̄ . I . uiłłm 7 I . borđ .   Val . V . foliđ . Leuuiñ tenuit de rege . E

Ibidē manſit q̄dā Altet qui tenuit de rege . E . ı̄ı̄ . acſ
in alodı̄u . 7 tenuit eas de Anſfrido . 7 app̄ciat̄ . VI . foliđ .

Rạdulf⁹ de cúrbeſp̄ine ten̄ *COLRET* de ep̄o . T̄ra . ē

         In dn̄io . I . car̄ 7 dim̄ . 7 VI . uiłti cū . VII . borđ
hn̄t . II . car̄ . Ibi . II . ſerui . 7 IIII . āc p̄ti . p̄ . II . folins ſe defđ .
T . R . E . ualeb̄ . VIII . lib̄ . 7 poſt.˸ XX . foliđ . Modo.˸ VI . lib̄ .
Molleue tenuit de rege . E .

Iſđē Radulf⁹ ten̄ *EWELLE* . p̄ III . folins ſe defđ . T̄ra . ē

         In dn̄io . ē uña car̄ . 7 V . uiłti cū . IIII . borđ
hn̄t . II . car̄ . Ibi ſilua . X . porc̄ .

De hoc c̄ō ten̄ q̄dā miles . I . folin de Radulfo . 7 ibi ht̄ . I . car̄
                                      ⌠ cū . III . borđ .

11 b

Totū c̄ō . T . R . E . ualeb̄ . XII . lib̄ . 7 poſt.˸ XX . fol . Modo.˸ XL . fol .
7 tam̄ qđ Radulf⁹ ht̄ . reddit . IIII . lib̄ .   ⌠ Hugo de montfort
ht̄ cap̄ manerii . 7 ibi . V . molin 7 dimiđ de . VI . lib̄ .

Iſđē Radulf⁹ ten̄ de ep̄o *SVANETONE* . ⌠ Molleue tenuit de rege . E .
. p̄ . II . folins ſe defđ . T̄ra . ē   In dn̄io . I . car̄ . 7 II . borđ cū
dimiđ car̄ .

De hac tra ten̄ Rob̄t⁹ de barbes . I . folin . 7 ibi ht̄ . III . uiłłos
cū dimiđ car̄ . 7 q̄dā Hugo ten̄ . I . folin 7 ht̄ ibi . I . car̄ in dn̄io .
7 uñ borđ . T . R . E . ualeb̄ . X . lib̄ . Qᵈo recep̄.˸ XXX . foliđ .
Modo.˸ XL . foliđ . 7 tam̄ redd . IIII . lib̄ . Coloen tenuit de rege . E .

Iſđē Radulf⁹ ten̄ de ep̄o *APLETONE* . p̄ uno folin ſe defđ .
T̄ra . ē   In dn̄io ſunt . II . car̄ . cū . VI . borđ .
T . R . E . ualeb̄ . C . fol . 7 poſt.˸ X . fol . Modo.˸ XL . foliđ .
Aſcored tenuit de rege . E .

188   Hugh holds a mill in DOVER which pays 48 measures of corn; it does not belong to any manor.

189   Ansfrid holds ½ yoke in *LEUEBERGE* from the Bishop's Holding. He has
     1 villager and 1 smallholder.
Value 5s.
     Leofwin held it from King Edward.

190   There also lived a certain Altet who held 2 acres in freehold from King Edward and held them from Ansfrid.
It is assessed at 6s.

191   Ralph of Courbépine holds COLDRED from the Bishop. Land for ... In lordship 1½ ploughs.
     6 villagers with 7 smallholders have 2 ploughs.
     2 slaves; meadow, 4 acres.
It answers for 2 sulungs.
Value before 1066 £8; later 20s; now £6.
     Molleva held it from King Edward.

192   Ralph also holds (Temple) EWELL. It answers for 3 sulungs. Land for ...
In lordship 1 plough.
     5 villagers with 4 smallholders have 2 ploughs.
     Woodland, 10 pigs.
     A man-at-arms holds 1 sulung of this manor from Ralph.
He has 1 plough, with
       3 smallholders.
Value of the whole manor before 1066 £12; later 20s; now 40s;   11 b
however, what Ralph has pays £4.
     Hugh de Montfort has the head of the manor and 5½ mills at £6.
Molleva held it from King Edward.

193   Ralph also holds SWANTON from the Bishop. It answers for 2 sulungs. Land for ... In lordship 1 plough;
     2 smallholders with ½ plough.
     Robert of Barbes holds 1 sulung of this land. He has
       3 villagers with ½ plough.
     Hugh holds 1 sulung. He has 1 plough in lordship, and
       1 smallholder.
Value before 1066 £10; when acquired 30s; now 40s; however, it pays £4.
     Colswein held it from King Edward.

194   Ralph holds APPLETON from the Bishop. It answers for 1 sulung. Land for ... In lordship 2 ploughs, with
     6 smallholders.
Value before 1066, 100s; later 10s; now 40s.
     Ashred held it from King Edward.

Herfrid ten de Hugone *BROCHESTELE* . 7 ē de feudo epī.

T.R.E.
ꝑ uno folin fe defð . Tra . ē   In dñio . ē . ɪ . car . 7 ɪɪ . ferui.

T . R . E . ualeƀ . ʟx . fot . 7 poſt: ʟx . Modo: xʟ . Q̇do herƀt recep:
ɪɪɪ . juga . Modo: ɪɪ . juga . Vlnod tenuit de rege . E.

Turſtin tinel 7 uxor ej ten ad firmā de rege . W . jn Leue
berge . ɪ . jugū 7 v . aĉs . 7 ibi funt . ɪɪ . uitti cū . ɪɪ . borð.
Vat 7 ualuit fēp . vɪɪɪ . foliđ . Boche tenuit de rege . E.

IN LEST DE ESTREI.   *IN ESTREI HVND.*

Ansfrid ten de eꝑo *GOLLESBERGE* . ꝑ . ɪɪ . folins 7 ɪɪɪ.
jugis fe defð . Tra . ē · In dñio funt . ɪL . car . 7 xxɪɪɪɪ.
uitti

T . R . E . ualeƀ . xɪɪ . liƀ . 7 poſt: xx . fot . Modo: ɪx . liƀ.

In Sanduuic hƀ Archieꝑs xxx.ɪɪ . mafuras . ad hoc ꝧ
ptinent 7 redð . xʟɪɪ . foliđ 7 vɪɪɪ . den . 7 Adeluuold
hƀ . ɪ . jugū qđ uat . x . foliđ.

Hoc ꝧ ten . . . teigni de rege . E . 7 ɪɪɪ . manebant
ibi affidu . . . . . tenebant inde . ɪɪ . folins . in paragio.
fed non . . . . . nt ibi . Q̇do Ansfrid recep: fecit uñ ꝧ.

Turſtin ten de eꝑo *CHENOLTONE* . ꝑ uno folin fe defð.
Tra . ē .   In dñio funt . ɪɪ . car . cū . ɪɪ . borð . T . R . E: 7 poſt
.ɪɪɪɪ . liƀ . Modo: vɪɪ . liƀ . 7 tañ reddit . vɪɪɪ . liƀ . Eduuarð

Osƀt fili Letardi ten de eꝑo *BEDESHAM* .   ſ tenuit de rege . E.
ꝑ uno jugo 7 dim fe defð . Tra . ē   In dñio . ē una car.
cū uno uitto 7 ɪɪɪɪ . borð . T . R . E: ualeƀ ʟx . fot . 7 poſt xxx . fot.
Modo: ʟ . foliđ . Godefa tenuit de rege . E.

In eoð ꝧ ten de ipfo osƀno . x . teigni . uñ folin 7 dim
jugū . 7 ibi hñt ipfi . ɪɪɪɪ . car 7 dimid . T . R . E . ualeƀ . c . foliđ.
7 poſt: xxx . foliđ . Modo . ʟx . foliđ.

195 Herfrid holds BOSWELL (Banks) from Hugh; it is from the Bishop's
Holding.   Before 1066 it answered for 1 sulung. Land for ...
In lordship 1 plough and 2 slaves.
Value before 1066, 60s; later 60[s]; now 40[s].
When Herbert acquired it, 3 yokes; now 2 yokes.
Wulfnoth held it from King Edward.

196 Thurstan Tinel and his wife hold 1 yoke and 5 acres in
LEUEBERGE at a revenue from King William.
2 villagers with 2 smallholders.
The value is and always was 8s.
Buck held it from King Edward.

In the Lathe of EASTRY
In EASTRY Hundred
197 Ansfrid holds WOODNESBOROUGH from the Bishop. It answers for 2
sulungs and 3 yokes. Land for ...   In lordship 2 ploughs;
24 villagers.
Value before 1066 £12; later 20s; now £9.

198 In SANDWICH the Archbishop has 32 dwellings which belong to
this manor and pay 42s 8d; Aethelwold has 1 yoke, value 10s.
. . . of King Edward's thanes held this manor; 3 remained
there permanently . . . they held 2 sulungs of it jointly, but
they do not [live] there.
When Ansfrid acquired it he made one manor.

199 Thurstan holds KNOWLTON from the Bishop. It answers for 1
sulung. Land for ...   In lordship 2 ploughs, with
2 smallholders.
Value before 1066 and later £4; now £7; however, it pays £8.
Edward held it from King Edward.

200 Osbern son of Ledhard holds BETTESHANGER from the Bishop.
It answers for 1½ yokes. Land for ...   In lordship 1 plough,
with
1 villager and 4 smallholders.
Value before 1066, 60s; later 30s; now 50s.
Godesa held it from King Edward.
In the same manor 10 thanes hold 1 sulung and ½ yoke
from Osbern himself. They themselves have 4½ ploughs.
Value before 1066, 100s; later 30s; now 60s.

Ansfrid ten de epo SOLES . p uno solin se defd . Tra . e

In dnio funt . II . car . 7 VIII . uilti cu dimid car.

T.R.E. ualeb . c . fol . 7 poft: xx . fol . Modo . VI . lib . Elmer

tenuit de rege . E.

Radulf fili Robti ten de epo HERTANGE . p uno folin

se defd . Tra . e   In dnio . e una car . 7 v . uilti cu . II . bord

hnt . II . car . T.R.E. ualeb . XL . folid . 7 poft: x . fol . Modo . LX . folid.

Eddid tenuit de Rege . E.

Osbn ten de epo . I . jug 7 dimid . In eod hund.

7 ibi ht . VII . bord.

T.R.E. ualuit . x . lib 7 poft: x . folid . Modo: xxx . folid.

Ernold tenuit de rege . E.

IN BEVSBERGE HVND.

Hugo de montfort ten de epo . I . folin uacuæ træ ext:

diuifione fua . 7 adjacuit NEVENTONE M qd ht intra

fua diuifione . 7 ibi ht . I . bord . Val 7 ualuit fep . LX . fol.

Wibtus ten dimid jugu   IN ESTREI HVND.

qd jacuit in gilda de DOVERE . 7 m defd fe cu tra Osbti

filii Letard . 7 ualet p annu . IIII . folid.

Osbn fili Letard ten de epo HAMA . p uno folin fe defd.

Tra . e.   In dnio . e . I . car . cu uno uilto 7 II . bord 7 II . feruis.

T.R.E. ualeb . L . fol . 7 poft: xx . fol . Modo . LX . fol.

Tres teigni tenuer de rege . E.

Ifde osbn ten de epo CILLEDENE . p uno folin 7 uno jugo

7 x . acris fe defd . Tra . e   In dnio nichil m . fed . IX .

uilti hnt ibi . II . car 7 dimid . T.R.E. ualeb . LX . fol . 7 poft:

xxx . fol . Modo: XL . folid . Goduin tenuit de rege . E.

7 alii . v . teigni.   Osbn mifit tras eoz in un M.

201   Ansfrid holds SOLES (Court) from the Bishop. It answers for 1
      sulung. Land for ...   In lordship 2 ploughs;
          8 villagers with ½ plough.
      Value before 1066, 100s; later 20s; now £6.
          Aelmer held it from King Edward.

202   Ralph son of Robert holds HARTANGER from the Bishop.
      It answers for 1 sulung. Land for ...   In lordship 1 plough.
          5 villagers with 2 smallholders have 2 ploughs.
      Value before 1066, 40s; later 10s; now 60s.
          Edith held it from King Edward.

203   Osbern holds 1½ yokes in the same Hundred from the Bishop.
      He has
          7 smallholders.
      Value before 1066 £10; later 10s; now 30s.
          Arnold held it from King Edward.

      In BEWSBOROUGH Hundred   11 c
204   Hugh de Montfort holds 1 sulung of vacant land from the Bishop
      outside his territory; it is attached to the manor of Newington.
      which he has inside his territory. He has
          1 smallholder.
      The value is and always was 60s.

      In EASTRY Hundred
205   Wibert holds ½ yoke which lay in (the lands of) the guild of
      Dover; now it answers with Osbern son of Ledhard's land.
      Value, 4s a year.

206   Osbern son of Ledhard holds HAM from the Bishop. It answers
      for 1 sulung. Land for ...   In lordship 1 plough, with
          1 villagers, 2 smallholders and 2 slaves.
      Value before 1066, 50s; later 20s; now 60s.
          3 thanes held it from King Edward.

207   Osbern also holds CHILLENDEN from the Bishop. It answers for
      1 sulung, 1 yoke and 10 acres. Land for ...   In lordship now
      nothing, but
          9 villagers have 2½ ploughs.
      Value before 1066, 60s; later 30s; now 40s.
          Godwin and 5 other thanes held it from King Edward.
      Osbern put their lands into 1 manor.

Alured ten de epo *MIDELEA* . p . III . jugis 7 XII . acs
se defd . Tra . e . III . car . In dnio . e una car 7 dim . 7 v . uitti
cu . IX . bord hnt . I . car . Ibi æccla . 7 x . ac pti . Silua . x .
porc . T . R . E . ualeb . LX . fot . 7 poft : XL . fot . Modo : LX . fot .
Godric tenuit de rege . E.   *IN SVMERDENE HVND.*

Rotbt Latin ten . VI . acs tre . 7 ibi ht dim car . Hanc
tra tenuit un focks . 7 De nouo dono epi ht in manu
regis de Ricardo filio Gitlebti . x . uittos cu . III . car . 7 filua
.L . porc . 7 inde reddit Rotbt de firma . VI . lib .

Turftin ten de epo *TICHETESTE* . p uno folin 7 dim
se defd . Tra . e   In dnio . e . I . car . cu . IIII . bord . 7
7 parua filuula . T . R . E . ualeb . IIII . lib . 7 poft . XL . fot . Modo :
c . fot . Edric de Alha tenuit de rege . E.

Isde Turftin ten de . epo . I . jugu in *WANESBERGE* .
7 ibi funt . II . bord .   Tochi tenuit de rege . E.

Isde Turftin ten de epo . I . jugu in *ECE* . 7 ibi fun . IIII . bord .
H . II . juga T . R . E . ualeb . xv . fot . 7 poft : x . fot . M . xx . fot .

Osbt ten de epo . I . jugu 7 x . acs . in *MASSEBERGE* .
7 ibi funt . II . uitti cu dimid car . Goduin tenuit de rege . E.

Isde osbt ten de epo . XV . acs . in *ESMETONE* : 7 ibi
manet un pbr . Hoc utrunq T . R . E . ualeb xxx . fot .
7 poft : xx . fot . Modo . xxx . fot . Sired tenuit de rege . E.

                    IN ESTREI HVND.

Radulf de Curbefpine ten de epo . II . folins in *WALWALESERE* .
Tra . e   In dnio . I . car 7 dim . 7 XIIII . uitti cu . II .
car 7 dim . De hac tra ht Rotbt dimid folin . 7 una car
ibi . T . R . E . ualeb . VII . lib 7 x . fot . 7 poft . L . fot . m . VII . lib .
Wluuard tenuit de rege . E.

Osbt fili Letard ten de epo . I . jugu in *ECE* . 7 ibi fun
III . uitti . T . R . E . ualeb . XII . fot . 7 poft : VI . fot . Modo : XVI . fot .
Bernolt tenuit de rege . E.

208   Alfred holds MIDLEY from the Bishop. It answers for 3 yokes and
12 acres. Land for 3 ploughs. In lordship 1½ ploughs.
   5 villagers with 9 smallholders have 1 plough.
   A church; meadow, 10 acres; woodland, 10 pigs.
Value before 1066, 60s; later 40s; now 60s.
   Godric held it from King Edward.

In SUMMERDENE Hundred
209   Robert Latimer holds 6 acres of land. He has ½ plough.
A Freeman held this land. He has it, by a new gift of the Bishop,
in the King's hands, from Richard son of Count Gilbert and
   10 villagers with 3 ploughs.
   Woodland, 50 pigs.
Robert pays from it £6 in revenue.

210   Thurstan holds TICKENHURST from the Bishop. It answers for 1½
sulungs. Land for ... In lordship 1 plough, with
   4 smallholders.
   A small wood.
Value before 1066 £4; later 40s; now 100s.
   Edric of Elham held it from King Edward.

211   Thurstan also holds 1 yoke in WOODNESBOROUGH from the Bishop.
   2 smallholders there.
   Toki held it from King Edward.

212   Thurstan also holds 1 yoke in EACH from the Bishop.
   4 smallholders there.
Value of these 2 yokes before 1066, 15s; later 10s; now 20s.

213   Osbert holds 1 yoke and 10 acres in MARSHBOROUGH from the
Bishop.
   2 villagers with ½ plough there.
   Godwin held it from King Edward.

214   Osbert also holds 15 acres in ELMTON from the Bishop.
   A priest lives there.
Value of both of these before 1066, 30s; later 20s; now 30s.
   Sired held them from King Edward.

In EASTRY Hundred
215   Ralph of Courbépine holds 2 sulungs in WALDERSHARE from the
Bishop. Land for ... In lordship 1½ ploughs, and
   14 villagers with 2½ ploughs.
   Robert has ½ sulung of this land. 1 plough there.
Value before 1066 £7 10s; later 50s; now £7.
   Wulfward held it from King Edward.

216   Osbern son of Ledhard holds 1 yoke in EACH from the Bishop.
   3 villagers there.
Value before 1066, 12s; later 6s; now 16s.
   Bernhold held it from King Edward.

Rad de curbespine ten de epo *Essewelle* . p . iii . so
lins se defd . Tra . e   In dnio sunt . iii . car . 7 un
uilts cu . vii . bord hnt dim car . Ibi un seru . Val . vi . lib.
·Molleue tenuit de rege . E.

Osbn ten de epo unu M qd tenuer . iii . libi hoes
de rege . E . p uno solin 7 dimid se defd . Tra . e
In dnio . e una car . 7 un uilts cu uno bord ht dim car.
T . R . E . 7 post . 7 modo: ual . iiii . lib.

Radulf de Colubers ten de epo *Selinges* . p uno
solin 7 dimid se defd . Tra . e   In dnio . e una car.
7 iiii . uilti cu . iii . bord hnt dimid car . 7 i . car 7 dim
T . R . E . ualeb . iiii . lib : 7 post: xl . sol . Modo: c . sol.
Vluuic tenuit de rege . E.

Radulf de curbespine ten *Danetone* de epo . p dimid
solin se defd . Tra . e . iii . car . In dnio . e una . 7 iiii . uilti cu
ii . bord hnt . i . car . Ibi æccla . 7 iiii . masuræ in cantuaria.
reddent . vi . sol un den min . T . R . E . ualeb . lx . sol . 7 post:
xx . sol . Modo: lx . sol . Molleue tenuit de rege . E.

Isde Radulf ten de epo . i . jugu in Brochestele . Qd
Molleue tenuit de rege . E . 7 ibi . e un uilts redd . xxx . den.

Radulf de curbespine ten . xl . acs træ . *In Bevsberge Hd*.
quas tenuit Molleue de rege . E . 7 ibi . e un uilts reddes
vi . solid . 7 tant ualet.

Rannulf de ualbadon ten dimid jugu in *Hamestede*.
qd tenuer . ii . libi hoes de rege . E . in Bochelande . 7 dicit
m Rannulf qd eps baiocsis dedit cuida suo fri.
Ibi est un uilts reddens vi . x . sol. xxx . denar . *In Nvniberg Hd*.

Anschitil de ros ten de feudo epi *Acres* . qd tenuer
duo frs . 7 qsq habuit haula . Modo . e p uno M . 7 p una
solin se defd . Tra . e . ii . car . In dnio . e una car 7 dim.

217 Ralph of Courbépine holds EASOLE from the Bishop. It answers
for 3 sulungs. Land for ... In lordship 3 ploughs.
1 villager with 7 smallholders have ½ plough. 1 slave.
Value £6.
Molleva held it from King Edward.

218 Osbern holds a manor from the Bishop which 3 free men held   11 d
from King Edward. It answers for 1½ sulungs. Land for ...
In lordship 1 plough.
1 villager with 1 smallholder has ½ plough.
Value before 1066, later and now £4.

219 Ranulf of Colombières holds SHELVING from the Bishop. It answers
for 1½ sulungs. Land for ... In lordship 1 plough.
4 villagers with 3 smallholders have ½ plough and 1½ ploughs.
Value before 1066 £4; later 40s; now 100s.
Wulfwy held it from King Edward.

220 Ralph of Courbépine holds DENTON from the Bishop. It answers
for ½ sulung. Land for 3 ploughs. In lordship 1.
4 villagers with 2 smallholders have 1 plough.
A church; 4 dwellings in Canterbury which pay 6s less 1d.
Value before 1066, 60s; later 20s; now 60s.
Molleva held it from King Edward.

221 Ralph also holds 1 yoke in BOSWELL (Banks) from the Bishop, which
Molleva held from King Edward.
1 villager who pays 30d.

In BEWSBOROUGH Hundred

222 Ralph of Courbépine holds 40 acres of land which Molleva held
from King Edward.
1 villager who pays 6s.
The value is as much.

223 Ranulf of Vaubadon holds ½ yoke in HEMSTED which 2 free
men held from King Edward in Buckland; now Ranulf says that
the Bishop of Bayeux gave it to a brother of his.
1 villager there who pays 30d.
Value 10s.

In LONINGBOROUGH Hundred

224 Ansketel of Rots holds ACRISE from the Bishop's Holding; two
brothers held it and each had a hall. Now it is one manor; it
answers for 1 sulung. Land for 2 ploughs. In lordship 1½ ploughs.

7 .v. uilli cu . v . bord hnt . i . car . Silua . x . porc . 7 æccła.

T.R.E. ualeb . xl . soł . 7 post. xxx . soł . Modo. lx . soł.

Rogeri fili Anfchitil ten de   *In Briceode Hd.*

feudo epi *Hastingelai* . qd tenuit Vlnod de rege . E.

7 tc defd se p uno solin . 7 m p . iii . jugis . qa Hugo

de montfort ten alia parte int diuisione suam.

Tra . e . iii . car . In dnio sunt . ii . 7 ii . uilli cu . vi . bord

hnt . i . car . Ibi . iiii . serui . 7 silua . i . porc.

T.R.E. ualeb . lx . soł . 7 post. xxx . soł . Modo . lx . solid.

Terra Æcclæ De Labatailge.

.VI. Abbas Sci Martini de Loco belli tenet co qd uocat *Wi.*

qd T.R.E. 7 m se defd p . vii . solins . Tra . e . lii . car.

In dnio . ix . car sunt . 7 cxiiii . uilli cu . xxii . bord hnt

xvii . car . Ibi æccła . 7 vii . serui . 7 iiii . molini de xxiii.

solid 7 viii . den . 7 cxxxiii . ac pti . 7 silua . ccc . porc de

pasnagio.

T.R.E. ualeb qt xx lib 7 . c . solid . 7 vi . soł 7 viii . den . Qdo recep

cxxv . lib 7 x . soł de . xx . in ora . Modo. c . lib ad numeru

7 Si abb habuisset sacas 7 socas. xx . lib plus appciaret.

Radulf de curbespina una dena 7 un jugu de tra sochoz

huj Manerii . redd de csuetud . vi . den . 7 Adelulf . ii . partes

uni solin . redd . xii . denar . 7 Hugo de montfort ht . ii . juga.

redd . ccc . Anguill 7 ii . solid . 7 saca 7 soca . in T.R.E. reddeban.

De . xxii . hund ptin isti co saca 7 soca . 7 oma forisfacta quæ

juste ptin regi.

5 villagers with 5 smallholders have 1 plough.
Woodland, 10 pigs; a church.
Value before 1066, 40s; later 30s; now 60s.

In BIRCHOLT Hundred

225 Roger son of Ansketel holds HASTINGLEIGH from the Bishop's
Holding; Wulfnoth held from King Edward. Then it answered
for 1 sulung, now for 3 yokes, because Hugh de Montfort holds
the other part in his territory. Land for 3 ploughs In lordship 2.
2 villagers with 6 smallholders have 1 plough.
4 slaves. Woodland, 1 pig.
Value before 1066, 60s; later 30s; now 60s.

6   LAND OF BATTLE CHURCH

1 The Abbot of St. Martin of the Battlefield holds a manor which
is called WYE, which answered for 7 sulungs before 1066 and now.
Land for 52 ploughs. In lordship 9 ploughs.
114 villagers with 22 smallholders have 17 ploughs.
A church; 7 slaves. 4 mills at 23s 8d; meadow, 133 acres;
woodland, 300 pigs from pasturage.
Value before 1066 £80 and 100s and 6s 8d; when acquired
£125 10s at 20 (pence) to the *ora*; now £100 at face value; if the
Abbot had had the full jurisdictions it would be assessed at £20
more.
Ralph of Courbépine holds 1 pig pasture and 1 yoke of
Freemen's land of this manor; he pays 6d as a customary due;
Aethelwulf (holds) 2 parts of 1 sulung; he pays 12d. Hugh de
Montfort has 2 yokes which pay 300 eels and 2s. Before 1066
they paid full jursidiction.

Full jurisdiction and all the penalties from 22 Hundreds
which rightly belong to the King belong to this manor.

TERRA ÆCCLÆ SCI AVGVSTINI

IN DIMIDIO LEST DE SVDTONE. IN LITELAI HVND.

.VII. ABBAS Sci Avgvstini ht uñ ꝏ nomine
PLVMSTÈDE . qd defd se ꝑ . II . solins 7 uno jugo.

Tra . e̅   In dñio . e̅ . I . car̅ . 7 xvII . uitti cũ
vI . cot hñt . vI . car̅ . Ibi silua . v . porc de pasnagio.

T . R . E . 7 post. ualuit . x . lib̅ . Modo. xII . lib̅ . 7 tam
reddit xIIII . lib̅ . 7 vIII . solid 7 III . den.

IN LEST DE ELESFORT.   *IN HAIHORNE HVND.*

Ipse abb̅ teñ LERTHA . qd se defd ꝑ . v . solins 7 dimid.

Tra . e̅ xvIII . car̅ . In dñio sunt . II . car̅ . 7 xL . uitti cũ
vII . bord hñt xvI . car̅ . Ibi . I . seru̅ . 7 II . molini de . vI .
solid 7 vIII . den . 7 vIII . ac̅ pti . 7 Silua . xL . porc.

T . R . E . ualeb̅ . xxvIII . lib̅ . 7 post. xvI . lib̅ . Modo. xxvIII . lib̅.

De hoc ꝏ teñ Robt Latin uñ jugũ . qd ualet . v . solid.

IN BOROART LEST.   *IN BRIGE HVND.*

Ipse abb̅ teñ BORNE . qd se defd ꝑ uno solin . Tra . e̅
II . car̅ . In dñio . e̅ una . 7 Ix . uitti cũ uno bord hñt . I . car̅.

Ibi . II . molini de . Ix . solid 7 vI . den . 7 III . ac̅ pti 7 dimid.

Silua de . v . porc . T . R . E . ualeb̅ . c . sot . 7 post. xL . solid.

Modo. c . solid.

Ipse abb̅ teñ ꝏ LANPORT . 7 ibi . e̅ uñ solin 7 uñ jug̅.
7 sep̅ q̅etu̅ fuit . 7 sine c̅s̅uetudine . 7 uñ jugũ jacet in alio
hund qd ptiñ isti ꝏ . 7 Lxx . burgenses erant in cantua
ria ciuit huic ꝏ ptinent . In hoc ꝏ sunt . II . car̅ 7 dim̅
in dñio . 7 xx . vIII . uitti cũ LxIII . bord hñt . vI . car̅.

Ibi . xvII . ac̅ pti.

T . R . E . ualeb̅ xx . lib . 7 post. xvIII . lib . Modo. xxxv . lib̅
7 IIII . solid:

In the Half-Lathe of SUTTON
In LITTLE Hundred

1   The Abbot of St. Augustine's has a manor named PLUMSTEAD, which
     answers for 2 sulungs and 1 yoke. Land for ... In lordship 1 plough.
         17 villagers with 6 cottagers have 6 ploughs.
         Woodland, 5 pigs from pasturage.
     Value before 1066 and later £10; now £12; however, it pays
     £14 8s 3d.

In the Lathe of AYLESFORD
In EYHORNE Hundred
The Abbot himself holds

2   LENHAM, which answers for 5½ sulungs. Land for 18 ploughs.
     In lordship 2 ploughs.
         40 villagers with 7 smallholders have 16 ploughs.
         1 slave; 2 mills at 6s 8d; meadow, 8 acres; woodland, 40 pigs.
     Value before 1066 £28; later £16; now £28.
         Robert Latimer holds 1 yoke of this manor, value 5s.

in BOROUGH Lathe
in BRIDGE Hundred

3   BEKESBOURNE which answers for 1 sulung. Land for 2 ploughs.
     In lordship 1.
         9 villagers with 1 smallholder have 1 plough.
         2 mills at 9s 6d; meadow, 3½ acres; woodland at 5 pigs.
     Value before 1066, 100s; later 40s; now 100s.

4   the manor of LANGPORT. 1 sulung and 1 yoke. It was always
     exempt and without customary dues. 1 yoke which belongs
     to this manor lies in another Hundred. 70 burgesses (who)
     were in the City of Canterbury belong to this manor. In this
     manor are 2½ ploughs in lordship.
         28 villagers with 63 smallholders have 6 ploughs.
         Meadow, 17 acres.
     Value before 1066 £20; later £18; now £35 4s.

Ipſe abb ten *Litebvrne* . qd ſe defd ꝓ . VII : ſolins.

Tra . e . XII . car . In dnio ſunt . III . car . 7 XXXV . uilli
cu . XIIJI . cot . hnt . VI . 7 dim . Ibi æccla . 7 XXXVIII . ac pti.
Silua . IrII . porc . T . R . E . ualeb . XX . lib . 7 poſt . XX . lib.
Modo : XXXII . lib.

De iſto ᴍ hr eps baioc in ſuo parco tant qd uat . LX . ſol.

Ipſe abb ten *Warwintone* 7 ded ei eps baiocſis
ꝓ excabio parci ſui . ꝓ dimid ſolin 7 XLII . acris træ ſe
defd . Tra . e: I . car : 7 ibi . e in dnio . cu . III . cotar . 7 XVI.
ac pti . T . R . E : ualeb . IIII . lib . 7 poſt : XL . ſol . Modo : IIII . lib.
Hoc ᴍ tenuit Edric de Sbern biga . 7 m ten Radulf

Ipſe abb ten *Estvrai* *In Estvrai Hvnd.* f de abbe.
qd ſe defd ꝓ . V . ſolins qetis . Tra . e . XII . car . In dnio
ſunt . II . car . 7 XXXIX . cu XXXII . bord hnt . XII . car . Ibi
æccla . 7 X . molini de . VIII . lib . 7 VII . piſcariæ de . V . ſol.
7 XX . VIII . ac pti . De paſnagio . XXX . porc.
T . R . E . ualeb . L . ſol . Qdo abb recep : XL . V . lib . Modo :
. L . lib . 7 tam redd . L . IIII . lib . *In Tanet Hvnd.*

Ipſe abb ten *Tanet* . ᴍ . qd ſe defd f S *Mildredæ.*
ꝓ . XLVIII . ſolins . Tra . e . LXII . car . In dnio ſunt . II.
7 CL . uilli cu . L . bord hnt . LXIII . car . Ibi æccla 7 un pbr

12 b

qui dat . XX . ſolid p ann . Ibi una ſalina . 7 II . piſcariæ:
de . III . den : 7 un molin.
T . R . E : ualeb qt . XX . lib : Qdo abb recep : XL . lib : Modo . c . lib.
De iſto ᴍ ten : III . milites tant de tra uillanoʒ . qd uat
IX . lib quando pax . e in tra . 7 ibi hnt : IIII : cari

Ipſe abb ten *Cistelet* : qd ꝓ . XII : *In Cistelet Hvnd.*
ſolins ſe defd . Tra . e . XXX . car . In dnio ſunt : V . car . 7 LXXII.
uilti cu . LXVIII . bord hnt . XXXIX . car . Ibi æccla de . XII . ſolid.
7 XIIII . ſerui . Ibi . L . ac pti . 7 XLVII : ſalinæ de . L . ſumis ſalis.

12 a, b

in DOWNHAMFORD Hundred

5   LITTLEBOURNE, which answers for 7 sulungs. Land for 12 ploughs.
In lordship 3 ploughs.
35 villagers with 14 cottagers have 6½ [ploughs].
A church; meadow, 38 acres; woodland, 4 pigs.
Value before 1066 £25; later £20 now £32.
The Bishop of Bayeux has in his park as much of this manor as is valued at 60s.

6   GARRINGTON. The Bishop of Bayeux gave it to him in exchange for his park. It answers for ½ sulung and 42 acres of land. Land for 1 plough. It is there, in lordship, with
3 cottagers.
Meadow, 16 acres.
Value before 1066 £4; later 40s; now £4.
Edric held this manor from Esbern Big; now Ralph holds it from the Abbot.

in STURRY Hundred

7   STURRY, which answers for 5 exempt sulungs. Land for 12 ploughs.
In lordship 2 ploughs.
39 [villagers] with 32 smallholders have 12 ploughs.
A church; 10 mills at £8; 7 fisheries at 5s; meadow, 28 acres; from pasturage, 30 pigs.
Value before 1066, 50s; when the Abbot acquired it £45; now £50; however, it pays £54.

in the THANET Hundred of St. MILDRED

8   the manor of MINSTER, which answers for 48 sulungs. Land for 62 ploughs. In lordship 2.
150 villagers with 50 smallholders have 63 ploughs. A church and a priest who gives 20s a year.
A salt-house; 2 fisheries at 3d; a mill.   12 b
Value before 1066 £80; when the Abbot acquired it £40; now £100.
3 men-at-arms hold as much of the villagers' land of this manor as is valued at £9 when there is peace in the land; they have 3 ploughs there.

in CHISLET Hundred

9   CHISLET, which answers for 12 sulungs. Land for 30 ploughs.
In lordship 5 ploughs.
72 villagers with 68 smallholders have 39 ploughs.
A church at 12s; 14 slaves. Meadow, 50 acres. 47 salt-houses at 50 packloads of salt; from pasturage, 130 pigs.

De paſnag̃ . cxxx . porc . T . R . E . ualeb̃ . L . III . lib̃ ; 7 poſt: xL . lib̃ . Modo: LXXVIII . lib̃ . Ibi ſunt . III . arpenni uineæ. De iſto c̃o ten . IIII . francig̃ miiites . qd̃ ual̃ .p ann̄ xII . lib̃. Ipſe abb̃ ten̄ unū paruū burgū *IN FOREVVIC HVND.* qd̃ uocat̃ *FOREWIC* . Huj burgi . II ; partes ded̃ rex . E . ſc̃o Auguſtino . T̃cia ū parte quæ fuerat Goduini: eps baioc̃ſis c̃ceſſit eid̃ ſc̃o annuente rege . W.

.p uno ſe jugo defd̃ . Ibi fuer̃ . c . maſuræ træ . IIII . min̄. reddt̃es . xIII . ſol̃ . Modo ſunt . LXXLIII . maſuræ . tntd̃ reddt̃. T . R . E . 7 poſt ualeb̃ . c . ſolid̃ . Modo: xI . lib̃ 7 II . ſolid̃. Ibid̃ē ſunt . xxIIII . ac̃ træ . quas ſep̃ habuit . S̃ Auguſtin̄. vbi fuer̃ 7 ſunt . vI . burg̃ſes reddt̃es . xxII . ſolid̃. In iſto burgo ten̄ archieps Lanfr̃ . vII ; maſuras træ . quæ T . R . E . ſeruieba̋t S̃ Auguſtino . m̄ arc̃h aufert ei ſeruitiū. Juxta ciuitate cantuar̃ h̃t S̃ Augtin̄

dimid̃ ſolin . qd̃ ſep̃ fuit quietū ; 7 ibi . ē . I . car̃ in dn̄io . cū xv . bord̃ . 7 vII . acræ p̃ti . 7 ibid̃ ſunt . IIII . ac̃ tre q̃s ten̄ . IIII . moniales in elemoſina de abb̃e . 7 reddt̃ ; II . ſol̃ 7 unā ſumā farinæ . Totū hoc T . R . E ; 7 poſt . 7 m̄: ual . IIII . lib̃. *IN LEST DE WIWARLET . IN FAVRESHÆNT HVND.* Ipſe abb̃ ten̄ *WIRENTONE* . qd̃ .p uno ſolin ſe defd̃. Tra . ē . II . car̃ . In dn̄io . ē una . 7 Ix . uiłłi cū . I . car̃ . Ibi . II. ac̃ p̃ti . 7 v . porc de paſnag̃ ſiluæ . T . R . E . ualeb̃ . Lx . ſol̃. Qdo recep̃: xL . ſol̃ . Modo: IIII ; lib̃ . *IN WI HVND.* Ipſe abb̃ ten̄ *ESMEREFEL* . 7 Anſchitil de eo . .p uno ſolin ſe defd̃ . Tra . ē . I . car̃ . 7 ibi . ē in dn̄io eū . v . bord̃ . 7 vI . ac̃ p̃ti. Silua . x . porc . T . R . E . xL . ſol̃ . 7 poſt: xx . ſol̃ . Modo: xL . ſol̃. In *DÆRENDEN* ten̄ Ada de abb̃e dimid̃ ſolin . Tra . ē dimid̃ car̃ . Ibi ſunt . II . ſerui . 7 vII . ac̃ p̃ti . Val 7 ſep̃ ualuit . xx . ſol̃.

Value before 1066 £53; later £40; now £78.
3 *arpents* of vines there.
Of this manor 4 French men-at-arms hold what is valued at
£12 a year.

in FORDWICH Hundred

10   a small Borough which is called FORDWICH. King Edward gave two
parts of this Borough to St. Augustine's; but the Bishop of Bayeux,
with King William's assent, also assigned to St. Augustine's the third
part, which had belonged to Earl Godwin.
    It answers for 1 yoke. There were 100 measures of land less 4
there which paid 13s. Now there are 73 dwellings, which pay as much.
Value before 1066 and later 100s; now £11 2s.
    There also are 24 acres of land which St. Augustine's always had,
where there were and are 6 burgesses who pay 22s.
    In this Borough Archbishop Lanfranc holds 7 measures of land
which served St. Augustine's before 1066; now the Archbishop
takes (their) service from it.

11   Near the City of Canterbury St. Augustine's has ½ sulung which was
always exempt. 1 plough there in lordship, with
    15 smallholders.
    Meadow, 7 acres.
    There are also 4 acres of land which 4 nuns hold in alms from the
Abbot; they pay 2s and 1 packload of flour.
Value of all this before 1066, later and now £4.

In the Lathe of WYE
In FAVERSHAM Hundred

12   The Abbot holds WILDERTON himself, which answers for 1 sulung.
Land for 2 ploughs. In lordship 1;
    9 villagers with 1 plough.
    Meadow, 2 acres; 5 pigs from woodland pasturage.
Value before 1066, 60s; when acquired 40s; now £4.

In WYE Hundred

13   The Abbot holds ASHENFIELD himself and Ansketel from him. It
answers for 1 sulung. Land for 1 plough. It is there, in lordship, with
    5 smallholders.
    Meadow, 6 acres; woodland, 10 pigs.
[Value] before 1066, 40s; later 20s; now 40s.

14   In DERNEDALE Adam holds ½ sulung from the Abbot. Land for
½ plough.
    2 slaves.
    Meadow, 7 acres.
The value is and always was 20s.

Ipſe abƀ ten̅ *SETLINGES* m̅   *In Boltone hvnd.*

ſine halla . qđ ſe defđ ℣ . vi . ſolins . Tra . ē . xi . car̅.

Nichil in dn̅io . Ibi xxx . uiƚƚi hn̅t . x . car̅ . Ibi æcc̅ƚa.

T . R . E . ualeƀ xv . liƀ . Q̊do recep̅: viii . liƀ . Modo: xiii . liƀ

Ipſe abƀ ten̅ dimiđ jugu̅   *In Caleheve hvnd.* ∫ 7 . v . ſoliđ.

in Rotinge . qđ T . R . E . ſe defđ ℣ dim̅ ſolin . Ibi fuit 7 eſt

una car̅ in dn̅io . Vaƚ 7 ualuit ſēp . xv . ſoƚ . *In Cert hđ.*

Ipſe abƀ ten̅ un̅ jugu̅ *Rapentone* . 7 ʼAnſered de eo.

7 ℣ uno jugo ſe defđ . Tra . ē . ii . car̅ . In dn̅io . ē una . cu̅ . iiii.

borđ . Ibi . xi . ac̅ p̅ti . 7 q̅rta pars molini de . xv . den̅ . 7 ſilua

. x . porc̅ . 7 adhuc h̅t . ii . juga quæ de ſuo dn̅io dedit ei abƀ.

7 ibi . ii . uiƚƚos cu̅ . viii . borđ . T . R . E . 7 poſt: ualuit . iii . liƀ.

∫ Modo . iiii . liƀ.

12 c

Ansfriđ ten̅ de abƀe *Cherincheuelle* . *In Ferleberg hđ.*

℣ dimiđ ſolin ſe defđ . Tra . ē . i . car̅ . In dn̅io ſunt . ii . 7 viii.

uiƚƚi hn̅t . i . car̅ 7 dimiđ . T . R . E . 7 poſt . ualuit . xx . ſoƚ . M: xxx . ſoƚ.

In Lest de Estrea.   *In Cornelest hvnd.*

Ipſe abƀ ten̅ *Norborne* . ℣ xxx . ſolins ſe defđ.

Tra . ē . liiii . car̅ . In dn̅io ſunt . iii . 7 lxxix . uiƚƚi cu̅

xl . ii . borđ hn̅t . xxxvii . car̅ . Ibi xl . ac̅ p̅ti . 7 ſilua . x.

porc̅ . T . |

T . R . E . ualeƀ q̅t xx . liƀ . Q̊do recep̅: xx . liƀ . M: lxxvi . liƀ.

De tra uillano₇ huj m̅ ten̅ Oidelard . i . ſolin . 7 ibi h̅t

. ii . car̅ . cu̅ . xi . borđ .   Vaƚ . iiii . liƀ.

∫ De eađ tra uillano₇ ten̅ Giſleƀt . ii . ſolins . dimiđ jugu̅

min̅ . 7 ibi h̅t . i . car̅ . 7 iiii . uiƚƚos cu̅ . i . car̅ . Vaƚ . vi . liƀ.

∫ Wadard ten̅ de iſto m̅ . iii . ſolins . lx . ac̅s min̅ de tra

uillano₇ . 7 ibi h̅t . i . car̅ . 7 viii . uiƚƚos cu̅ . i . car̅ . 7 ii . ſeruos.

Vaƚ . ix . liƀ . Ipſe u̅ nullu̅ ſeruitiu̅ reddit abƀi . niſi . xxx . ſoƚ

quos p̅ſoluit in an̅no.

In BOUGHTON Hundred

15 The Abbot holds SELLING manor himself without a hall, which answers for 6 sulungs. Land for 11 ploughs. In lordship nothing.
   30 villagers have 10 ploughs. A church.
   Value before 1066 £15; when acquired £8; now £13 5s.

In CALEHILL Hundred

16 The Abbot holds ½ yoke in ROOTING himself, which answered for ½ sulung before 1066. There was and is 1 plough in lordship. The value is and always was 15s.

In CHART Hundred

17 The Abbot holds 1 yoke (in) RIPTON himself and Ansered from him. It answers for 1 yoke. Land for 2 ploughs. In lordship 1, with
   4 smallholders.
   Meadow, 11 acres. ¼ mill at 15d; woodland, 10 pigs.
Further, he has 2 yokes which the Abbot gave him from his lordship and
   2 villagers with 8 smallholders.
Value before 1066 and later £3; now £4.

In FELBOROUGH Hundred   12 c

18 Ansfrid holds SHILLINGHAM from the Abbot. It answers for ½ sulung. Land for 1 plough. In lordship 2.
   8 villagers have 1½ ploughs.
Value before 1066 and later 20s; now 30s.

In the Lathe of EASTRY
In CORNILO Hundred

19 The Abbot holds NORTHBOURNE himself. It answers for 30 sulungs. Land for 54 ploughs. In lordship 3.
   79 villagers with 42 smallholders have 37 ploughs.
   Meadow, 40 acres; woodland, 10 pigs.
Value before 1066 £80; when acquired £20; now £76.
   Odilard holds 1 sulung of villagers' land of this manor; he has
2 ploughs, with
   11 smallholders.
Value £4.
   Gilbert holds 2 sulungs less ½ yoke of the same villagers' land;
he has 1 plough and
   4 villagers with 1 plough.
Value £6.
   Wadard holds 3 sulungs less 60 acres of the villagers' land of this manor; he has 1 plough,
   8 villagers with 1 plough and 2 slaves.
Value £9.
   But he himself renders no service to the Abbot except 30s which he pays in full in a year.

Odelin̄ ten̄ de ead̄ t̄ra uillano₂ . ı . ſolin . 7 ibi h̄t . ı . car̄.
cū . ııı . bord̄.   Val . ııı . lib̄.

Marcheri ten̄ de ead̄ t̄ra uillano₂ qd̄ ual . vııı . ſolid.

Osbn̄ fili Letardi ten̄ dimid̄ ſolin 7 xı . ac̄s p̄ti . de t̄ra
uillano₂ . qd̄ ual . xxv . ſol . Ipſe redd̄ abbi . xv . ſolid.

Rannulf̄ de colūbers ten̄ un̄ jugū.   Val . ʟ . den̄.

Rannulf̄ de ualbadon ten̄ un̄ jugū . 7 redd̄ inde . ʟ . den̄.

It̄e ſup̄dict̄ Oidelard ten̄ de hoc m̄ . un̄ ſolin . 7 uocat̄
BEVESFEL . 7 ibi h̄t . ıı . car̄ . cū . x . bord̄ . Val . vı . lib̄.

Ipſe abb̄ ten̄ MVNDINGEHA . p̄ duob̄ ſolins 7 dimid̄
ſe defd̄ . Tra . ē . v . car̄ . In hoc m̄ t̄ra quā tenent
monachi nunq̄ geldauit . 7 Wadard ten̄ ibi t̄ra
quæ T . R . E . ſēp geldauit . 7 illo t̄pr erat m̄ inſimul.
Modo h̄nt monachi in dn̄io . ıııı . car̄ . 7 xx . bord̄
cū una car̄ . 7 un̄ molin̄ de . xvı . ſolid . 7 ſiluā . ıııı . porc.
Ibi æccta . T . R . E . ualeb̄ . xxıı . lib̄ . 7 poſt . x . lib̄ . Pars
abbis . xxvı . lib̄.

Wadard h̄t in dn̄io ibi . ı . car̄ . 7 vııı . uiłłos cū . ıı.
bord̄ h̄ntib̄ . ıııı . car̄ . Val 7 ualuit . x . lib̄.
nullū ſeruitiū inde reddit niſi . xxx . ſolid p̄ ann̄ū abbi.

Ipſe abb̄ ten̄ SIBERTESWALT   IN BEVSBERG HVND.
p̄ duob̄ ſolins ſe defd̄ . Tra . ē . ıııı . car̄ . In dn̄io . ē una 7 dim.
7 xı . uiłłi cū . vı . bord̄ . h̄nt . ıı . car̄ 7 dim̄ . Ibi æccta.
T . R . E . ualeb̄ . vııı . lib̄ . Q̄do recep̄ . xʟ . ſol . Modo . vı . lib̄.
7 tam̄ redd̄ . vııı . lib̄.

Ipſe abb̄ ten̄ PLATENOVT . p̄ uno ſolin ſe defd̄ . Tra . ē
          In dn̄io nichil . ſed . ıııı . uiłłi cū . ııı . bord̄ h̄nt
car̄ 7 dimid̄ . Ibi ſilua minuta . Radulf̄ de curbeſpina
h̄t xxv . ac̄s de hac t̄ra . T . R . E . 7 poſt . 7 m̄ . ual . xx . ſolid.
tam̄ app̄ciat̄ . xʟ . ſolid . eo qd̄ ſit ad firmā.

Odelin holds 1 sulung of the same villagers' land; he has 1 plough there, with
3 smallholders.
Value £3.
Marcher holds what is valued at 8s from the same villagers' land.
Osbern son of Ledhard holds ½ sulung and 11 acres of meadow of villagers' land, value 25s. He pays the Abbot 15s himself.
Ranulf of Colombières holds 1 yoke.
Value 50d.
Ranulf of Vaubadon holds 1 yoke; he pays 50d from it.
Also the above Odilard holds 1 sulung of this manor, called Beauxfield; he has 2 ploughs, with
10 smallholders
Value £6.

20 The Abbot also holds (Great and Little) MONGEHAM. It answers for 2½ sulungs. Land for 5 ploughs. In this manor the land which the monks hold never paid tax. Wadard holds land there which always paid tax before 1066. At that time the manor was all one. Now the monks have 4 ploughs in lordship, and
20 smallholders with 1 plough.
A mill at 16s; woodland, 4 pigs. A church.
Value before 1066 £22; later £10; the Abbot's part £26.
Wadard has 1 plough in lordship, and
8 villagers with 2 smallholders who have 4 ploughs.
The value is and was £10.
He pays no service from it except 30s a year to the Abbot.

In BEWSBOROUGH Hundred
21 The Abbot holds SIBERTSWOLD himself. It answers for 2 sulungs. Land for 4 ploughs. In lordship 1½.
11 villagers with 6 smallholders have 2½ ploughs. A church.
Value before 1066 £8; when acquired 40s; now £6; however, it pays £8.

22 The Abbot holds WADHOLT himself. It answers for 1 sulung. Land for ... In lordship nothing, but
4 villagers with 3 smallholders have 1½ ploughs.
Underwood.
Ralph of Courbépine has 25 acres of this land.
Value before 1066, later and now 20s; however, it is assessed at 40s because it is at a revenue.

Ipſe abb̄ ten̄ PRESTETVNE .p̄ . v . ſolins IN PRESTETVN

ſe defd̄ . Tra . ē . viii . car̄ . In dn̄io ſunt . ii . car̄ . 7 xxv.

uiłłi cū . xvii . bord̄ . hn̄t ix . car̄ . Ibi parūa ſiluula.

12 d
De hoc M̄ ten̄ Vitał . i . ſolin 7 dim̄ jugū . 7 ibi h̄t in dn̄io . ii . car̄.

7 xvii . bord̄ cū dim̄ car̄ . Totū M̄ T . R . E . ualeb̄ . x . lib̄.

Q̄do recep̄: vi . lib̄ . Modo uał . xiiii . lib̄ . q̄d h̄t abb̄.

Q̄d Vitalis tenet: c . ſolid̄ ualet.

Ansfrid ten̄ de abb̄e ÆLVETONE . p̄ dimid̄ ſolin 7 dim̄

jugo ſe defd̄ . Tra . ē .   In dn̄io . ē una car̄ . 7 iii.

uiłłi cū . iii . bobʒ in car̄.

In iſto M̄ ten̄ Ansfrid dimid̄ ſolin de dn̄io monachoʒ.

7 reddit inde S̄ Auguſtino . c . denar̄ p̄ annū.

Godeſſa tenuit in alodiū . 7 ded̄ inde S̄ Auguſtino . xxv.

denar̄ in elemoſina . unoq̄qʒ anno.

T . R . E . ualeb̄ . xl . ſoł . 7 poſt: x . ſoł . Modo: lx . ſolid̄.

IN LEST 7 in hund̄ de ESTREI . h̄t S̄ Auguſtin̄ . iii . uirg tre.

7 ibi . ē in dn̄io . i . car̄ . cū v . bord̄ . T . R . E . ualeb̄ . x . ſolid̄.

7 poſt: v . ſoł . Modo: xx . ſolid̄.

IN LIMOWART LEST.   IN STOTINGES HVND.

Gaufrid ten̄ BODESHA de abb̄e . p̄ uno ſolin ſe defd̄.

Tra . ē . ii . car̄ . 7 ibi ſunt cū . viii . bord̄ . Silua . xv . porc̄.

T . R . E . ualeb̄ . iiii . lib̄ . 7 poſt: xx . ſoł . Modo: iiii . lib̄.

Ipſe abb̄ ten̄ in LANPORT   ᚠ Quidā uiłłs tenuit.

ii . ſolins 7 uñ jugū . Tra . ē . vi . car̄ . Ibi ſunt . ix . uiłłi cū

iiii . bord̄ . hn̄tes . vi . car̄ . Ibi . x . ac̄ p̄ti . 7 ſilua . ii . porc̄.

T . R . E . ualeb̄ . vi . lib̄ . 7 poſt: iiii . lib̄ . Modo: viii . lib̄.

IN LEST DE WIWARLET.   IN LANGEBRIGE HVND.

Ipſe abb̄ ten̄ CHENETONE . T . R . E . ſe defd̄ p̄ . iiii . ſolins.

7 jacuit in BORCHEMERES . Tra . ē . x . car̄ . Ibi ſunt xxx.

uiłłi hn̄tes . x . car̄ . Ibi eccła.   Viłłi tenuer̄ . T . R . E.

In PRESTON Hundred

23   The Abbot holds PRESTON himself. It answers for 5 sulungs.
Land for 8 ploughs. In lordship 2 ploughs.
    25 villagers with 17 smallholders have 9 ploughs.
    A small wood.
    Vitalis holds 1 sulung and ½ yoke of this manor. He has   12 d
2 ploughs in lordship, and
    17 smallholders with ½ plough.
Value of the whole manor before 1066 £10; when acquired £6;
now value of what the Abbot has £14; value of what Vitalis
holds 100s.

24   Ansfrid holds ELMSTONE from the Abbot. It answers for ½ sulung
and ½ yoke. Land for ... In lordship 1 plough, and
    3 villagers with 3 oxen in a plough.
    In this manor Ansfrid holds ½ sulung from the monks'
lordship; from it he pays St. Augustine's 100d a year. Godesa held
it in freehold; from it she gave St. Augustine's 25d in alms each year.
Value before 1066, 40s; later 10s; now 60s.

In the Lathe and Hundred of EASTRY

25   St. Augustine's has 3 virgates of land. 1 plough in lordship, with
    5 smallholders.
Value before 1066, 10s; later 5s; now 20s.

In LYMPNE Lathe
In STOWTING Hundred

26   Geoffrey holds BODSHAM from the Abbot. It answers for 1 sulung.
Land for 2 ploughs. They are there, with
    8 smallholders.
    Woodland, 15 pigs.
Value before 1066 £4; later 20s; now £4.
    A villager held it.

27   The Abbot holds 2 sulungs and 1 yoke in LANPORT himself.
Land for 6 ploughs.
    9 villagers with 4 smallholders who have 6 ploughs.
    Meadow, 10 acres; woodland, 2 pigs.
Value before 1066 £6; later £4; now £8.

In the Lathe of WYE
In LONGBRIDGE Hundred

28   The Abbot holds KENNINGTON himself. Before 1066 it answered
for 4 sulungs and lay in (the lands of) Burmarsh. Land for 10
ploughs.
    30 villagers who have 10 ploughs. A church.
The villagers held it before 1066.

Cū his .iiii. folins h̅t̅ Ṡ Auguſtin̅.i. jugū q̄etū ab om̅i
ſcoto regio. 7 ibi tant̅ ſiluæ unde exeunt de paſnagio.
xl. porci. aut. liiii. denar̅ 7 un̅ obot̅.
Totū hoc T.R.E. ualeb̄.x. lib̄. 7 poſt viii. lib̄. Modo:́
xii. lib̄ 7 x. fot̄. *IN MARESS DE ROMENEL.*

Ipſe abb̄ ten̅ *BVRWARMARESC*. p̄. ii. ſolins 7 iii. jugis
ſe defd̄.Tra.e̅.xii. car̅. In dn̅io ſunt.iiii. 7 xl.iiii. uitt̅i
cū.v. bord hn̅t.x. car̅.
T.R.E. ualeb̄.xx. lib̄. 7 poſt:́ x. lib̄. Modo:́ xxx. lib̄.
Scẏra teſtificat̄ q̄d Bedeneſmere fuit Ṡ Auguſtini
T.R.E. 7 de illo qui eā teneb̄ habeb̄ abb̄ ſacā 7 ſocā.

TERRA SC̄I PETRI DE GAND. *IN GRENVIZ HVND̄.*

.VIII Abbas de Gand ten̅ de rege *LEVESHĀ*.7 de rege.E.
tenuit. 7 t̅c̅ 7 m̊ p̄.ii. ſolins ſe defd̄.Tra.e̅.xiiii. car̅.
In dn̅io ſunt.ii. car̅.7 l. uitt̅i cū.ix. bord hn̅t xvii. car̅.
Ibi.iii. ſerui. 7 xi. molini cū gablo ruſticoꝝ.viii. lib̄ 7 xii.
ſolid reddt̄. De exitu port:́xl. ſolid. Ibi.xxx.ac̅ pti.
De ſilua:́ l. porci de paſnag.
Totū m̅ T.R.E. ualeb̄.xvi. lib̄. 7 poſt:́xii. lib̄. Modo:́xxx̄. lib̄.

TERRA HVGONIS DE MONTFORT.

.IX. Hvgo de montfort ten̅ un̅ m̅ *ESTWELLE*. q̄d tenuit Fre
deric de rege. E. 7 p̄ uno ſolin ſe defd̄. Tria juga ſunt
infra diuiſion̅e Hugonis. 7 q̄rtū jugū.e̅ extra. 7 e̅ de feudo.epi Baioc̄.
Tra.e̅.iii. car̅ int totū. In dn̅io ſunt.ii. car̅. 7 v. uitt̅i cū.v. bord
hn̅t.i. car̅ 7 dim̅. Ibi.x. ſerui. 7 xii. ac̅ pti. 7 ſilua
T.R.E. ualeb̄ lxx. ſot̄. 7 poſt:́ xxx. ſot̄. Modo:́ lxx. ſolid.
Ipſe Hugo ten̅ *HAINTONE*. de rege. q̄d Vlſi prb̄r tenuit de rege.E.
7 p̄ uno ſolin ſe defd̄. Tra.e̅.i. car̅. 7 ibi.e̅ cū.i. uitt̅o 7 iiii. bord. 7 iii.
ac̅ pti. T.R.E. 7 poſt:́ 7 modo. uat̄. xx. ſolid.

With these 4 sulungs St. Augustine's has 1 yoke exempt from all royal levy, and as much woodland as produces an income from pasturage of 40 pigs or 54½d.
Value of all this before 1066 £10; later £8; now £12 10s.

In the MARSH of ROMNEY
29   The Abbot holds BURMARSH himself. It answers for 2 sulungs and 3 yokes. Land for 12 ploughs. In lordship 4.
    44 villagers with 5 smallholders have 10 ploughs.
Value before 1066 £20; later £10; now £30.

30   The Shire testifies that BADLESMERE was St. Augustine's before 1066. The Abbot had the full jurisdiction of its holder.

8   LAND OF ST. PETER'S OF GHENT

In GREENWICH Hundred
1   The Abbot of Ghent holds LEWISHAM from the King. He held it from King Edward. Then and now it answers for 2 sulungs. Land for 14 ploughs. In lordship 2 ploughs.
    50 villagers with 9 smallholders have 17 ploughs.
    3 slaves; 11 mills with the countrymen's tribute pay £8 12s;
       from the income of the port 40s. Meadow, 30 acres;
       from the woodland 50 pigs from pasturage.
Value of the whole manor before 1066 £16; later £12; now £30.

9   LAND OF HUGH DE MONTFORT   13 a

1   Hugh de Montfort holds a manor, EASTWELL, which Frederick held from King Edward. It answers for 1 sulung. There are 3 yokes inside Hugh's territory; a fourth yoke is outside; it is of the Bishop of Bayeux' Holding. Land for 3 ploughs in total. In lordship 2 ploughs.
    5 villagers with 5 smallholders have 1½ ploughs.
    10 slaves; meadow, 12 acres; woodland ......
Value before 1066, 70s; later 30s; now 70s.

2   Hugh holds HAMPTON from the King himself. Wulfsi the priest held it from King Edward. It answers for 1 sulung. Land for 1 plough. It is there, with
    1 villager and 4 smallholders.
    Meadow, 3 acres.
Value before 1066 later and now 20s.

Maigno ten de Hug *Seivetone* . Brefibalt tenuit de rege . E.

7 p dimid folin fe defd . Tra . e . I . car . 7 ibi . e in dnio . cu . I . uitto 7 VI.

bord . Ibi æccta 7 pbr . 7 un molin de . x . den . 7 VIII . ac pti.

T.R.E . ualeb . xxx . fot . 7 poft: xx . fot . Modo: xxx . folid.

Ifde Maigno ten de Hugone *Estefort* . Turgifus tenuit de Goduino

7 p uno folin fe defd . Tra . e dimid car . In dnio tam . e una car . 7 II.

uitti hnt . I . car . Ibi . II . ferui . 7 VIII . ac pti.

T.R.E . ualeb . xxv . folid . Q̇do recep: xx . fot . Modo: xxx . folid.

Ipfe Hugo ten *Essella* . Tres hoes tenuer de rege . E . 7 potuer ire

quolibʒ cu tris fuis . p . III . jugis fe defd . Tra . e . I . car 7 dimid.

Ibi m . IIII . uitti cu . II . bord hnt . I . car . 7 VI . acs pti.

Totu T.R.E . ualeb . xx . folid . 7 poft: xv . folid . Modo: xx . folid.

Alia *Essetesford* ten Maigno de hugone . Wirelm tenuit

de rege . E . p uno folin fe defd . Tra . e . IIII . car . In dnio fuʒ . II .

7 II . uitti cu . xv . bord hnt . III . car . Ibi æccta 7 pbr . 7 III . ferui.

7 II . molin de x . folid 7 II . den.

T.R.E . ualeb . Lxx . fot . 7 poft: Lx . fot . Modo: c . fot.

Ifde Hugo ten in Marefc de Romenel . I . jugu . Tra . e

Medietate huj træ tenuer . II . fochi . 7 II . uitti alia.

Ibi funt m . IIII . uitti . hntes . I . car.

Ħ tra ualuit 7 uat . xII . folid.

Ifd Hugo ten dimid jugu . qd tenuit un focħs . Ibi . II . bord funt m.

Ħ tra appciat in Titentone . q̇a illuc arata . e cu dnicis carrucis.

Hoc teftat hund 7 burgenfes de Doure . 7 hoes abbis S Auguftini.

7 Eftrea left: qd tra *Etretone* qua caluniant canonici S Martini

de Doure fup Hugone de montfort . qd Vluuile Wilde ea tenuit

in alodio . T.R.E . 7 defd fe p uno jugo . 7 ibi ħt . I . car in dnio . 7 v . bord

cu . I . car . 7 un molin de . xx . folid .　　　Vat 7 ualuit . x . lib.

13 a

In the Lathe of WYE

In LONGBRIDGE Hundred

3   Maino holds SEVINGTON from Hugh. Bresibalt held it from King
Edward. It answers for ½ sulung. Land for 1 plough. It is there,
in lordship, with
> 1 villager and 6 smallholders.
> A church and a priest; a mill at 10d; meadow, 8 acres.

Value before 1066, 30s; later 20s; now 30s.

4   Maino also holds (South) ASHFORD from Hugh. Thorgils held it
from Earl Godwin. It answers for 1 sulung. Land for ½ plough.
In lordship, however, 1 plough.
> 2 villagers have 1 plough.
> 2 slaves; meadow, 8 acres.

Value before 1066, 25s; when acquired 20s; now 30s.

5   Hugh holds ESSELLA himself. Three men held it from King Edward;
they could go wherever [they would] with their lands. It answers
for 3 yokes. Land for 1½ ploughs.
> Now 4 villagers with 2 smallholders have 1 plough.
> Meadow, 6 acres.

Value of the whole before 1066, 20s; later 15s; now 20s.

6   Maino holds the other ASHFORD from Hugh. Wirelm held it from
King Edward. It answers for 1 sulung. Land for 4 ploughs.
In lordship 2.
> 2 villagers with 15 smallholders have 3 ploughs.
> A church and a priest, 3 slaves; 2 mills at 10s 2d.

Value before 1066, 70s; later 60s; now 100s.

In LYMPNE Lathe

In NEWCHURCH Hundred

7   Hugh also holds 1 yoke in ROMNEY MARSH. Land for ... 2 Freemen
held half of this land; 2 villagers the other.
> Now 4 villagers who have 1 plough.

The value of this land was and is 12s.

8   Hugh also holds ½ yoke which a Freeman held.
> Now there are 2 smallholders.

This land is assessed in Tinton, because it is ploughed with the
lordship ploughs from there.

9   The Hundred and the Burgesses of Dover and the Abbot of St.
Augustine's men and of Eastry Lathe testify this; that the land of
ATTERTON which the Canons of St. Martin's of Dover claim from
Hugh de Montfort which Wulfy Wilde held in freehold before 1066
answers for 1 yoke. He has 1 plough in lordship, and
> 5 smallholders with 1 plough.
> A mill at 20s.

The value is and was £10.

Ipſe Hugo ten̄ *ESTBRIGE* . in dn̄io.

Alſi tenuit de Goduino . 7 p uno ſolin ſe defđ . Tra . ē . vi . car̄.

In dn̄io ſunt . iii . car̄ . 7 ii . uiłłi cū . xxxvi . borđ hn̄t . iiii . car̄ . Ibi . viii.

ſalinæ cū tcia parte nouæ ſalinæ de . xx . ſoliđ . Dimiđ piſcaria . viii.

den̄ . Silua de . iii . porc̄ de paſnaḡ . Ibi . ii . æcclæ.

T.R.E. 7 poſt . ualuit . x . liƀ . Modo . xv . liƀ.

Bertrann̄ ten̄ de Huḡ dimiđ juḡ 7 dimiđ uirḡa . p tanto ſe defđ.

Adelelm̄ tenuit de rege . E . Tra . ē ad . i . car̄ . T.R.E. ualeƀ . xx . ſoliđ.

Herueus ten̄ de Hugone *BLACHEMENESTONE* . Blacheman

13 b

tenuit T.R.E. 7 p dimidio ſolin ſe defđ . Tra . ē . ii . car̄.

In dn̄io ſunt ibi . 7 iii . uiłłi cū . x . borđ cū . i : car̄ . Ibi æccła

7 un̄ ſeruus.

T.R.E. ualeƀ . iiii . liƀ . 7 poſt . iii . liƀ . Modo . vi . liƀ.

Iſđ Hugo ten̄ in Mareſc de Romenel uñ ſolin dimiđ

uirga min . p tanto ſe defđ . Tra . ē . iii . car̄ . Ibi . xiiii . ſochi

hn̄t . iii . car̄ . T.R.E. ualeƀ . iiii . liƀ . 7 poſt . iii . liƀ . M̄ . c . ſoł.

Rogeri ten̄ de Hugone uñ jugū in Mareſc de Romenel.

p uno jugo ſe defđ . Duo ſochi tenuer̄ . Tra . ē . i . car̄ . 7 ibi : ē

cū . iii . borđ . T.R.E. ualeƀ . xxx . ſoł . 7 poſt . xv . ſoł . Modo.

Rotƀt ten̄ de Hugone in eođ Mareſch   £ xxx . ſoliđ.

ſextā parte uni jugi . Vn̄ ſochis tenuit.

Vał 7 ualuit . v . ſoliđ.

Rogeri ten̄ de Hugone *POSTINGES* . Sbern tenuit.

p duobz ſolins 7 dimiđ ſe defđ . Tra . ē . xiii . car̄ . In dn̄io

ſunt . iii . 7 xvi . uiłłi cū . vii . borđ hn̄t . vii . car̄.

Ibi . ii . æccleſiolæ . 7 ii . molini de . vi . ſoliđ . 7 xl . ac̄ p̄ti.

Silua . xl . porc̄.

T.R.E. ualeƀ . x . liƀ . 7 poſt . c . ſoliđ . Modo . xiiii . liƀ.

De iſto m̄ ten̄ Radulf de curbeſpine . iii . denas . ex̄

diuiſion̄ ſunt . 7 ual . xv . ſoliđ.

In WORTH Hundred

10 Hugh holds EAST BRIDGE in lordship himself. Alfsi held it from Earl
Godwin. It answers for 1 sulung. Land for 6 ploughs. In lordship
3 ploughs.
2 villagers with 36 smallholders have 4 ploughs.
8 salt-houses with a third part of a ninth salt-house at 20s;
½ fishery, 8d; woodland at 3 pigs from pasturage. 2 churches.
Value before 1066 and later £10; now £15.

11 Bertram holds ½ yoke and ½ virgate from Hugh. It answers for as
much. Aethelhelm held it from King Edward. Land for 1 plough.
Value before 1066, 20s.

12 Harvey holds BLACKMANSTONE from Hugh. Blackman held it   13 b
before 1066. It answers for ½ sulung. Land for 2 ploughs. They
are there in lordship, and
3 villagers with 10 smallholders with 1 plough.
A church; a slave.
Value before 1066 £4; later £3; now £6.

13 Hugh also holds 1 sulung less ½ virgate in ROMNEY MARSH. It answers
for as much. Land for 3 ploughs.
14 Freemen have 3 ploughs.
Value before 1066 £4; later £3; now 100s.

14 Roger holds 1 yoke in ROMNEY MARSH from Hugh. It answers for
1 yoke. 2 Freemen held it. Land for 1 plough. It is there, with
3 smallholders.
Value before 1066, 30s; later 15s; now 30s.

15 Robert holds the sixth part of a yoke, also in the MARSH , from Hugh.
A Freeman held it.
The value is and was 5s.

In HAYNE Hundred

16 Roger holds POSTLING from Hugh. Esbern Big held it. It answers
for 2½ sulungs. Land for 13 ploughs. In lordship 3.
16 villagers with 7 smallholders have 7 ploughs.
2 small churches; 2 mills at 6s; meadow, 40 acres; woodland,
40 pigs.
Value before 1066 £10; later 100s; now £14.
Ralph of Courbépine holds 3 pig pastures of this manor; they are
outside his territory.
Value 15s.

Isdē Hugo ten dimid solin . qđ Aldret tenuit de
rege . E . sine halla . p dimid solin se defđ . Tra . ē . iii.
car. Ibi un uilts cū . iiii . borđ man . nulla ibi car.
Vn molin de . xxv . denar . 7 v . ac pti.

Isdē Hugo ten BELICE . Turgis tenuit de rege . E.
7 p uno solin se defđ . Tra . ē   In dnio . ē una car . 7 ii.
uilti cū uno borđ hnt . i . car . Ibi . iii . ac pti.

Hæ duæ træ T . R . E . ualeb . lx . sol . 7 post. xx . sol . M. lx . sol.

Ipse Hugo ten unā trā quā   IN NEVVECERCE HĐ.
Azor tenuit de rege . E . sine halla . p uno solin se
defđ . Tra . ē . v . car . Ibi . viii . uilti cū . iii . borđ hnt . ii.
car . T . R . E 7 post. ualuit . viii . lib . Modo. ix . lib.

Ipse Hugo ten dimid solin in Maresch de Romenel.
p tanto se defđ . Tra . ē . iiii . car . Duodeci sochi te
nuer 7 tenent hntes . iiii . car . Val 7 ualuit . lx . soliđ.

Isdē Hugo ten in ipso Maresch   IN ADELOVESBRIGE HĐ.
un jugu . p tanto se defđ . Tra . ē . ii . car . Ibi sunt
xii . sochi cū . viii . borđ hntes . ii . car.

Hæ duæ træ T . R . E . ualeb . c . x . sol . 7 post 7 m similit.

                    IN BLACHEBVRNE HĐ.
Ipse Hugo ten TINTENTONE . Vlnod tenuit de
rege . E . 7 tc defđ se p uno solin . Modo p dimidio.
qa foris diuisione . ē . Tra . ē . v . car . In dnio sunt
ii . car . 7 xxi . uilts cū . vi . borđ hnt . vii . car.
Ibi æccla 7 ix . serui . 7 iii . piscariæ de . v . soliđ.
7 xxxviii . ac pti . Silua . xl . porc.
T . R . E . ualeb . xii . lib . 7 post. vi . lib . Modo. vii . lib.

Isdē Hugo ten dimid jugu qđ tenuer . v . sochi
7 m tenen. hntes . i . car ibi cū . iiii . borđ . Val 7 ualuit

                    semp . v . soliđ.

13 b

17 Hugh also holds ½ sulung which Aethelred Bot held from King
Edward, without a Hall. It answers for ½ sulung. Land for
3 ploughs.
>1 villager with 3 smallholders lives there; no ploughs.
>A mill at 25d; meadow, 5 acres.

18 Hugh also holds *BELICE*. Thorgils held it from King Edward.
It answers for 1 sulung. Land for ... In lordship 1 plough.
>2 villagers with 1 smallholder have 1 plough.
>Meadow, 3 acres.
Value of these two lands before 1066, 60s; later 20s; now 60s.

In NEWCHURCH Hundred
19 Hugh holds a land himself which Azor Roote held from King
Edward, without a Hall. It answers for 1 sulung. Land for 5
ploughs.
>8 villagers with 3 smallholders have 2 ploughs.
Value before 1066 and later £8; now £9.

20 Hugh holds ½ sulung in ROMNEY MARSH himself. It answers for
as much. Land for 4 ploughs.
>12 Freemen who have 4 ploughs held and hold it.
The value is and was 60s.

In ALOESBRIDGE Hundred
21 Hugh also holds 1 yoke in the MARSH. It answers for as much.
Land for 2 ploughs.
>12 Freemen with 8 smallholders who have 2 ploughs.
Value of these two lands before 1066, 110s; later and now
the same.

In BLACKBURN Hundred
22 Hugh holds TINTON himself. Wulfnoth held it from King Edward.
It answered for 1 sulung then; now for ½, because it is outside his
territory. Land for 5 ploughs. In lordship 2 ploughs.
>21 villagers with 6 smallholders have 7 ploughs.
>A church; 9 slaves; 3 fisheries at 5s; meadow, 38 acres;
>>woodland, 40 pigs.
Value before 1066 £12; later £6; now £7.

23 Hugh also holds ½ yoke which 5 Freemen held, and now hold, who
have 1 plough, with
>4 smallholders.
The value is and always was 5s.

Herueus teń de Hugoné   *IN ESTRAITES HD.*

SEDLINGES . Oſuuard tenuit de rege . E . p̄ uno

ſolin ſe defđ . Tra . ē . vii . car̄ . In dn̄io ſunt . iii . car̄.

7 viii . uiłłi cū . xxv . borđ hn̄t . iiii . car̄ . Ibi . ii . æcclæ.

7 uñ molin de . xxx . deń . 7 xxxvi . ac̄ p̊ti . 7 ſilua

de . vi . porc̄.

T.R.E. ualeb̄ . viii . lib̄ . 7 poſt. c . ſoliđ . Modo. vii . lib̄.

Alnod teń de Hugone *HORTONE.*   *IN STOTINGES HD.*

Leuuiń tenuit de rege . E . 7 p̄ dimidio ſolin ſe

defđ . Tra . ē . iii . car̄ . In dn̄io ſunt . ii . car̄ . 7 v.

uiłłi cū . vi . borđ hn̄t . i . car̄ 7 dimiđ . Ibi æcclᵃ.

7 uñ moliñ de . xxv . deń . 7 xxiiii . ac̄ p̊ti . Silua.

x . porc̄ . T.R.E. ualeb̄ . xl . ſoł . 7 poſt. xx . Modo. lx . ſoł.

Ibiđ teń Alnod . i . jugū de Hugone . ſed nil ibi eſt.

Ipſe Hugo teń . iii . uirḡ 7 dimiđ in eođ *LEST.*

quas tenueŕ . iii . ſochi de rege . E.

Ibi m̄ uń uiłłs h̄ dimiđ car̄ cū . iii . borđ.

Vał 7 ualuit ſēp . x . ſoliđ .   *IN HAME HVND.*

Wiłłs teń de Hugone . iii . juga 7 dimiđ uirga in

ORLAVESTONE . Hanc tr̄a tenueŕ xi . ſochi . Tra ē . iii . car̄.

Ibi m̄ . ii . car̄ in dn̄io . 7 xv . uiłłi cū . ix . borđ hn̄t . iii.

car̄ 7 dim . Ibi . ii . æcclæ . 7 xx . ac̄ p̊ti . Silua . vi . porc̄.

T.R.E. ualeb̄ . lx . ſoł . 7 poſt. xxx . ſoł . Modo. c . ſoliđ.

Radulf fili Ricardi teń de Hugone dimiđ ſolin

in Rochinges . qđ Leuret tenuit de rege . E . p̄ dimiđ

ſolin ſe defđ . Tra . ē . ii . car̄ . Ibi m̄ . xii . uiłłi hn̄t unā

car̄ 7 dimiđ . de ſilua. i . porc̄.

T.R.E. ualeb̄ . l . ſoł . 7 poſt. xxx . ſoł . Modo. l . ſoliđ.

Radulf teń de huḡ *HORTVN.*   *IN STOTINGES HD.*

Duo ſochi tenueŕ de rege . E . 7 p̄ uno jugo 7 dim ſe defđ.

Tra i . car̄ 7 dim . In dn̄io . ē una . cū . iiii . uiłłis . 7 uñ

In STREET Hundred

24 Harvey holds SELLINDGE from Hugh. Osward held it from King
Edward. It answers for 1 sulung. Land for 7 ploughs. In
lordship 3 ploughs.
   8 villagers with 25 smallholders have 4 ploughs.
   2 churches; a mill at 30d; meadow, 36 acres; woodland at
      6 pigs.
Value before 1066 £8; later 100s; now £7.

In STOWTING Hundred

25 Alnoth holds (Monk's) HORTON from Hugh. Leofwin held it from
King Edward. It answers for ½ sulung. Land for 3 ploughs. In
lordship 2 ploughs.
   5 villagers with 6 smallholders have 1½ ploughs.
   A church; a mill at 25d; meadow, 24 acres; woodland, 10 pigs.
Value before 1066, 40s; later 20[s]; now 60s.

26 There Alnoth also holds 1 yoke from Hugh; but there is nothing there.

27 Hugh holds 3½ virgates himself in the same Lathe, which 3 Freemen
held from King Edward.
   Now 1 villager has ½ plough, with 3 smallholders.
The value is and always was 10s.

In HAM Hundred

28 William holds 3 yokes and ½ virgate in ORLESTONE from Hugh.
11 Freemen held this land. Land for 3 ploughs. Now 2 ploughs
in lordship.
   15 villagers with 9 smallholders have 3½ ploughs.
   2 churches; meadow, 20 acres; woodland, 6 pigs.
Value before 1066, 60s; later 30s; now 100s.

29 Ralph son of Richard holds ½ sulung from Hugh in RUCKINGE, which
Leofred held from King Edward. It answers for ½ sulung. Land for
2 ploughs.
   12 villagers have 1½ ploughs.
   From the woodland, 1 pig.
Value before 1066, 50s; later 30s; now 50s.

In STOWTING Hundred

30 Ralph holds (Monk's) HORTON from Hugh. Two Freemen held it
from King Edward. It answers for 1½ yokes. Land for 1½ ploughs.
In lordship 1, with
   4 villagers.

molin̄ de . xxx . den̄ . 7 x . ac̄ p̄ti . De ſilua . vi . porc̄.

T.R.E. ualeƀ . xl . ſol . 7 poſt.' xx . ſol . Modo.' xxx . ſolid̄.

Hugo de manneuile ten̄ de Hug   IN ESTRAITES HD̄.

ESTRAITES . Vlnod tenuit de rege . E . p̄ . ii . ſolins ſe
defd̄ . Tra .e̅ . viii . car̄ . In dn̄io ſunt . ii . 7 xi . uiłłi cū
xxv . bord̄ hn̄t . v . car̄ . Ibi æccła . 7 vii . ſerui . 7 xxx . ac̄
p̄ti . T.R.E. ualeƀ x . ſol . 7 poſt.' iiii . ſol . Modo.' viii . liƀ.'

Ansfrid ten̄ de Huḡ . i jugū qd̄ tenuit in eod̄ hund̄
un̄ ſocħs de rege . E . 7 p̄ uno jugo ſe defd̄ . Tra .e̅ . i . car̄.
Ibi .e̅ cū uno uiłło 7 ii . bord̄ . 7 un̄ molin̄ de . xxvi . den̄.
7 viii . ac̄ p̄ti . T.R.E. 7 m̄ ual . xl . ſol.

Rotƀt coc̄ ten̄ de Hugone . i . jugū qd̄ tenuit un̄ ſocħs
7 p̄ tanto ſe defd̄ . Ibi .e̅ una car̄ cū uno bord̄ . 7 iiii . ac̄
p̄ti . T.R.E. 7 m̄ ual . xxx . ſolid̄.

Gisłeƀt ten̄ de Hugone un̄ jugū IN LANGEBRIGE HD̄.
qd̄ tenuit qdā ſocħs de rege . E . Val 7 ualuit . iiii . ſol.
Nil ibi fuit nec .e̅.

De Etwelle q̄ ten̄ Herƀt fili̓ Iuonis ext̄ diuiſion̄ē Hugon̄.
ten̄ ipſe Hugo . xiiii . ac̄s træ . jnfra ſuā diuiſione . 7 ual . ii . ſol.

IN ESTREA LEST.   IN BEVSBERGE HVND̄.

Ipſe Hugo de montfort ten̄ ETWELLE . Molleue tenuit
p̄ . iii . ſolins ſe defd̄ . 7 M.' p̄ . i . ſolin.
Tra .e̅ . i . car̄ . 7 ibi .e̅ in dn̄io . 7 xix . bord̄ hn̄t . i . car̄ . Ibi
æccła . 7 iiii . molini {de . iiii . liƀ . 7 xvii ſol 7 iiii . den̄ . 7 iiii . ac̄
p̄ti . T.R.E. ualeƀ . xi . liƀ . 7 poſt.' iiii . liƀ . Modo.' viii . liƀ.

Ipſe Hugo ten̄ NEVENTONE . Ederic̄ tenuit de rege . E.
7 p̄ . ii . ſolins ſe defd̄ tc̄ . 7 m̄ p̄ uno q̄a alius .e̅ ext̄ diuiſion̄ē.
Tra .e̅ . ii . car̄ . 7 ibi ſunt in dn̄io . Ibi æccła 7 xxi . bord̄ . 7 iii.
ſerui cū . iii . car̄ . Ibi . iii . molini 7 dimid̄ de . c.v . ſolid̄.
Totū T.R.E. ualeƀ . xii . liƀ . 7 poſt.' iii . liƀ . Modo.' xii . liƀ.
qd̄ ħt Hugo int̄ diuiſione ſuā.

A mill at 30d; meadow, 10 acres; from the woodland, 6 pigs.
Value before 1066, 40s; later 20s; now 30s.

In STREET Hundred

31 Hugh de Mandeville holds (Court at) STREET from Hugh. Wulfnoth held it from King Edward. It answers for 2 sulungs. Land for 8 ploughs. In lordship 2.
    11 villagers with 25 smallholders have 5 ploughs.
    A church; 7 slaves; meadow, 30 acres.
Value before 1066, 10s; later 4s; now £8.

32 Ansfrid holds 1 yoke from Hugh, which a Freeman held from King Edward in the same Hundred. It answers for 1 yoke. Land for 1 plough. It is there, with
    1 villager and 2 smallholders.
    A mill at 26d; meadow, 8 acres.
Value before 1066 and now 40s.

33 Robert Cook holds 1 yoke from Hugh which a Freeman held. It answers for as much. 1 plough there, with
    1 smallholder.
    Meadow, 4 acres.
Value before 1066 and now 30s.

In LONGBRIDGE Hundred

34 Gilbert holds 1 yoke from Hugh which a Freeman held from King Edward.
The value is and was 4s.
    There was and is nothing there.

35 From (Temple) EWELL, which Herbert son of Ivo holds outside Hugh's territory, Hugh holds 14 acres of land himself inside his territory.
Value 2s.

In EASTRY Lathe   13 d
In BEWSBOROUGH Hundred

36 Hugh de Montfort holds (Temple) EWELL himself. Molleva held it. It answered for 3 sulungs; now for 1 sulung. Land for 1 plough. It is there, in lordship.
    19 smallholders have 1 plough.
    A church; 4½ mills at £4 17s 4d; meadow, 4 acres.
Value before 1066 £11; later £4; now £8.

37 Hugh holds NEWINGTON himself. Edric held it from King Edward. Then it answered for 2 sulungs; now for 1, because the other is outside his territory. Land for 2 ploughs. They are there, in lordship.
    A church; 21 smallholders and 3 slaves with 3 ploughs.
    3½ mills at 105s.
Value of the whole before 1066 £12; later £3; now what Hugh has in his territory £12.

Int̃ diuifionẽ hanc eſt uñ ſocħs teneʒ . xvi . acs̃ træ . 7 ipſe
idẽ tenuit de rege . E.

In eođ hunđ teñ iđ Hugo unã partẽ Jaonei . quæ nichil redđ
nec reddiđ . nec ad ullũ m̃ jacuit . ſed . ẽ int̃ diuifionẽ ſuã . 7 fuit
de dñio regis.   Aluuiñ tenut

In eođ hunđ ħt Fulƀt de Hugone uñ moliñ . 7 redđ . xxiiii . ſoł.

Herfrid teñ de Hugone POLTONE . Vluuiñ tenuit de rege . E.
7 p̃ uno ſolin ſe defđ . Tra . ẽ . ii . car̃ . Ibi ſunt . iii . uitti 7 æcclefiola.

T . R . E . ualeƀ . xl . ſoł . 7 poſt:́ xv . ſoł . M:́ xxx . ſoł.

IN WIWART LEST .   IN BERISOVT HVNĐ.

Ipſe Hugo teñ BREBVRNE . Godric̃ de burnes tenuit de rege . E.
7 p̃ . vii . ſolins ſe defđ tc̃ . 7 m̃ p̃ . v . ſolins 7 dimiđ . 7 dim̃ jugo.
q̃a alia pars . ẽ ext̃ diuifionẽ hug̃ . 7 eã teñ eps̃ baiocenſis.

T̃ra . ẽ . xv . car̃ . In dñio ſunt . ii . 7 xxxi . uitts cũ . x . borđ
hñt . x . car̃ . Ibi æcc̃ła 7 viii . ſerui . 7 ii . molini de . vii . ſoliđ.
7 xx . ac̃ p̃ti . Silua de . xxv . porc̃.

T . R . E :́ ualeƀ . xx . liƀ . 7 poſt:́ viii . liƀ . Modo:́ xvi . liƀ.

In Hund de Certh teñ quædã femina de Hugone . i . uirgã.
quã uñ ſocħs tenuit de rege . E.   Vał . iii . ſoliđ.

Ipſe Hugo teñ dimiđ jugũ in TEPINDENE . IN BLACHEBVRNE HĐ.
qđ tenuit Norman de rege . E . 7 p̃ dim̃ jugo ſe defđ . Ibi ſux̃
ii . uitti cũ dim̃ car̃ . Valuit ſemp 7 uał . c . denar̃.

IN LIMOWART LEST .   IN ESTRAITES HĐ.

Ipſe Hugo teñ SIBORNE . Oſiar tenuit de rege . E . 7 p̃ uno
ſolin ſe defđ tc̃ 7 m̃ . Tra . ẽ . ii . car̃ . In dñio . ẽ una . 7 uñ uitts
cũ . iiii . borđ ħt . i . car̃ . 7 ibi uñ ſeruus.

T . R . E . ualeƀ . lx . ſoliđ . 7 poſt:́ xx . ſoł . Modo:́ iiii . liƀ.

Iſđẽ Hugo ħt   dimiđ ſolin SVANETONE . Tra . ẽ . i . car̃.
Norman tenuit de rege . E . p̃ tanto ſe defđ.

Ibi . iiii . uitti hñt . i . car̃ . Ibi ſilua de . v . porc̃.

T . R . E . ualeƀ . xxv . ſoł . 7 poſt:́ xv . ſoł . Modo:́ xxx . ſoł.

38 In this territory is a Freeman who holds 16 acres of land. He also held it himself from King Edward.

39 In the same Hundred Hugh also holds one part of *JAONEI* which pays and paid nothing, and did not lie in (the lands of) any manor, but it is in his territory and was of the King's lordship. Alwin the priest held it.

40 In the same Hundred Fulbert has a mill from Hugh which pays 24s.

41 Herfrid holds POULTON from Hugh. Wulfwin held it from King Edward. It answers for 1 sulung. Land for 2 ploughs.
  3 villagers and a small church.
Value before 1066, 40s; later 15s; now 30s.

In WYE Lathe
In BIRCHOLT Hundred

42 Hugh holds BRABOURNE himself. Godric of (Bishops)bourne held it from King Edward. Then it answered for 7 sulungs; now for 5½ sulungs and ½ yoke, because the other part is outside Hugh's territory. The Bishop of Bayeux holds it. Land for 15 ploughs. In lordship 2.
  31 villagers with 10 smallholders have 10 ploughs.
  A church; 8 slaves; 2 mills at 7s; meadow, 20 acres;
    woodland, 25 pigs.
Value before 1066 £20; later £8; now £16.

In the Hundred of CHART

43 A woman holds 1 virgate from Hugh which a Freeman held from King Edward.
Value 3s.

In BLACKBURN Hundred

44 Hugh holds ½ yoke himself in TIFFENDEN which Norman held from King Edward. It answers for ½ yoke.
  2 villagers with ½ plough.
The value always was and is 100d.

In LYMPNE Lathe
In STREET Hundred

45 Hugh holds *SIBORNE* himself. Osgeard held it from King Edward. Then and now it answered for 1 sulung. Land for 2 ploughs. In lordship 1.
  1 villager with 4 smallholders has 1 plough. 1 slave.
Value before 1066, 60s; later 20s; now £4.

46 Hugh also has ½ sulung (in) SWANTON. Land for 1 plough. Norman held it from King Edward. It answers for as much.
  4 villagers have 1 plough.
  Woodland at 5 pigs.
Value before 1066, 25s; later 15s; now 30s.

Nigellus ten̅ de Hugone un̅ jugu̅ . 7 in Aia . VII . acræ.

Vn̅ soċħs tenuit de rege . E . Tra̅ . e̅ . I . caŕ.

In dn̅io . e̅ dimidia caŕ . 7 VI . borđ 7 II . serui . 7 V . ac̅ p̅ti.

T.R.E . ualeƀ . xx . soliđ . 7 poſt:̅ x . soł . Modo:̅ xxv . soł.

Witts fili̅ Groſſe ten̅ de Hugone *BONINTONE*.

Norman tenuit de rege . E . 7 ꝑ uno solin se defđ Tra̅ . e̅

.IIII . caŕ . In dn̅io . e̅ una . 7 IX . uitti cu̅ . IIII . borđ hn̅t . II.

⌐ car.

Ibi æccła 7 VIII . serui . 7 silua . VIII . porc̅.

T.R.E . ualeƀ . IIII . liƀ . 7 poſt:̅ III . liƀ . Modo:̅ c . soliđ.

Herueus ten̅ de Hugone *OBTREPOLE* . Alrebot tenuit

de rege . E . 7 ꝑ uno solin se defđ . Tra̅ . e̅ . VI . caŕ . In dn̅io eſt

una . 7 XI . uitti cu̅ . II . caŕ . 7 un̅ seru̅ . 7 x . ac̅ p̅ti . 7 silua

redđ . v . denar de paſnagio . T.R.

T.R.E . ualeƀ . L . soliđ . 7 poſt:̅ xx . soł . Modo:̅ IIII . liƀ.

IN BLACHEBVRNE HVND 7 IN NEVCERCE HVND.

Herald ten̅ dimiđ solin una̅ uirga̅ min̅

Sex soċħi tenueŕ de rege . E . 7 ꝑ tanto se defđ . Tra̅ . e̅ . v . caŕ.

In dn̅io sunt . II . 7 xxxI . borđ hn̅t . III . caŕ . Ibi un̅ seruus.

T.R.E . ualeƀ . Lx . soł . 7 poſt:̅ xxx . soł . Modo:̅ IIII . liƀ . 7 xv . soł.

7 Adhuc h̅t una̅ dena̅ quæ jacuit in *FANE* manerio Ađa̅.

Ibi sunt . II . borđ . redđtes . xxx . denar̅ . Vał 7 ualuit ſep̅ . v . soł.

Ipse Hugo ten̅ dimiđ solin   *IN BERISCOLT HVND.*

in *HASTINGELIE* . Vlnod tenuit de rege . E . 7 ꝑ tanto se defđ.

Modo ten̅ q̅da̅ homo de Hugone . 7 h̅t ibi . II . borđ . red

dentes . IIII . soliđ . Valuit ſep̅ 7 uał . x . soł.

⌐hđ.
Ipse Hugo ten̅ in dn̅io un̅ jugu̅ 7 dimiđ *IN LANGEBRIGE*

in *TEVEGATE* . God tenuit de rege . E . Ibi . e̅ m̅ un̅ uitts

cu̅ . I . caŕ . 7 ibi . VIII . ac̅ p̅ti.

T.R.E:̅ ualeƀ . xx . soł . 7 poſt:̅ x . soł . Modo:̅ xx . soliđ.

In eođ Hund eſt una uirga træ in *SVESTONE* . qua̅ te

nuit un̅ soċħs de rege . E . Ibi m̅ eſt un̅ borđ . xII . denar̅

redđ . T.R.E . ualeƀ xxx . den̅ . 7 poſt:̅ xvIII . Modo:̅ III . soliđ.

47 Nigel holds 1 yoke and 7 acres from Hugh in *AIA*. A Freeman
held them from King Edward. Land for 1 plough. In lordship ½
plough;
  6 smallholders; 2 slaves.
  Meadow, 5 acres.
Value before 1066, 20s; later 10s; now 25s.

48 William son of Gross holds BONNINGTON from Hugh. Norman held
it from King Edward. It answers for 1 sulung. Land for 4 ploughs.
In lordship 1.
  9 villagers with 4 smallholders have 2 ploughs.
  A church; 8 slaves; woodland, 8 pigs.   14 a
Value before 1066 £4; later £3; now 100s.

49 Harvey holds OTTERPOOL from Hugh. Aethelred Bot held it from King
Edward. It answers for 1 sulung. Land for 6 ploughs. In lordship 1;
  11 villagers with 2 ploughs; a slave.
  Meadow, 10 acres; woodland which pays 5d from pasturage.
Value before 1066, 50s; later 20s; now £4.

In BLACKBURN Hundred and in NEWCHURCH Hundred
50 Harold holds ½ sulung less 1 virgate. 6 Freemen held it from King
Edward. It answers for as much. Land for 5 ploughs. In lordship 2.
  31 smallholders have 3 ploughs. 1 slave.
Value before 1066, 60s; later 30s; now £4 15s.

51 Further, he has a pig pasture which lies in (the lands of) Fanscombe,
a manor of Adam's.
  2 smallholders there who pay 30d.
The value is and always was 5s.

In BIRCHOLT Hundred
52 Hugh holds ½ sulung in HASTINGLEIGH himself. Wulfnoth held it from
King Edward. It answers for as much. Now a man holds it from Hugh.
He has
  2 smallholders who pay 4s.
The value was and always is 10s.

In LONGBRIDGE Hundred
53 Hugh holds in lordship 1½ yokes in EVEGATE himself. Goda held it
from King Edward.
  Now 1 villager with 1 plough.
  Meadow, 8 acres.
Value before 1066, 20s; later 10s; now 20s.

54 In the same Hundred 1 virgate of land in *SUESTONE* which a Freeman
held from King Edward.
  Now 1 smallholder, who pays 12d.
Value before 1066, 30d; later 18[d]; now 3s.

TERRA COMITIS EVSTACHII.

IN DIMIDIO LEST DE SVDTONE . IN OSTREHÁ HVND.

Comes Evstachivs ten de rege OISTREHAM . Goduin

tenuit de rege . E . 7 ᵱ . IIII . folins fe defđ tē 7 modo.

Tra . ē   In dñio funt . II . cař . 7 XLII . uiłti cū . VII .

borđ hñt xxx . cař . Ibi . x . ferui . 7 uñ molin de . v . foliđ .

7 XVI . ãc ᵱti . 7 de filua . c . porč .

T . R . E . ualeƀ . xxx . liƀ . Qdo recep . xxIIII . liƀ . Modo . XL . liƀ .

IN LEST DE WIWARLET.   IN WI HVNDRET.

Ipfe comes ten BOLTVNE . Goduin com tenuit . 7 ᵱ . VII .

folins fe defđ tē 7 m̃ . Tra . ē xxx.III . cař . In dñio funt . III .

7 LXVII . uiłti cū . v . borđ hñt . xxx . cař . Ibi æccła . 7 XVII .

ferui . 7 II . molini de . VII . foliđ 7 II . denař . 7 xxVI . ãc ᵱti .

Silua . cc . porč .

T . R . E . ualeƀ . xx . liƀ . 7 poſt . xxx . liƀ . Modo . XL . liƀ .

14 b
TERRA RICARDI . F . GISLEƀTI IN TVIFERDE HVND.

.XI Ricard de Tonebrige ten HALLINGES . 7 Aldret

tenuit de rege . E . 7 tē 7 m̃ defđ fe ᵱ . II . folins . Tra . ē xvI .

cař . In dñio . ē una 7 dimidia . 7 XVI . uiłti cū XII . borđ

hñt . VI . cař . Ibi . II . æcclæ . 7 xv . ferui . 7 II . molini de xxv .

foliđ . 7 IIII . pifcariæ de mille 7 feptingent anguiłł . xx min .

Ibi . v . ãc ᵱti . 7 Silua . c.L . porč .

. T . R . E . 7 poſt . ualuit . xxx . liƀ . Modo . xx . liƀ . eo qđ tra

uaſtata . ē a pecunia .   IN MEDESTAN HVND.

Ifđ Ricard . ten BERMELINGE . Alret tenuit de rege . E .

7 tē 7 m̃ ᵱ uno folin fe defđ . Tra . ē . IIII . cař . In dñio

II . cař . 7 v . uiłti cū . vIII . borđ hñt . v . cař . Ibi . XIII . ferui .

7 uñ moliñ de . v . foliđ . 7 IIII . ãc ᵱti . Silua . x . porč .

T . R . E . ualeƀ . IIII . liƀ . 7 poſt . c . foliđ . Modo . IIII . liƀ .

LAND OF COUNT EUSTACE

In the Half-Lathe of SUTTON
In WESTERHAM Hundred

1   Count Eustace holds WESTERHAM from the King. Earl Godwin held it from King Edward. It answered for 4 sulungs then and now. Land for ...   In lordship 2 ploughs.
      42 villagers with 7 smallholders have 30 ploughs.
      10 slaves; a mill at 5s; meadow, 16 acres; from the woodland, 100 pigs.
      Value before 1066 £30; when acquired £24; now £40.

In the Lathe of WYE
In WYE Hundred

2   The Count holds BOUGHTON (Aluph) himself. Earl Godwin held it. It answered for 7 sulungs then and now. Land for 33 ploughs. In lordship 3.
      67 villagers with 5 smallholders have 30 ploughs.
      A church; 17 slaves; 2 mills at 7s 2d; meadow, 26 acres; woodland, 200 pigs.
      Value before 1066 £20; later £30; now £40.

11   LAND OF RICHARD SON OF GILBERT   14 b

In TWYFORD Hundred

1   Richard of Tonbridge holds YALDING. Aethelred held it from King Edward. It answered for 2 sulungs then and now. Land for 16 ploughs. In lordship 1½.
      16 villagers with 12 smallholders have 6 ploughs.
      2 churches; 15 slaves; 2 mills at 25s; 4 fisheries at 1,700 eels less 20. Meadow, 5 acres; woodland, 150 pigs.
      Value before 1066 and later £30; now £20, because the land has been despoiled of livestock.

In MAIDSTONE Hundred

2   Richard also holds (East) BARMING. Alfred held it from King Edward. Then and now it answered for 1 sulung. Land for 4 ploughs. In lordship 2 ploughs.
      5 villagers with 8 smallholders have 5 ploughs.
      13 slaves; a mill at 5s; meadow, 4 acres; woodland, 10 pigs.
      Value before 1066 £4; later 100s; now £4.

TERRA HAMONIS VICECOMITIS.

In Lest de Wiwarlet.   *In Wit hvnd.*

.XII. **H**aimo uicecom tẽ de rege uñ Maneꝛ.

qđ T.R.E. ſe deſđ ꝓ . ɪɪ . ſolins 7 dimiđ . 7 m̂ ꝓ uno
ſolin 7 ɪɪɪ . jugis . Tra . ē . vɪɪɪ . caꝛ . In dñio . v . bou arantes.
7 xvɪ . uiɫɫi cū . xv . borđ hñt . x . caꝛ . Ibi æccɫa . 7 vɪɪ . ſerui.
7 uñ moliñ de . ɪx . ſoliđ . 7 ɪx . anguiɫɫ . Ibi . xx . ãc p̃ti.
7 ſilua . xxx . porc̄.   £ 7 . vɪ . deñ.

T.R.E. ualeƀ . x . liƀ . 7 poſt.́ vɪɪ . liƀ . Modo.́ xɪɪɪɪ . liƀ . 7 vɪ . ſoliđ
De iſto m̃ tẽ Hugo de montfort . ɪɪɪ . juga 7 dim̄ . Vaɫ . ɪx . ſoɫ.

In Dimidio Lest de Svdtone.   *In Grenviz hvnd.*

Ibi h̄ Haimo . ɪxɪɪɪ . acs̃ træ . quæ ptiñ in *Hvlviz.*
Wiɫɫs accipitrari tenuit de rege . E . Ibi ſunt . xɪ . borđ
redđtes xɪɪ . denaꝛ.   Totũ uaɫ . ɪɪɪ . liƀ.

In Lest de elesford.   *In Litefel hvnd.*

Ipſe Haimo tẽ *Marovrde* . Norman tenuit de rege . E.
7 tc̄ 7 m̂ ꝓ . ɪɪ . ſolins ſe deſđ . Tra . ē . ɪx . caꝛ . In dñio ſunt . ɪɪ.
7 xxvɪɪɪ . uiɫɫi cū . xv . borđ hñt . x . caꝛ . Ibi æccɫa . 7 x.
ſerui . 7 ɪɪ . molini de . x . ſoliđ . 7 ɪɪ . piſcaꝛ . de . ɪɪ . ſoliđ.
Ibi . xx . ãc p̃ti . 7 tant̄ ſiluæ unde exeunt . ɪx . porc̄ . de paſnag.
T.R.E. ualeƀ . xɪɪ . liƀ . 7 poſt.́ x . liƀ . Modo.́ xɪx . liƀ.

In Lest de Borowart.   *In Witestaple hvnd.*

Ipſe Haimo tẽ *Blehem* . Norman tenuit de rege . E.
7 tc̄ 7 m̂ ſe deſđ ꝓ uno ſolin . Tra . ē . ɪɪɪɪ . caꝛ . 7 xɪɪ . uiɫɫi
hñt ibi . ɪɪ . caꝛ . In dñio . ē una caꝛ . Ibi æccɫa . 7 ɪɪ . ãc p̃ti.
7 de paſnag . ɪx . porc̄ . Ibi una piſcaria.
T.R.E. ualeƀ . vɪɪɪ . liƀ . 7 poſt 7 modo.́ uaɫ . vɪ . liƀ.

LAND OF HAMO THE SHERIFF

In the Lathe of WYE

In WYE Hundred

1   Hamo the Sheriff holds a manor from the King which answered
for 2½ sulungs before 1066; now for 1 sulung and 3 yokes. Land
for 8 ploughs. In lordship 5 ploughing oxen.
    16 villagers with 15 smallholders have 10 ploughs.
    A church; 7 slaves; a mill at 9s and 60 eels. Meadow, 20 acres;
      woodland, 30 pigs.
  Value before 1066 £10; later £7; now £14 6s 6d.
    Hugh de Montfort holds 3½ yokes of this manor.
  Value 60s.

In the Half-Lathe of SUTTON

In GREENWICH Hundred

2   Hamo has 63 acres of land which belong in WOOLWICH. William
the Falconer held them from King Edward.
    11 smallholders who pay 41d.
  Value of the whole £3.

In the Lathe of AYLESFORD

In LITTLEFIELD Hundred

3   Hamo holds MEREWORTH himself. Norman held it from King Edward.
Then and now it answered for 2 sulungs. Land for 9 ploughs. In
lordship 2.
    28 villagers with 15 smallholders have 10 ploughs.
    A church; 10 slaves; 2 mills at 10s; 2 fisheries at 2s.
      Meadow, 20 acres; as much woodland as produces
      60 pigs in pasturage.
  Value before 1066 £12; later £10; now £19.

In the Lathe of BOROUGH

In WHITSTABLE Hundred

4   Hamo holds BLEAN himself. Norman held it from King Edward.
Then and now it answered for 1 sulung. Land for 4 ploughs.
    12 villagers have 2 ploughs.
  In lordship 1 plough.
    A church; meadow, 2 acres; from pasturage, 60 pigs;
      a fishery.
  Value before 1066 £8; value later and now £6.

TERRA ALBERTI CAPELLANI.

IN DIMIDIO LEST DE MILDETONE . IN MILDETONE HD.

.XIII. A LBERTVS capellan̄ ten̄ de rege *NEWETONE*.

Sidgar tenuit de regina Eddid . 7 tc̄ 7 m̄ se defd̄

p̄ . VII . solins 7 dimid̄ . Tra . ē

Terra quæ fuit in dn̄io est ad firmā p̄ . LX . solid̄.

In ipso M̄ . x . uitti cū . XLVIII . bord̄ hn̄t . v . car̄.

Ibi . XII . ac̄ p̄ti . 7 IIII . denæ de silua redd̄t . xxx . porc̄.

de pasnaḡ . Ibi una piscaria seruie s Hallæ . 7 II . serui.

Siluula parua ad clausurā.

Ad hoc M̄ p̄tin̄ in cantuaria ciuitate . IIII . hagæ . 7 ī i . in

Roueceftre . quæ reddeb̄ . LXIIII . denar̄.

7 de M̄ Mildentone reddit in Neuuetone una c̄suetudo

idest . XXVIII . pensæ caseo₂ . 7 de XXVIII . solins de Mildentone

p̄tin̄ in Neuuetone . x . lib̄ 7 x . sot̄ . 7 de alia parte de noue

solins de Middeltone p̄tin̄ in Neutone XXVIII . pensæ caseo₂.

7 dimidia . 7 LVIII . solid̄ de gablo ex his noue solins.

7 de his . IX . solins reddeb̄ S̄igar ap̄ Mildetone Auerā.

De hoc M̄ sunt foris . III . denæ . quæ ibi fuer̄ T.R.E. sicut

hund̄ teftificat̄.

Tot̄ M̄ T.R.E. ualeb̄ XL . lib̄ . 7 post̄ xxxvi . lib̄ . Modō xxxiiii or̄ . lib̄.

Archiep̄s inde h̄t̄ . VI . lib̄ . 7 ep̄s baioc̄ . III . denas h̄t̄ . Val . XL . sot̄.

De tra huj M̄ ten̄ Goisfrid unū jugū . 7 uat . x . sot̄.

Adā fili Hubti tant̄ siluæ unde exeunt . XL . den̄ p̄ ann̄.

In the Half-Lathe of MILTON
In MILTON Hundred
1   Albert the Chaplain holds NEWINGTON from the King. Sigar
held it from Queen Edith. Then and now it answered for 7½
sulungs. Land for ... The land which was in lordship is at a
revenue for 60s. In this manor
        10 villagers with 84 smallholders have 5 ploughs.
        Meadow, 12 acres; 4 woodland pig pastures pay 30 pigs
            from pasturage. A fishery which serves the Hall;
            2 slaves; a small wood for fencing.
To this manor belong 4 sites in the City of Canterbury and 2 in
Rochester which paid 64d. From the manor of Milton a customary
due is paid in Newington, that is 28 weys of cheeses; from the 28
sulungs of Milton £10 10s belong in Newington; from the other
part of 9 sulungs of Milton which belong in Newington 28½ weys
of cheeses; 58s of tribute from these 9 sulungs; from these 9 sulungs
Sigar paid cartage to Milton.
        3 pig pastures of this manor which were there before 1066, as the
Hundred testifies, are outside it.
Value of the whole manor before 1066 £40; later £36; now £34.
        The Archbishop has £6 from it; the Bishop of Bayeux has 3 pig
pastures.
Value 40s.
        Geoffrey of Rots holds 1 yoke of the land of this manor;
value 10s.
        Adam son of Hubert has as much woodland as produces 40d
a year.

NOTES

ABBREVIATIONS used in the notes. Birch ... *Cartularium Saxonicum*, ed. W. de G. Birch, 3 vols. (1885–93). Colvin, 'A list of the archbishop of Canterbury's tenants by knight service in the reign of Henry II', *Documents Illustrative of Medieval Kentish Society* (*Kent Archaeological Society*, xviii 1964). DB ... Domesday Book. DG ... H. C. Darby and G. R. Versey, *Domesday Gazetteer* (Cambridge 1975). Dom.Mon. ... *The Domesday Monachorum of Christ Church Canterbury* ed. David C. Douglas (1944). Excerpta ... 'An Eleventh-Century Inquisition of St. Augustine's Canterbury', Adolphus Ballard (ed), *The British Academy Records of the Social and Economic History of England and Wales*, iv (1920). Förstemann PN ... E. Förstemann, *Altdeutsches Namenbuch*, Band I, *Personennamen* (2nd ed. Bonn 1900). Hasted ... Edward Hasted, *The History and Topographical Survey of Kent*, 4 vols. (Canterbury 1778–1799). KPN ... J. K. Wallenberg, *Kentish Place Names* (*Uppsala Universitets arsskrift*, 1931). MS ... Manuscript. NoB ... *Namn och Bygd*. OEB ... G. Tengvik, *Old English Bynames* (*Nomina Germanica* iv, Uppsala 1938). PNDB ... O. von Feilitzen, *The Pre-Conquest Personal Names of Domesday Book* (*Nomina Germanica* iii, Uppsala 1937). PNK ... J. K. Wallenberg, *The Place-Names of Kent* (Uppsala 1934). Regesta ... *Regesta Regum Anglo-Normannorum 1066–1100* ed. H. W. C. Davis (1913). Sawyer ... P. H. Sawyer, *Anglo-Saxon Charters* (1968). VCH ... *The Victoria History of the County of Kent*, iii (1932), with Domesday and Domesday Monachorum translations by N. Neilson. WS ... *Winchester Studies*, I, ed. M. Biddle et al., (Winchester 1976).

The manuscript is written on either side of leaves, or folios, of parchment (sheepskin) measuring about 15 by 11 inches (38 by 28 cms.). On each side, or page, are two columns, making four to each folio. The folios were numbered in the 17th century, and the four columns of each are here lettered a, b, c, d. Red ink was used to emphasize words and to distinguish most chapters and sections. Underlining was used to indicate deletion.

KENT. In red, across the top of the page, spread above both columns, with the exception of 11 a,b, *CHENTH*.

ASSOCIATED TEXTS

In common with other counties a number of Domesday-like texts survive for Kent which appear to bear some relation to DB itself. The most notable are the *Domesday Monachorum* of Christ Church Canterbury, a Domesday-like account of some ecclesiastical estates, with a different order and different information to DB; and an eleventh-century Inquisition of St. Augustine's Canterbury, commonly referred to as the *Excerpta*, which likewise contains information presented in the fashion of DB and refers to the Survey in its own heading. Both texts omit much of the manorial detail to be found in DB.

The *Domesday Monachorum* is in reality a group of 4 texts, only one of which is claimed as a Domesday satellite. The manuscript survives in a hand of *c.* 1100 but is itself a copy of an earlier document, which its editor, David Douglas, argues was compiled in 1087 from the original returns of the Domesday Survey. Robert S. Hoyt ('A Pre-Domesday Kentish Assessment List'), *A Medieval Miscellany for Doris Mary Stenton*, Patricia M. Barnes & C. F. Slade (eds), *Pipe Roll Society*, New Series 36, 1960, 189–202) has more recently argued that part at least of another text is an assessment list independent of and earlier than the Domesday Survey itself.

The *Excerpta* survives only in an emended thirteenth-century copy but is derived from an independent compilation made in or before 1087. This compilation is likewise argued to have been based on the information of the original returns. The thirteenth-century heading of the document refers both to the *King's Domesday* and to an *account of the sulungs of the County of Kent*, perhaps an assessment list of the kind which appears as part of the *Domesday Monachorum*.

In recent years the significance of these texts and of the Kent folios in general has assumed a great importance in the debate dealing with the making of the Domesday Book. In outline the debate revolves around the question as to whether such texts as the *Excerpta* and *Domesday Monachorum* are to be seen as products of the Domesday Survey itself, the conclusion of the editors of both texts, or else as part of the framework of Anglo-Norman governance to which the Domesday Survey was the immediate heir. An account of the major theories is to be found in

V. H. Galbraith, *The Making of Domesday Book* (1961), 146–155; *idem*, *Domesday Book: Its Place in Administrative History* (1974); Sally Harvey, 'Domesday Book and its Predecessors', *English Historical Review*, lxxxvi (1971), 753–66 and *idem*, 'Domesday Book and Anglo-Norman Governance', *Transactions of the Royal Historical Society*, 5th Series, 25 (1975), 175–93. Since, however, both theories admit the contemporary eleventh-century nature of the information in these sources, full reference to variants and amplifications of the DB text is given in these notes.

D1   DOVER. *Excerpta* 23 adds 'is the King's Borough'.
D2   20 SHIPS. *Excerpta* 24 adds 'for the keeping of the sea'.
D7   ORA. Literally an ounce, in Scandinavia a monetary unit and coin still in use; in DB valued at 16 (assayed) or 20 (unassayed) pence, see S. Harvey, 'Royal revenue and Domesday terminology', *Economic History Review*, 2nd series, xx (1967), 221–8.
D8   WADARD. One of Odo of Bayeux's knights, named and depicted on the Bayeux Tapestry where he is shown during the foraging near Hastings, see *The Bayeux Tapestry*, ed. Sir Frank Stenton (2nd ed. 1965), plate 47.
     MODBERT'S SON. *Excerpta* 24–5 identifies him as Geoffrey son of Modbert.
D10   A MILL. From the description it would appear that this was a tidal mill.
D11   FOUR LATHES. See the Introduction to the Index of Places.
D17   DEATH DUTY. The *relevatio, relevum*, the 'relief' or 'heriot', was paid by the heir on taking up his inheritance. The scale of rates was laid down in the law codes, especially 2 Canute 71 and the 'Laws of King William' 20. The *villanus* paid an ox, cow or horse, the *censarius* a year's tribute.
D18   *SCHILDRICHEHAM*. An unlocated place which appears later in 5,146 as *Cildresham*. The first element is the personal-name *Cildrīc*, rare in Old English.
D23   PENENDEN Heath. The site of the Shire court and the scene of Lanfranc's claim against Odo of Bayeux in 1072 concerning the losses from the Canterbury estate sustained, it now appears, as a result of encroachments made by the Godwine family in the years before 1066, see David R. Bates, 'The Land Pleas of William I's Reign: Penenden Heath Revisited', *Bulletin of the Institute of Historical Research*, ii (1978), 1–19. DB refers to the claim at 2,5; 43.4,16. See also note 2,30.
M   LAND OF THE CANONS OF ST. MARTIN'S OF DOVER. Entered here as an appendix to the account of Dover, but interrupted by the account of the City of Canterbury on folio 2a. The account of the lands of the Canons of St. Martin's of Dover thus breaches the custom of beginning each County with the land of the King, and their name is omitted from the list of landholders on folio 2b. The information in these sections differs from the formula employed elsewhere in DB in omitting ploughlands and retaining, apparently, only the Edwardian assessment. Sally Harvey, 'Domesday Book and Anglo-Norman Governance', *Transactions of the Royal Historical Society*, 5th series, 25 (1975), 175–93, argues that these features are indicative of a pre-1085 date for the St. Martin's entries and suggests that Rannulf Flambard, who had been master of the house, had conducted a survey of the estate which, on the failure of the 1085 re-assessment, he recommended as a model for the Domesday Inquest.
M1   21 SULUNGS. Listed below in M2–24. The total here is 17 sulungs, 4½ yokes, 3 virgates and 235 acres. The 3 sulungs in Lympne Lathe are entered below in P2–4.
     PREBENDS IN COMMON. DB records that Bishop Odo of Bayeux had distributed the prebends individually, although in the following entries the former occupant is given.
M3   1 MONASTERY. *Excerpta* 26 calls it a church, *unam ecclesiam*.
M5   25 ACRES. See note M18.
M7   VALUE 60s AND 9s 2d. *Excerpta* 27 gives £3 10s 2d.
M9   VALUE 30s. *Excerpta* 27 gives 60s.
M10   WALTER. *Excerpta* 27 identifies him as Walter of Cambremer.
M11   ROBERT. *Excerpta* 27–8 has 'In the Hundred of Bewsborough and Cornilo Robert Trublet has 1 sulung in prebend which two men, Sigar and Goldstan, held before 1066'.
M13   85 ACRES. *Excerpta* 28 gives 80 acres.
     VALUE £3; BEFORE 1066, £4. *Excerpta* 28 gives 'Value then £12; now 60s'.
M14   ARCHDEACON ANSKETEL HOLDS. *Excerpta* 28 has 'In Cornilo Hundred the Archbishop of Canterbury has 1 sulung in prebend of St. Martin's. Value £6 10s'.
M15   ½ SULUNG AND 12 ACRES. *Excerpta* 28 gives as '½ sulung and 12½ acres' and reduces the holding in Deal to '½ sulung less 11½ acres'.
M17   3 VIRGATES. Perhaps in error. *Excerpta* 29 renders as 3 yokes.
     THE VALUE IS AND ALWAYS WAS 60s. *Excerpta* 29, 'Value £4'.
M18   IN DEAL. *Excerpta* 29 places part of the holding in Guston, perhaps the 25 acres referred to in M5.

M20   VALUE 25s: BEFORE 1066, 35s. *Excerpta* 29, 'The value was 30s; now 25s'.

M21   1½ YOKES. *Excerpta* 29 gives 1 yoke.

VALUE BEFORE 1066, 25s. *Excerpta* 29 gives it as 20s.

SPIRITES. Favourite of Harold Harefoot (1037–40) and Harthacnut (*c.* 1040–42) who was banished by Edward the Confessor in 1065 and whose lands were forfeited, *Hemingi Chartularium* i, 254.

M23   EDWIN. *Excerpta* 29–30 identifies him as Baldwin's brother.

M24   GODRIC. *Excerpta* 30 identifies him as Godric Latimer, whose predecessor was Oswy Wild the priest.

51 BURGESSES WHO PAID TRIBUTE. £3 7s 5d, *Excerpta* 7.

C1   212 BURGESSES. *Excerpta* 9 calls them free men (*liberi homines*) and adds 'The cobblers and drapers pay 30s, the porter 5s'.

8 ACRES OF MEADOW. *Excerpta* 7 adds 'on which the King's horses graze, coming and going'.

1000 ACRES OF UNPRODUCTIVE WOODLAND. '1000 acres of underwood where the men of the district (*patria*) and the burgesses of the City paid 20s to the King's Sheriff', *Excerpta* 7.

C2   TWO HOUSES. *Excerpta* 10 adds 'The monks of Holy Trinity destroyed one, and have forbidden the other to be repaired. They paid 16d in tribute to the King'.

C3   TRIBUTE. *Excerpta* 10 adds that it was worth 53s.

THESE HOUSES. *Excerpta* 10 adds 'Now Ranulf of Colombières and Vitalis of Canterbury hold all these from the Bishop of Bayeux's Holding, but they only acknowledge 26'.

5 ACRES. *Excerpta* 10 adds 'with a Church'.

C6   IF ANYONE DIGS. *Excerpta* 9 gives 'If anyone makes a ditch, or puts up a pigsty or narrows the King's highway'.

C8   BISHOP OF BAYEUX. *Excerpta* 7–8 adds 'and Hugh de Montfort and the Count of Eu and Richard son of Gilbert'. These were presumably the King's barons whom DB refers to as having tried the case.

P6   NORWOOD. Not entered under any Hundred. The place was later in the Hundred of Newchurch PNK 470. See also P18.

P11   MEDERCLIVE. Not entered under any Hundred, although geographcally within Bewsborough Hundred in Eastry Lathe.

P16   400½ ACRES, WHICH MAKE 2½ SULUNGS. The statement, taken literally, would make the Kentish sulung contain a little over 160 acres. Paul Vinogradoff, 'Sulung and Hide', *English Historical Review*, xix (1904), 282–6, argued that the Domesday clerk had meant 400 and ½ (a hundred) acres, which would give a sulung of roughly 180 acres. Comparison of the entries for Northbourne in DB and the *Excerpta* gives a much more precise figure of 200 acres. See note 7,19.

P19   MS. The manuscript omits the gallows-like section sign, added by Farley.

P20   HAWKHURST. A *dene* of Wye Lathe. The place was later in Great Barnfield Hundred which, it is argued, may have been in existence by 1086, PNK 335 and the Introduction to the Index of Places.

1,1   DARTFORD. Later in its own Hundred, PNK 31.

PIG PASTURES. An area of woodland pasture located in the Weald but still dependent on its parent manor in the upland of north Kent. Identification of these Wealden settlements, which appear anonymously in DB, is often possible from later records. K. P. Witney, *The Jutish Forest* (1976) contains full reference to these identifications.

1,2   THE CASTLE. The original motte and bailey castle at Rochester, sited on Boley Hill outside the south-west angle of the city walls.

1,3   HUGH OF PORT HOLDS. *Excerpta* 3 adds 'from the Bishop of Bayeux. Edward held it'.

THE ABBOT OF ST. AUGUSTINE'S HOLDS. *Excerpta* 3 adds 'From these sulungs (the Abbot of) St. Augustine has his part which was proved in the Hundred of Milton and in the County (court) of Kent in the time of William I'.

CHURCHES AND TITHES. *Excerpta* 4 gives '8 prebends and a church'.

1,4   LATER £60. Farley error, *ix* for *lx*.

2,1   LATHE RUBRIC. In BOROUGH Lathe. Omitted in the MS.

THE CLERGY OF THE TOWN. *Dom.Mon.* 82 adds '32 dwellings and a mill which the clergy of St. Gregory hold near their Church'. The Church was the Priory of Augustinian canons founded in 1084 by the Archbishop Lanfranc.

2,2   SANDWICH. *Dom.Mon.* 89 adds 'Sandwich is Holy Trinity's manor for the monks' clothing. It is in its own Lathe and Hundred'. There is no evidence that Sandwich was a

Lathe and the reference would seem to be an error. See the Introduction to the Index of Places. *Excerpta* 20 adds 'In this Borough St. Augustine's has 1 acre. In this acre St. Augustine's also has a Church'. Cf. 5,189.

2,3   LATHE RUBRIC. In the Half-Lathe of Sutton. Omitted in the MS.

VALUE £15 10s. *Dom.Mon.* 88 adds 'It is assessed at £15. Richard has 10s in his castle (*infra castellum*)'. The castle is that at Tonbridge, the centre of Richard of Tonbridge's territory. See note 2,4.

2,4   3 THANES. *Dom.Mon.* 87 identifies them and the value of their holdings. 'What Hamo holds is assessed at 60s and 10s. What Robert Latimer and Geoffrey of Rots hold at £8 10s'.

WHAT RICHARD OF TONBRIDGE HOLDS IN HIS TERRITORY. Richard of Tonbridge, son of Count Gilbert of Brionne held what was later to become the Lowy of Tonbridge. This was not a compact block of land and has no clear boundary. Its primary purpose was the maintenance of Tonbridge castle in the aftermath of the Conquest, an offensive role shared with other compact lordships such as the Sussex Rapes, and in Kent the *divisio* or territory of Hugh de Montfort, see note 5,130. Richard held the manors of Yalding, East Barming, Hadlow and Tudeley but the greater part of his holdings consisted of the *denes* of upland manors located in the Weald around the castle and manor of Tonbridge. DB surveys 24 of them in the accounts of the manors to which they were formerly dependent, usually prefacing the entry with the formula 'What Richard of Tonbridge holds in his territory'. See Richard Mortimer, 'The beginnings of the Honour of Clare', *Proceedings of the Battle Conference 1980*, ed. R. Allen-Brown (1981), 119–41 and Jennifer C. Ward, 'The Lowy of Tonbridge and the Lands of the Clare Family in Kent, 1066–1217', *Archaeologia Cantiana*, xcvi (1980), 119–31.

2,5   SUNDRIDGE. *Dom.Mon.* 87 adds 'which Godwin held unjustly before 1066. The Archbishop, that is Lanfranc, gained it justly by the King's grant in a plea against the Bishop of Bayeux'. See note D23.

SUNDRIDGE AND OTFORD. *Dom.Mon.* 87 adds 'these manors were in Codsheath Hundred'. The Hundred is not otherwise mentioned in DB.

13s 6d. MS *xiii solid. 7 dim.* interlined *id est vi d.*

2,7   CRAYFORD. *Dom.Mon.* 86 adds 'Osward held it from the Archbishop before 1066'.

2,10   WROTHAM. *Dom.Mon.* 87 gives the taxable value of the men-at-arms' holdings:
William the Bursar. 'It is assessed at £3'.
Geoffrey of Rots. 'It is assessed at £3'.
Farman. 'It is assessed at 100s'.

GEOFFREY HOLDS 1 SULUNG. Perhaps at Yaldham, Colvin 30.

1½ YOKES. *Dom.Mon.* 87 gives '1½ sulungs'.

2,11   3 MEN-AT-ARMS. *Dom.Mon.* 86 adds 'Ralph holds 1 sulung which is assessed at 50s. William, brother of Bishop Gundulf holds 2 sulungs. They are assessed at £10. Ansketel of Rots holds 1 sulung which is assessed at 60s'. The sulung belonging to Ansketel was perhaps at Cossington, Colvin 21.

2 MEN OF THIS MANOR. *Dom.Mon.* 86 adds '2 men have 1 sulung which pays 16s to the altar of Holy Trinity. Value of this sulung however, 20s'.

MAIDSTONE. *Dom.Mon.* 95 adds 'Wulfric and Cola hold *Burgericestune*. ½ sulung there. It pays 100d to the altar of Holy Trinity. This ½ sulung is from the 10 sulungs in Maidstone'.

2,12   TOTAL VALUE OF THIS MANOR. *Dom.Mon.* 85 gives 'What the Archbishop has in lordship is assessed at £18; what Ansketel of Rots and Robert Brutin hold, 40s; however, it pays the Archbishop £25 18s'.

2,13   LATHE RUBRIC. In BOROUGH Lathe. Omitted in the MS.

TOTAL VALUE OF THIS MANOR. *Dom.Mon.* 84 gives 'It is assessed at £42 5s less 3 farthings'. Farthing appears only once in DB, see DB Cheshire S3,2.

2,14   IT PAYS £50 14s 2d. 'It is assessed at £51 5s', *Dom.Mon.* 84.

VITALIS. Of Canterbury, *Dom.Mon.* 84. Named and depicted in the Bayeux Tapestry where he is shown being questioned by Duke William as to the location of Harold's army, see *The Bayeux Tapestry*, ed. Sir Frank Stenton (2nd ed., 1965), plate 56.

3 SULUNGS, 1 YOKE AND 12 ACRES. '1 sulung and 1 yoke and 1½ sulungs in Thanet. He also has 12 acres and ½ sulung in Makinbrook and Stourmouth from the Archbishop', *Dom.Mon.* 84.

2,15   GODFREY AND NIGEL HOLD 1½ SULUNGS. *Dom.Mon.* 83 adds 'From these sulungs Godfrey the Steward holds ½ sulung which belongs to the monks' clothing. That is Swarling. Nigel has 1 sulung and 1 yoke which is assessed at 40s'. *Dom.Mon.* 95 adds that Godfrey held Swarling '*at farm*'.

2,16   THERE ARE ONLY 25. *Excerpta* 12 and *Dom.Mon.* 81 add '25 burgesses who pay 10s in tribute'.
NEW LODGING. MS *Inoua* for *In noua*, corrected by an interlined *n*.
OF THIS MANOR 5 OF THE ARCHBISHOP'S MEN. *Dom.Mon.* 81-2 adds 'Godfrey the Steward holds 1 sulung from the Archbishop in Thanington. It is assessed at 100s. Vitalis has 1 yoke from the Archbishop. It is assessed at 20s. Robert of Hardres holds 1 yoke. It is assessed at 30s. Alfward holds 3 yokes in Nackington which before 1066 paid and still pays 12s to the altar of Holy Trinity. It is assessed at 40s. Aethelwold holds 1 yoke at *Wic*. It is from the land of the monks of Holy Trinity which is assessed at 30s'.
HAMO THE SHERIFF HOLDS. *Dom.Mon.* 82 adds 'Hamo likewise holds ½ sulung which Alfred Big held from the Archbishop before 1066. It is assessed at 100s'. It was perhaps at Milton, near Canterbury, Colvin 2.

2,17   BARHAM HUNDRED. Later Kinghamford Hundred, PNK 552.

2,18   LATHE RUBRIC. In WYE Lathe. Omitted in the MS.
5 SULUNGS. *Dom.Mon.* 84 gives '5½ sulungs'.
TOTAL VALUE. *Dom.Mon.* 84 adds 'Before 1066 it was assessed at £10 and the Archbishop has 100s and 15 and 3d in tribute; now, however, the value is £20 but it pays £25 at a revenue and the Archbishop has his tribute as before'.

2,19   IT ANSWERS FOR 8 SULUNGS. *Dom.Mon.* 85 adds 'Before 1066 it answered for 8 sulungs, now for 7 because the Archbishop has the other for his plough'.
TOTAL VALUE BEFORE 1066. *Dom.Mon.* 85 gives 'Value before 1066, £20; the Archbishop has £4 7s in tribute. Now the value is £30 but it pays £40 at a revenue and the Archbishop has tribute as before'.

2,21   VALUE OF THE WHOLE 40s. *Dom.Mon.* 83 gives 'Value £6'.
5 OF THE ARCHBISHOP'S MEN. *Dom.Mon.* 83 identifies them: 'Vitalis has 1 sulung. Value 45s'. Probably Walmestone in Wingham, Colvin 14. 'Wibert and Arnold have 3 sulungs. Value £12'. Perhaps Ratling in Nonington, Colvin 23. 'Heringod has 1 sulung less 10 acres. Value 40s'. Probably Knell and Goss Hall in Ash, Colvin 25. 'Godfrey the Arblaster has 1½ sulungs. Value 100s'. Probably Overland in Ash, Colvin 26.

2,22   IT ANSWERED FOR 6 SULUNGS. MS *p vi . solins se defd.* Judging by the position of the full stop and a greyish patch it once read *vii.*, but the second minim has been scratched out. Farley renders as *p vii. solins se defd.*, although *Dom.Mon.* 91 supports a reading of the MS as corrected and suggests that the alteration was made by the Domesday copyist.
LATHE RUBRIC. In WYE Lathe. Omitted in the MS.
NOW FOR 3. *Dom.Mon.* 91 adds 'When the Archbishop acquired it for 5½. Hugh de Montfort has the moiety of them. Value £18'.

2,23   NOW FOR 15 SULUNGS. *Dom.Mon.* 83 gives '20'.

2,24   1½ SULUNGS. Probably in error for 1 sulung, as suggested by the value clause. *Excerpta* 14 and *Dom.Mon.* 82 give '1 sulung'. *Dom.Mon.* 82 adds that this land was part of the 7 sulungs of Westgate, in which case the DB entry would appear to duplicate information given earlier in 2,16 under the holdings of the Archbishop's men.
RALPH. The Chamberlain, *Dom.Mon.* 82.

2,25   85 BURGESSES. *Dom.Mon.* 84, 'In Romney Marsh 25 burgesses who belong to Aldington'.
STOWTING. *Dom.Mon.* 83 gives 'William of Argues has 1 manor, Stowting, which Alfhere held from the Archbishop. Then it answered for 1½ sulungs; now for 1. Value £10'.

2,26   3 OF THE ARCHBISHOP'S MEN. 'Robert son of Watson has 2 sulungs as a Holding; Robert of Hardres, ½ sulung and Osbern Paisforiere, ½ yoke', *Dom.Mon.* 84.

2,27   NEWENDEN. *Dom.Mon.* 92 refers to the Archbishop's manor of *Niuuendene* in Selbrittenden Hundred in Lympne Lathe which would seem to be this holding. On the basis of additional information given in the *Dom.Mon.* entry David Douglas' footnote raised the possibility that the entry referred to the holding of Hugh de Montfort in Newington (5,204; 9,37-8), although in the context this would seem less likely. The full *Dom.Mon.* entry is here reproduced: 'Newenden. In Lympne Lathe. In Selbrittenden Hundred. The Archbishop has 1 manor from the monks' land in lordship Newenden. Before 1066 Leofric held it from the former Archbishop. It answers for 1 sulung with Saltwood. Now it is assessed at £8 1s in gifts'.

2,28   LATHE RUBRIC. In the Half-Lathe of Sutton. Omitted in the MS.
ANSGOT. Of Rochester, *Dom.Mon.* 95.
FARNINGHAM. 'It is for the monks' clothing', *Dom.Mon.* 95.

2,29	RICHARD OF TONBRIDGE HOLDS. 'Richard has as much as is assessed at £3', *Dom.Mon.* 88.
2,30	HUNDRED RUBRIC. In Ruxley Hundred. Omitted in the MS. 3 YOKES. 'These 3 yokes did not pay tax with this manor. They are from the pleading which the Archbishop made against the Bishop of Bayeux with the King's agreement', *Dom.Mon.* 94. See note D23.
2,31	BRASTED. 'This manor is in the Hundred of Westerham', *Dom.Mon.* 86, PNK 70. ABBOT ALNOTH HELD THIS MANOR. 'Young Wulfnoth held Brasted from the Archbishop before 1066', *Dom.Mon.* 86.
2,32	LATHE AND HUNDRED RUBRIC. In Aylesford Lathe. In Eyhorne Hundred. Omitted in the MS. VALUE NOW £9. 'It is assessed at £11', *Dom.Mon.* 88.
2,33	BOUGHTON (MALHERBE). 'Ratel held Boughton (Malherbe) from the Archbishop of Canterbury before 1066', *Dom.Mon.* 91.
2,34	LATHE RUBRIC. In Wye Lathe. Omitted in the MS. RICHARD. The Constable, *Dom.Mon.* 93. LEAVELAND. 'The Deacon of Canterbury had and held this land', *Dom.Mon.* 93.
2,35	GRAVENEY. 'It is from the monks' clothing', *Dom.Mon.* 95. RICHARD. The Constable, *Dom.Mon.* 95.
2,37	IN TEYNHAM HUNDRED. Not otherwise mentioned in DB. Teynham itself is not surveyed, although the following detail appears in *Dom.Mon.* 85 as a preface to the entry for Sheppey. 'Teynham is the Archbishop's manor. Before 1066 it answered for 5½ sulungs; now the same. It is assessed at £50.' GODFREY. Of Malling, *Dom.Mon.* 85. SHEPPEY. 'Osward held it from the Archbishop before 1066', *Dom.Mon.* 85.
2,38	LATHE RUBRIC. In Eastry Lathe. Omitted in the MS.
2,39	FINGLESHAM. Later in Cornilo Hundred, although the place lies close to the Hundred boundary with Eastry, PNK 570. 'Leofnoth held it from the Archbishop before 1066. Value 20s', *Dom.Mon.* 89. STATENBOROUGH. 'Godwin held it from Archbishop Edsi before 1066. Value 30s', *Dom.Mon.* 89. Edsi had been Archbishop from 1035 to 1050.
2,40	WILLIAM. Follet, *Dom.Mon.* 89.
2,41	SALTWOOD. 'Earl Godwin held it. It answered for 7 sulungs; now there are 5; however, it is not taxed except for 3', *Dom.Mon.* 93. 225 BURGESSES. 'From whom Hugh de Montfort has nothing except 3 forfeitures', *Dom.Mon.* 93. Probably robbery, breach of the peace and highway robbery. IN THE BOROUGH OF HYTHE. *Dom.Mon.* 93 describes Saltwood as lying in Lympne Lathe, in the Hundred of Hythe. DB nowhere refers to Hythe as a Hundred which, if it existed in 1086, makes no further appearance in the records, PNK 459. It is possible that the copyist of *Dom.Mon.* wrote *Hede* in error for *Hen*, Hayne Hundred, in which Saltwood lay. LATHE RUBRIC. In Lympne Lathe. Omitted in the MS.
2,42	BERWICK. 'Godric the Deacon held it', *Dom.Mon.* 92.
2,43	LANGPORT. 'Which the Archbishop proved against the Bishop of Bayeux. Earl Godwin held it', *Dom.Mon.* 92. See note D23. *Dom.Mon.* 92 adds '1 yoke belongs elsewhere'.
3,1	LATHE RUBRIC. In the Half-Lathe of Sutton. Omitted in the MS. ORPINGTON. 'A freeman held it before 1066', *Dom.Mon.* 94. 2½ SULUNGS. 'From these sulungs Derman has ½ sulung at Keston', *Dom.Mon.* 94.
3,2	ONE OF THE ARCHBISHOP'S MEN HOLDS ½ SULUNG. 'In Stokenbury which Edric held from King Edward', *Dom.Mon.* 94. The place, now lost, is perhaps commemorated by Stocking Lane in the adjoining parish of East Farleigh, PNK 166. The field-names Stockenbury Meadows, Stockenbury Wood Field, Little Stockenbury Field and Stockbury Wood are recorded in 1578 on the site of Borough's Oak Farm (TQ 671497) in East Peckham. I am grateful to Mrs. Margaret Laurence for this reference. See also 5,61.
3,4	MEOPHAM. 'It is from the monks' food', *Dom.Mon.* 94. WHAT IS VALUED AT 18s 6d. '18s 8d', *Dom.Mon.* 94.
3,5	WHAT ABEL NOW HOLDS. 'Loose is the monks' manor for their clothing. It answers for 1 sulung. Abel the Monk holds it and pays a revenue to the monks. This sulung lies in the 6 sulungs of Farleigh', *Dom.Mon.* 95. WHAT GODFREY (HOLDS). 'Hunton is the monks' manor for their clothing. It answers for ½ sulung which Godfrey the Steward holds and pays a revenue. This ½ sulung is from the 6 sulungs of Farleigh', *Dom.Mon.* 95.

3,6   CLIFFE. 'It is from the monks' clothing. Before 1066 it answered for 2½ sulungs', *Dom.Mon.* 94.

3,7   MONKTON. 'For their food', *Dom.Mon.* 89.

3,8   WILLIAM. 'William of Adisham holds 1 sulung at Ruckinge. Value £7', *Dom.Mon.* 90.

3,9   NORTHWOOD. Thus DB and *Dom.Mon.* 88. *Excerpta* 12 gives *Norgate*, Northgate.
100 BURGESSES LESS 3. *Excerpta* 12 gives 100 burgesses less 19.
WHO PAY £8 4s. *Dom.Mon.* 88 £8 0s 6d, *Excerpta* 12 £9 0s 6d.

3,10   BLIZE. *Blittaere, Dom.Mon.* 90. Perhaps a garbled Anglo-Norman attempt at the rare OE personal-name *Blithhere* (NoB 33 (1945), 75; WS I, 151 note 3), or OG *Blithgaer* (Förstemann PN 313).
SEASALTER. *Dom.Mon.* 90 adds 'Land for 2 ploughs. This manor is in no Hundred'. It was later in Whitstable Hundred, PNK 100.

3,11   (SOUTH) PRESTON. 'For their clothing', *Dom.Mon.* 93.

3,12   CHARTHAM. 'For their clothing', *Dom.Mon.* 90.

3,13   GODMERSHAM. 'For their clothing', *Dom.Mon.* 90.

3,14   (GREAT) CHART. 'For their clothing', *Dom.Mon.* 90.

3,15   LITTLE CHART. 'For their food. Before 1066 it answered for 3 sulungs; now for 2½', *Dom.Mon.* 90.
2½ HIDES. Probably in error for 2½ sulungs as in *Dom.Mon.* 90.
WILLIAM HOLDS. 'William son of Hermenfrid has ½ sulung in Pett from the Archbishop as a holding. It pays 25d to the altar of Holy Trinity for all customs', *Dom.Mon.* 90.

3,17   GIDDINGE. The DB entry would appear to locate this place in Eastry Hundred, although, like Denton, it was later in Kinghamford Hundred, similarly entered under Eastry in DB, see note 5,220.
VALUE £36 10s 4¼d. *Dom.Mon.* 88 gives £37 10s 3d.

3,18   ADISHAM. Later in Downhamford Hundred in Borough Lathe. *Dom.Mon.* 89-90 records that 'This manor is itself a Hundred and is in Eastry Lathe'. The DB indentification is retained here.
ADISHAM. 'Adisham is the monks' of Holy Trinity's manor for their food', *Dom.Mon.* 89.
2 MEN-AT-ARMS. 'Robert son of Watson has 2 sulungs. That is Eythorne. Value £7. Roger holds 1 sulung at Barham. Value £4', *Dom.Mon.* 90.
IT PAYS £46 16s 4d. *Dom.Mon.* 90 gives £16 16s 4d.

3,19   LATHE RUBRIC. In Lympne Lathe. Omitted in the MS but added at 3,20.

3,21   LATHE RUBRIC. In Wye Lathe. Omitted in the MS.
ONE MANOR. 'Robert of Romney holds one manor, Brook, at a revenue for the monks' food', *Dom.Mon.* 92.

3,22   LATHE RUBRIC. In Lympne Lathe. Omitted in the MS.
ALMS-LAND. *Dom.Mon.* 84 associates this sulung with Lyminge but then adds, 'In Romney Marsh lies 1 sulung of *Aelmesland* from the alms of the monks of Holy Trinity. It is not from the above mentioned sulungs. From that sulung William Follet has 1 yoke, that is *Sturtune*. From that same sulung Robert has 3 yokes, that is Orgarswick, Castweazel and *Eadruneland*.' From this entry it is clear that DB *Asmelant, Dom.Mon.* *Aelmesland* is not a place-name, but a sulung of alms-land belonging to Holy Trinity, the four yokes of which lay in *Sturtune*, Orgarswick, Castweazel and *Eadruneland*. A reference to alms-land, OE *almeslond*, appears also in a charter of Athelstan to Milton abbey, Birch 738, Sawyer 391. In transcribing a minuscule *Almeslant*, the DB clerk clearly misread a long 's' for 'l'. The identification of *Asmelant* in DG as Gammons in Orgarswick is based on a misreading of KPN 267-9.

4,1   LATHE AND HUNDRED RUBRIC. In the Half-Lathe of Sutton. In Axton Hundred. Omitted in the MS. *Dom.Mon.* 96 assigns 4,1-4 to Axton Hundred.
IN TONBRIDGE. In the territory of Richard of Tonbridge.

4,2   NOW FOR 4 SULUNGS. *Dom.Mon.* 96 gives it as 3 sulungs.

4,6   LATHE AND HUNDRED RUBRIC. In Aylesford Lathe. In Larkfield Hundred. Omitted in the MS. *Dom.Mon.* 97 assigns 4,6-9 to Larkfield Hundred.
VALUE NOW £12. 'It is assessed at £13', *Dom.Mon.* 96.

4,10   VALUE NOW £10 10s. 'It is assessed at £10', *Dom.Mon.* 97.

4,11   VALUE NOW £7 15s. 'It is assessed at £6 10s', *Dom.Mon.* 97.

4,15   THEY PAY £11 13s 4d. *Dom.Mon.* 97 gives £11 13s 3d.

4,16   LANFRANC PROVED (HIS CLAIM). A reference to the land plea at Penenden Heath in 1072, see note D23.
VALUE NOW £8 0s 20d. 'It is assessed at £8', *Dom.Mon.* 98.

5,2   OF THE WOODLAND. MS *De silva*. Farley renders it as *De Silva*.

5

5,2–3	MS. The manuscript leaves a gap in the value clause, probably for an intermediate value when acquired.
5,6	ADAM SON OF HUBERT. Adam of Ryes near Bayeux, brother of Eudo the Steward, D. Douglas (ed), *The Domesday Monachroum of Christ Church Canterbury* (1944), 29.
5,7	'SONNINGS'. A lost place, surviving as a field-name in the modern parish of Horton Kirby (TQ 580683), Zena Bamping, 'A Domesday Name Identified?', *Kent Archaeological Review*, 61 (1980), 6–7.
5,13	½ MILL AT 5s. MS *½ mill at 5 sulungs*, obviously in error. ANSKETEL. Of Rots, *Dom.Mon.* 101.
5,18	ALFWARD HELD IT FROM HAROLD. MS *tenuit de Heraldo. H.* The meaning of the *H.* is not apparent.
5,20	ANSGOT. Of Rochester. *Dom.Mon.* 103 associates this land with others held by Ansgot of Rochester. HOWBURY. A lost place surviving as Howbury Lane in Crayford. PNK 30.
5,24	(ST. MARY) CRAY. MS South Cray. The place was known as St. Mary Cray from at least the mid-thirteenth century, after the dedication of the parish church, PNK 20.
5,26	SEAL. Later in Codsheath Hundred, PNK 63.
5,27	(NORTH) CRAY. Thus PNK 19.
5,31	THOROLD OF ROCHESTER'S SON. Ralph son of Thorold, *Dom.Mon.* 102.
5,34	(FOOTS) CRAY. Thus PNK 18.
5,35	ANSKETEL. Of Rots, *Dom.Mon.* 107.
5,38	SANDLINGS. 'Alfgeat held Sandlings from the Archbishop before 1066', *Dom.Mon.* 94.
5,41	ANSKETEL. Of Rots, *Dom. Mon.* 107.
5,48	NASHENDEN. Entered by DB in Larkfield Hundred, although the place was later in Rochester Hundred, PNK 126. It lies close to the Hundred boundary.
5,53	MS *Rouecest.*, 'corrected' by Farley to *Roucest.*
5,56	ANSKETEL. Of Rots, *Dom. Mon.* 107.
5,61	'STOKENBURY'. See note 3,2.
5,62	IN THE LATHE OF AYLESFORD. The rubric would appear to be redundant, as that at 5,40 still applies. See note 5,90.
5,67	Farley error, *ten epo* for *ten de epo*. LEEDS. 'Earl Leofwin held Leeds from King Edward. It answered for 3 sulungs; now it answers for 2 sulungs. Aethelwold held it from the Bishop of Bayeux but now King William has it in his hand', *Excerpta* 2. BISHOP OF BAYEUX'S PARK. *Excerpta* 2 locates it at Wickhambreux (*Wicham*). 4 PIG PASTURES. 'Count Robert of Eu holds 4 pig pastures from this manor in Sussex', *Excerpta* 2.
5,70	Farley error, *ten de ALNOITONE* for *ten ALNOITONE*.
5,71	SUTTON (VALENCE). The identification here follows Hasted II, 409.
5,88	HUNDRED RUBRIC. In Chatham Hundred. Not entered in the MS until 5,89.
5,90	IN THE LATHE OF AYLESFORD. The rubric would appear to be redundant, as that at 5,40 still applies. See note 5,62.
5,94	PIMP'S COURT. Later in Maidstone Hundred but entered here under Twyford, PNK 138. The place is close to the Hundred boundary.
5,96	HAMO. The Sheriff, *Dom.Mon.* 103.
5,99–100	AETHELWOLD. The Chamberlain, *Dom.Mon.* 101.
5,103	HUNDRED HEADING. In Wrotham Hundred. Omitted in the MS.
5,104	HUNDRED HEADING. In Shamwell Hundred. Not entered in the MS until 5,107.
5,115	MS repeats *solins* at the start of the second line, corrected by Farley with the gap indicated by a line of dots.
5,117	STUPPINGTON. Interlined. Later in Faversham Hundred but entered here under Milton, PNK 289. The place lies close to the Hundred boundary.
5,121	STELLING. Later partly in Loningborough Hundred and partly in Stowting Hundred in Wye Lathe, but entered here under Bridge Hundred, PNK 437. The place is close to the Hundred boundary.
5,122	BEKESBOURNE. The place was also known as *Lyvyngisbourn*, after a descendant of the *TRE* holder, as late as the sixteenth century. The modern form commemorates a twelfth-century holder, PNK 540–1, P. H. Reaney, 'A Survey of Kent Place-Names', *Archaeologia Cantiana*, LXXIII (1959) 64.
5,124	ALFRED BIG HELD THIS MANOR FROM KING EDWARD. The MS originally read *Hoc M tenuit Alured' biga tenuit de rege.E.* but the second and redundant *tenuit* has been scratched out and is not reproduced by Farley.

5

5,124   ALFRED BIG. OE *Bigga*, used here as a byname. The personal-name appears in Surrey 5,22, PNDB 202, OEB 290.

GEOFFREY SON OF MALLETERRE. *Excerpta* 16 identifies him further as Geoffrey son of Roger of Malleterre, OEB 349.

5,126   NACKINGTON. Later in Bridge and Petham Hundred but entered here under Canterbury Hundred, PNK 544. The place is close to the Hu ⟩dred boundary. The identification retained here and followed by VCH 233, DG ana *Dom.Mon.* 103 note, and applied also to the 3 yokes which appear in *Dom.Mon.* 103 as dependent on Westgate, see note 2,16. Nackington was later in Bridge hundred. PNK 496-7 argued that this place was Hackington, as suggested by Hasted III, 594.

HAMO THE SHERIFF. 'Hamo the Steward holds Nackington from the Bishop of Bayeux. The Burgesses of the City claim this ½ sulung', *Excerpta* 14.

5,127   HAMO ALSO HOLDS ½ SULUNG. The location of this holding is not clear, although the lands which the Burgesses of Canterbury claimed from the Bishop of Bayeux would seem to have been between Westgate and Nackington, *Dom.Mon.* 82, *Excerpta* 14. See also note 2,16.

5,128   VALUE OF THE WHOLE OF FOLKESTONE. Farley adds the gallows-like section sign omitted in the MS.

5,130   HUGH DE MONTFORT'S TERRITORY. Some of Hugh de Montfort's holdings in Kent are described as lying either within (*infra*), or without (*extra*) his territory (*divisio*), see 5,130; 169; 182, 9,1; 22; 35; 37-39; 42. VCH 188-190 suggests that this was an arrangement, analogous to the Lowy of Tonbridge, which served to maintain the castle at Saltwood. Hugh's *divisio* was likewise not a compact block of lands, but its detail, as recorded in DB, suggests a significant re-organisation in the pattern of assessment in Kent in the years immediately after the conquest. DB also uses the same term to describe the holdings of the Bishop of Bayeux, Ralph of Courbépine and the Count of Eu on three occasions, see 5,171; 175, 9,16.

5,131   ANSFRID. Male the clerk, ... *Male* is a Norman French man's name, see OEB 351, s.v. *Masculus*; P. H. Reaney, *Dictionary of British Surnames*, 229.

5,133   1 YOKE. *Dom.Mon.* 101 assigns this holding to Ralph of Courbépine.

5,134   AETHELWOLD. The Chamberlain, *Dom.Mon.* 101.

EASOLE. Entered here and at 5,217 in Eastry Hundred but later in Wingham Hundred, PNK 534. The place lies close to the Hundred boundary.

5,135   1 SULUNG IN SHELVING. *Dom.Mon.* 102 gives '1 yoke'.

5,136   HUNDRED RUBRIC. In Bewsborough Hundred. Omitted in the MS but added at 5,137.

A MAN-AT-ARMS OF HIS. The Latin is equivocal and might refer either to Osbern or to Odo of Bayeux, although in the context the latter is perhaps more likely.

5,138   LATHE RUBRIC. In Borough Lathe. Omitted in the MS.

1 SULUNG TO OSBERN PAISFORIERE. *Dom.Mon.* 101 gives 1½ sulungs.

5,146-51 ANSFRID. Male the clerk, *Dom.Mon.* 101.

5,146   *CILDRESHAM*. *Dom.Mon.* 101, *Cyldresham*. See note D18.

5,149   BADLESMERE. 'Godric Wisce held the manor of Badlesmere from King Edward. It answers for 1 sulung. Now Ansfrid holds it from the Bishop of Bayeux. It is assessed at £4. The monks of St. Augustine claim back this manor through the charter and seal of King Edward', *Excerpta* 4-5. The claim is entered below at 7,30. Godric Wisce was undoubtedly the 1066 landholder, now dead, whose son provided evidence for the Domesday enquiry, see V. H. Galbraith, *The Making of Domesday Book* (1961), 153-5.

5,152   OSBERN. Paisforiere, *Dom.Mon.* 101.

5,156   NORTH EASTLING. *Dom.Mon.* 102 credits this land to Herfrid, see also 5,183.

5,159   30 VILLAGERS. The MS would seem to have been amended from *xxx* to *xxix* in heavy black ink. Farley retained what appeared to have been the original entry. Whether the alteration was a contemporary one is not apparent from close examination of the MS.

5,162   ANSFRID. Male the Clerk, *Dom.Mon.* 101.

5,163   IN [WYE] HUNDRED. The MS is damaged at this point. The following places were all in Wye Hundred.

5,166   HUNDRED RUBRIC. In Felborough Hundred. Omitted in the MS.

5,167   HUNDRED RUBRIC. In Calehill Hundred. Omitted in the MS.

WAUA. Probably from an OE *Wafa*, which may be associated with OE *wafian* 'to wave', PNDB 409. Farley misreads as *Wana*.

5,169   POSTLING. Entered here under Calehill Hundred in Wye Lathe, probably in error. It appears correctly under Hayne Hundred in Lympne Lathe at 9,16.

5,171   OSBERT. *Dom.Mon.* 101, makes it clear that this is Osbern Paisforiere.

5,171 ALDGLOSE. Now in Bircholt Hundred, KPN 425. DB associates it with Brabourne, also in Bircholt Hundred, see 9,42.

5,173 12 ACRES. *Dom.Mon.* 101 infers that these too, were at Palstre.

5,181 ½ YOKE. *Dom.Mon.* 103 places this in Benenden.
A WIDOW WHO PAYS 22d. Farley error, *xiii* for *xxii*, apparently following the abbreviation *ci* (*tresdecim*) interlined. The figures in the MS are clearly *xxii*.

5,182 HUNDRED RUBRIC. In Blackburn Hundred. Omitted in the MS. Tinton is entered in Blackburn Hundred at 9,22. The name survives in Warehorne parish in Ham Hundred, parts of which are known to have lain in Aloesbridge and Blackburn Hundreds, PNK 474-5.

5,183 RINGLETON. *Dom.Mon.* 102 credits this land to Herfrid; see also 5,156.

5,185-188 HUGH. Of Port, *Dom.Mon.* 102.

5,189-90 ANSFRID. Male the Clerk, *Dom.Mon.* 101.

5,189 *LEUEBERGE*. Unidentified, Cf. 5,210-212 note. *Dom.Mon.* 101-102, *Endleueberga*, *Endleuaberga*. See PNK 561 where Wallenberg relates the DB form to the name of the *TRE* tenant *Leuuinus*, (OE *Leofwine*), and discounts the *Dom.Mon.* form as a subsequent rationalisation. However, in this section *Dom.Mon.* is independent of and antecedent to DB, and it shows the name to be OE *endleofan beorga* or (*aet*) *endleofan beorgum* '(at) eleven barrows'. Wallenberg *loc.cit.* may well be correct in supposing that DB *in leueberge* may represent a development of the OE place-name to **indlefenbeorga* > **inleveberge*, whence the metanalysis *in leveberge*, especially likely in a context where the Latin preposition *in* preceded the name.

5,192 A MAN-AT-ARMS. VCH 239 suggests that this is Hubert son of Ivo, who is recorded as holding land in Ewell at 9,35.

5,194 ASHRED. MS *Ascored*. Possibly from OE *Aescraed*, PNDB 165.

5,196 BUCK. OEB 359-60, PNDB 210.

5,197 ANSFRID. Male the Clerk, *Dom.Mon.* 101.

5,198 SANDWICH. 'It is in its own Lathe and Hundred', *Dom.Mon.* 89. See 2,2.

5,200 OSBERN SON OF LEDHARD. The MS calls him Osbert but refers in the same entry to *Osbern himself*. DB refers to Osbern son of Ledhard at 2,38; 5,135; 136; 200; 206-7. 7,19 and to Osbert son of Ledhard at 5,200; 205; 216, but they are clearly the same man as is made apparent in *Dom.Mon.* 102. The translation gives Osbern throughout.

5,201 ANSFRID. Male the Clerk, *Dom.Mon.* 101.

5,203 1½ YOKES IN THE SAME HUNDRED. VCH 240 suggests Buckland in Woodnesborough.

5,204 NEWINGTON. Entered here, and at 9,37-8, in Bewsborough Hundred in Eastry Lathe. The place was later in Folkestone Hundred in Lympne Lathe, PNK 453.

5,208 MIDLEY. Later in St. Martin's Hundred in Lympne Lathe, PNK 479.

5,209 IN SUMMERDENE HUNDRED. Taken literally the DB Hundred of Summerdene would include Robert Latimer's anonymous 6 acres and lands in Tickenhurst, Woodnesborough, Each, Marshborough and *Esmetone* in Eastry Lathe. Both Each (5,216) and Woodnesborough (5,197) are also entered by DB under Eastry Hundred, and all these places, with the exception of Robert Latimer's anonymous 6 acres, were later in that Hundred, PNK 574-88. Most authorities have therefore assumed that this entry refers to the Hundred of Somerden in the Half-Lathe of Sutton. K. P. Witney, *The Jutish Forest* (1976) 120, locates the 6 acres in Cowden (TQ 465404). That Robert held from Richard son of Count Gilbert might also be taken as circumstantial evidence that this holding lay in south-west Kent. The DB clerk, unfamiliar with this recent subinfeudation, was therefore unsure which Hundred the following five places were in and did not enter the next rubric until 5,215. Alternatively, it is possible that these places did lie in Summerdene Hundred in Eastry Lathe, although the Hundred was later absorbed into Eastry Hundred. The parish of Woodnesborough contains the place names Denne Court and Summer Field, PNK 587, 590. The translation and indices preserve the DB view of the situation for want of better evidence.

5,210-12 THURSTAN. Presumably Thurstan Tirel whom DB records as the holder of *LEUBERGE* 5,196 (cf. 5,189 note). *Dom.Mon.* 102 associates that holding with those at Tickenhurst, Woodnesborough and Each.

5,212 EACH. See note 5,209.

5,213-4 OSBERT. *Dom.Mon.* 101, makes it clear that this was Osbern Paisforiere.

5,214 ELMTON. DB *Esmetone*, *Dom.Mon.* 101 *Emmetune*. This place was identified by Hasted IV, 195, and followed by PNK 582-3 and DG, as Elmton in Eythorne. VCH and the editor of *Dom.Mon.* retained the eleventh-century form. *Esmetone* could represent a mis-copied minuscule script *Elmetone* OE *elmen-tune* 'village at the elms'; and *Emmetune* a poor translation of a mis-written form *elmne-tune*. Elmton is therefore a credible suggestion.

5,217   EASOLE. See note 5,134.
5,218   OSBERN. Son of Ledhard, *Dom.Mon.* 102.
5,220   DENTON. Entered here in Eastry Hundred, but later in Kinghamford Hundred, PNK 556.
5,221   HUNDRED RUBRIC. In Bewsborough Hundred. Not entered in the MS until 5,222.
5,222   40 ACRES. 'And near there (Boswell Banks) in a manor, 40 acres', *Dom.Mon.* 101.
5,223   LATHE AND HUNDRED RUBRIC. In Lympne Lathe. In Loningborough Hundred. Not entered in the MS until 5,224.
5,224   LATHE RUBRIC. In Lympne Lathe. Omitted in the MS.
6,1   LATHE AND HUNDRED RUBRIC. In Wye Lathe. In Wye Hundred. Omitted in the MS.
7,1   PLUMSTEAD. 'Sorag held it before 1066', *Excerpta* 1. The unintelligible personal-name of this *TRE* holder appears in a thirteenth-century MS copy of a 1087 text, so there is a possibility of scribal error. The origin may have been an OE by-name, *Strang* 'the strong' (not in OEB); or a variant form of the Anglo-Norman by-name *Sorz* 'the deaf' (*Winchester Studies* I (1976), 216).
     IT PAYS £14 8s 3d. 'It pays £14', *Excerpta* 1.
7,2   LENHAM. 'It is for the monks' food', *Excerpta* 2.
     1 YOKE OF THIS MANOR, VALUE 5s. 'St. Augustine has ½ yoke in *Bromfeld* which lies in this manor. It is assessed at 5s', *Excerpta* 2. Despite the discrepancy in the number of yokes this would appear to be the same holding.
7,4   LANGPORT. 'It lies in the Hundred of Canterbury', *Excerpta* 11.
     70 BURGESSES. '. . . who paid £4 10s in tribute. The villagers and smallholders who dwell outside the City pay £8 10s 8d in tribute and one sester of honey. 4 mills which pay 29s 4d', *Excerpta* 11.
     1 YOKE. 'Value 4s', *Excerpta* 11.
     VALUE NOW £35 4s. 'It is assessed at £35', *Excerpta* 11.
7,6   RALPH. Of St. Wandrille, *Excerpta* 16.
7,7   IT PAYS £54. 'It is assessed at £56', *Excerpta* 17.
7,9   IN CHISLET HUNDRED. 'In Blengate Hundred', *Excerpta* 17. See the Introduction to the Index of Places.
     12 SULUNGS. '6 are in Margate', *Excerpta* 17.
     WITH WILLIAM'S ASSENT. Odo's grant and King William's confirmation dated 1077, Regesta 99–100.
7,10   24 ACRES. 33 acres, *Excerpta* 17.
     SERVICE. 'At sea', *Excerpta* 18, *Dom.Mon.* 82.
7,11   VALUE NOW £4. 'It is assessed at £4 2s and one sester of flour', *Excerpta* 11.
7,12   WILDERTON. 'It is for the monks' food', *Excerpta* 4.
7,13   ANSKETEL. The Marshal, *Excerpta* 11. *Dom.Mon.* 101 adds 'of Rots'.
7,14   ADAM HOLDS ½ SULUNG FROM THE ABBOT. 'For a tribute', *Excerpta* 5.
7,15   ANSWERS FOR 6 SULUNGS. 'It answered for 7 sulungs', *Excerpta* 6.
7,16   ROOTING. 'Now a villager holds from the Abbot. It is assessed at 40s', *Excerpta* 6.
     1 YOKE IN RIPTON. *Excerpta* 5 and *Dom.Mon.* 100 give it as 1 sulung.
7,17   FURTHER, HE HAS 2 YOKES. 'Further, the Abbot gave him 3 villagers with 2 yokes. It is assessed at £4 5s', *Excerpta* 5–6.
7,18   ANSFRID. Male the clerk, *Excerpta* 5.
7,19   MS. *T.* probably for *T.R.E* which begins the next line.
     ODILARD. The Steward, *Excerpta* 21.
     VALUE £4. 100s, *Excerpta* 21.
     2 SULUNGS LESS ½ YOKE. '2 sulungs less 25 acres', *Excerpta* 21. On this evidence the Kentish yoke contained 50 acres, the sulung 200 acres, see note P16.
7,20   WADARD HOLDS LAND. 'Wadard holds all the villagers' land', *Excerpta* 22.
7,21   SIBERTSWOLD. 'It is for the monks' clothing', *Excerpta* 23.
7,23   PRESTON. 'It belongs to the monks' chamber', *Excerpta* 19.
     VITALIS HOLDS 1 SULUNG AND ½ YOKE. 'As a Holding', *Excerpta* 19.
7,24   ANSFRID. Male the clerk, *Excerpta* 19.
     IT ANSWERS FOR ½ SULUNG AND ½ YOKE. 'Before 1066 it answered for ½ sulung, 1 yoke and 20 acres', *Excerpta* 19.
7,25   3 VIRGATES. Probably in error for 3 yokes as in *Excerpta* 19, although *Dom.Mon.* 100 repeats 3 virgates.
     VALUE NOW 20s. 'Value 9s', *Excerpta* 19.
7,27   *LANPORT. Dom.Mon.* 100 renders as *Langeport* which David Douglas suggested might be Old Langport in Lydd, although the reference to Stowting Hundred would therefore be an error. In what is apparently the same entry *Excerpta* 30 places this holding at Elmsted and Monk's Horton.

7,29   BURMARSH. 'In the Hundred of Blackburn', *Excerpta* 30.

8,1   LATHE RUBRIC. In the Half-Lathe of Sutton. Omitted in the MS.

9,1   LATHE RUBRIC. In Wye Lathe. Omitted in the MS.

9,9   ATTERTON. DB enters Atterton with the rest of Hugh de Montfort's holding in Newchurch Hundred in Lympne Lathe but records the claim of the Canons of St. Martin's of Dover supported by the men of Eastry Lathe. The place was later in Bewsborough Hundred in Eastry Lathe, PNK 563.

9,10   MS. *'nove saline'*, corrected by Farley to *novae salinae*.

9,12   BLACKMANSTONE. Named after the pre-1066 holder, Blackman, PNK 461.

9,19   A LAND. *Dom.Mon.* 103 places this at *Belice*.
    BELICE. The name would appear to be identical in origin to that of Belce Wood, Sturry parish, PNK 514, although the hundred heading is an obstacle to its identification as that place.

9,27   IN THE SAME LATHE. *Dom.Mon.* 104 adds 'in Street Hundred'.

9,34   LATHE RUBRIC. In Wye Lathe. Omitted in the MS.

9,35   LATHE AND HUNDRED RUBRIC. In Eastry Lathe. In Bewsborough Hundred. Not entered in the MS until 9,36. The entry was perhaps added at the foot of column 13c.

9,41   POULTON. Later in Folkestone Hundred, PNK 454. The place lies close to the Hundred boundary.

9,44   LATHE HEADING. In Lympne Lathe. Not entered in the MS until 9,45. Farley omits 7 (*et*) between *de rege.E.* and *p tanto*.

9,47   *AIA. Aie, Dom.Mon.* 104. VCH 250 suggests Hythe. DB places it in Lympne Lathe in Street Hundred, adjacent to Hythe. But *Aia, Aie* probably represent a name other than *Hythe*, identical with that represented by those spellings recorded by Wallenberg under the name *Hythe* in PNK 459–460 which are formally unlikely for *Hythe*, viz.: *Hee* 1199, *Hei* 1206, *Hea* 1206, *Heia* 1224, *Heiā, Heyā* 1225. This other place-name was probably OE *(aet) Haege*, ME *Haye* from OE *hæg* 'hedged enclosure'. The spelling *Heiā, Heyā* are ambiguous; but read as *Heian, Heyan*, they would suggest comparison with the name Heane (Hundred meeting-place) in Saltwood parish, PNK 457, derived from the cognate OE *haegen* 'an enclosure'. However, the Hundred affiliation is an obstacle.

9,49   MS. *T.R.* Probably for *T.R.E.* which begins the next line. See note 7,19.

9,53   LATHE RUBRIC. In Wye Lathe. Omitted in the MS.

9,54   *SUESTONE.* Hasted iii, 388, followed by VCH and DG, identified this as Swetton in Cheriton in Folkestone Hundred. The DB reference to the same Hundred, that is Longbridge Hundred, would seem to militate against this suggestion, and the DB form is retained here. *Dom.Mon.* 103 gives *Westtune*, which may well represent the correct form.

10,1   IN WESTERHAM HUNDRED. MS *IN OSIREHA HUND* corrected by Farley *IN OSTREHA HUND*.

11,1   LATHE RUBRIC. In Aylesford Lathe. Omitted in the MS.

12,1   A MANOR. Hamo the Sheriff is recorded as holding 2½ sulungs at Trimworth in *Dom.Mon.* 103, probably the manor referred to here, see PNK 383 and Robert S. Hoyt, 'A Pre-Domesday Kentish Assessment List', in *A Medieval Miscellany for Doris Mary Stenton* ed. Patricia M. Barnes & C. F. Slade, *Pipe Roll Society*, New Series 36 (1960), 194.

13,1   2 IN ROCHESTER WHICH PAID 64d. *Excerpta* 4 gives 'which pay 2s to this manor'.
    £10 10s BELONG IN NEWINGTON. *Excerpta* 3 gives £11 10s.
    THE ARCHBISHOP HAS £6 FROM IT. From the customs of the Church, Regesta 176.
    3 PIG PASTURES, VALUE 40s. *Excerpta* 4 gives 60s.

INDEX OF PERSONS

Familiar modern spellings are given where they exist. Unfamiliar names are usually given in an approximate late 11th century form, avoiding variants that were already obsolescent or pedantic. Spellings that mislead the modern eye are avoided where possible. Two, however, cannot be avoided; they are combined in the name 'Leofgeat', pronounced 'Leffyet', or 'Levyet'. The definite article is used before bynames where there is a probability that they described the individual, rather than one of his ancestors. While an attempt has been made, with the aid of additional information supplied by *Dom.Mon.* and the *Excerpta*, to differentiate individuals with the same name, there remain many individuals who cannot be so differentiated. Readers are therefore advised that a group of references given under a single name (e.g. Aethelwold) do not necessarily refer to the same individual. References are to persons named in the text of DB. All names or name-forms which are not contained in DB itself, but are supplied from *Dom.Mon.* and the *Excerpta*, are printed in italics, as are the chapter numbers of listed landholders.

Churches and Clergy

Secular Titles and Occupational Names

INDEX OF PLACES

As in most counties some Hundred rubrics are missing. Others seem to be wrongly entered, as occasionally elsewhere, notably in Staffordshire. In most counties these omissions and errors are easily corrected, since the Hundreds were often geographical units, and their boundaries remained unchanged, apart from amalgamation, subdivision and the transfer of some monastic holdings to the Hundred of the Church concerned. In others, e.g. Buckinghamshire (see Bucks. note 1,1) the Hundred order is often the same within each chapter and throughout the County.

In Kent, however, the primary divisions of the County were the Lathes (see below) which were themselves subdivided into a large number of smaller Hundreds. DB frequently omits both Lathe and Hundred rubrics, or fails to refer to Hundreds which are known from other texts to have existed in 1086. The nature of Wealden settlement also ensured that many places there were annexed to Hundreds with which they had not a geographical connection. In the 13th century both the Lathes and the Hundreds were rearranged and renamed. Therefore, although it is possible that many of the anomalies are, as elsewhere, the result of errors and omissions in the MS, there is not always sufficient evidence to prove such errors. The authority of the MS in the location of places in their respective Lathes and Hundreds is therefore retained in the translation, and discussion of anomalies is reserved to the Notes. This index and the following maps do, however, reflect the incorporation of amendments to the MS as suggested in the Notes.

LATHES
The primary divisions of the County were the Lathes. These had originally been the provinces of the Jutish kingdom in Kent, each with its *villa regalis* at the centre and its share of Wealden forest. They first appear in written documents of the 6th century and have some parallels in the Sussex Rapes. DB mentions 7 in all: Aylesford, Wye, Lympne, Borough, Eastry and the half-Lathes of Sutton and Milton, although it is probable that there had once been several others. J. E. A. Jolliffe argued for the existence of two more, and K. P. Witney added another. The *Domesday Monachorum* of Christ Church Canterbury calls Sandwich a Lathe, but this is an isolated reference and would seem to be an error. The jurisdiction of the Lathe was originally comprehensive but its subdivision into Hundreds detracted from its judicial and administrative competence. At the time of the Domesday Survey, however, the men of the four east Kent Lathes, Borough, Eastry, Lympne, and Wye, were recorded as agreeing to royal laws (D11), although in the settlement of disputes the men of the Hundred gave evidence as was customary elsewhere in England (5,149. 9,9).

In the 13th century the number of Lathes in east Kent was reduced from 5 to 3: the half-Lathes of Milton and Wye were joined to form the Lathe of Scray, Borough and Eastry were joined to form the Lathe of St. Augustine, and Lympne was renamed as the Lathe of Shepway.

HUNDREDS
The division of the Kentish Lathes into Hundreds would seem to have been effected at some time after the kingdom lost its independence, probably during the 10th century (J. E. A. Jolliffe, 'The Origin of the Hundred in Kent', in J. G. Edwards, V. H. Galbraith & E. F. Jacob (eds.), *Historical Essays in Honour of James Tait* (1933), 155-68). The DB record of these Hundreds may, however, be in some respects incomplete. The *Domesday Monachorum* of Christ Church Canterbury refers to the Hundred of Codsheath in the half-Lathe of Sutton, and adds that Brook in Wye Lathe, Adisham in Eastry Lathe and the Borough of Hythe in Lympne Lathe were themselves Hundreds. The *Excerpta* of St. Augustine's Canterbury also contains a reference to the later Hundred of Blengate, although this would seem to be an interpolation by the 13th century copyist. In the Weald settlements were often dependent on parent manors elsewhere in the north of the County. They appear anonymously in DB as pig pastures or *denes*, although a number of places had been separated from their parent manors and are surveyed separately in DB and entered under an appropriate Wealden Hundred. Since reference to a Wealden Hundred in DB might be dependent on the chance that it contained some settlement which had been separated from its parent manor, it is conceivable that some of the later Hundreds in this area were in existence by 1086. An early date has been put forward for both Barclay Hundred and Great Barnfield Hundred in Wye Lathe (K. P. Witney, *The Jutish Forest* (1976), 124).

A number of Kentish Hundreds were reorganized, chiefly in the 13th century, and a few may have been created at the same time. At the time of DB Lympne Lathe contained the Hundreds of Stowting (Sw), Loningborough (Lo), Folkestone (F), Bircholt (Bi), Hayne (Ha), Street (St), Blackburn (Bl), Ham (Hm), Newchurch (N), Worth (Wo), Rolvenden (Rl), Selbrittenden (Se), Oxney (O), Aloesbridge (Al), and Langport (La). The Borough of Hythe lay within this Lathe and a number of places are described as being 'in Romney Marsh'. In the 13th century Blackburn, Rolvenden and Selbrittenden Hundreds were added to the Lathe of Scray, formerly Wye. Lympne Lathe, now Shepway, acquired the Hundreds of Felborough, Wye, Calehill, Chart and Longbridge. St. Martin's Hundred does not seem to have existed before the 13th century.

At the time of DB Eastry Lathe contained the Hundreds of Preston (P), Wingham (Wi), Sandwich (Sa), Eastry (E), Bewsborough (B), Cornilo (C), and perhaps also *Summerdene* (Su), see note 5,209.

At the time of DB Borough Lathe contained the Hundreds of Whitstable (Wh), Reculver (Re), Chislet (Ch), Sturry (Sy), Fordwich (Fo), Westgate (We), Bridge (Br), Petham (Pe), Barham (Ba), Downhamford (D), Thanet (Th) and Canterbury (Ca). In the 13th century Reculver, Sturry and Chislet Hundreds were joined to form the Hundred of Blengate; Bridge and Petham Hundreds were amalgamated, and the Hundreds of Barham and Thanet were renamed as Kinghamford and Ringslow respectively.

At the time of DB Wye Lathe contained the Hundreds of Teynham (T), Faversham (Fa), Boughton (Bo), Calehill (Ca), Chart (Ct), Longbridge (Lo), Wye (W), Felborough (Fe), and Bircholt (Bi). DB gives no authority for the existence of the 5 Wealden Hundreds of Marden, Cranbrook, Barclay, Great Barnfield and Tenterden, some or all of which may not have been created until the 13th century when Wye Lathe also acquired the Hundreds of Selbrittenden and Rolvenden.

At the time of DB the half-Lathe of Milton contained the Hundred of Milton (M).

At the time of DB Aylesford Lathe contained the Hundreds of Toltingtrough (To), Shamwell (S), Hoo (H), Rochester (R), Chatham (C), Eyhorne (E), Maidstone (M), Larkfield (La), Wrotham (Wr), Littlefield (Li), Twyford (Tw), and Washlingstone (Wa). Chatham Hundred was later known as Chatham and Gillingham Hundred. DB gives no authority for the existence of the Wealden Hundreds of Little Barnfield or Brenchley and Horsmonden which were probably not created before the 13th century.

At the time of DB the half-Lathe of Sutton contained the Hundreds of Greenwich (G), Bromley (Br), Ruxley (R), Little (Le), Axton (A), Westerham (Wm), and Codsheath (Co). Somerden Hundred, which was later part of this Lathe, may also have been in existence at the time of DB, see note 5,209. In the 13th century Greenwich Hundred was renamed as Blackheath, Bromley as Bromley and Beckenham, and Little as Little and Lesnes. At the same time Westerham Hundred was separated into the Hundreds of Brasted, and Westerham and Edenbridge; and Axton became the Hundreds of Axton, and Dartford and Wilmington.

The editor is grateful to Dr. Alexander Rumble for his advice on the place-names and Hundreds of Kent.

The name of each place is followed by (i) the initial of its Lathe and Hundred, and its location on the Map in this volume; (ii) its National Grid Reference; (iii) chapter and section reference in DB. Bracketed figures denote mention in sections dealing with a different place. Italic figures refer to places or information mentioned only in the notes. Unless otherwise stated the spellings of the Ordnance Survey are followed for places in England, of OEB for places abroad. Inverted commas mark lost places with known modern spellings; unidentifiable places are given in DB spelling, in italics. The National Grid reference system is explained on all Ordnance Survey maps, and in the Automobile Association Handbooks; the figures reading from left to right are given before those reading from bottom to top of the map. Places marked with (⁺) are in the 100 kilometre grid square lettered TR; all others are in square TQ.

	Map	Grid	Text
Burham	A La 5	72 62	5,58
Burgericestune	A M	—	*2,11*
Burmarsh[+]	L Rm 1	10 32	7,28–29
Canterbury[+]	B Ca 1	15 57	C. (D22;24. 1,4.) 2,1;*16*;(24. 3,9. 5,76;78;81;124)–125; (127;144–145;147;151;155; 160;220. 7,4;) 11. (13,1)
Castweazel	L Rm 4	83 37	*3,22*
Chalk	A S 4	68 72	5,104
Charing	W Ca 2	95 49	2,19
Charlton (near Dover)[+]	E B 18	31 42	M2–3
Charlton (near Greenwich)	S G 2	41 77	5,33
Chartham[+]	W Fe 2	10 55	3,12
(Great) Chart	W Ct 1	97 41	3,14
(Little) Chart	W Ca 6	94 45	3,15
Chart Sutton	A E 23	80 49	5,72
Chatham	A C 1	75 68	5,89
Chelsfield	S R 12	47 63	5,23
Chilham[+]	W Fe 4	06 53	5,144
Chillenden[+]	E E 9	26 53	5,207
Chislet[+]	B Ch 1	22 64	7,9
Cildresham, see also *Shildriceham*	W Fa	—	5,146
Cliffe	A S 1	73 76	3,6. 5,110
Coldred[+]	E B 2	27 47	5,191
Cooling	A S 2	75 75	5,106;113
Coombe(Grove)[+]	W W 10	07 46	5,165
(Court-at-) Street[+]	L St 5	09 35	9,31
(Foots) Cray	S R 3	47 71	5,34
(North) Cray	S R 2	49 72	5,27
(St. Mary) Cray	S R 6	47 67	5,24
(St. Pauls) Cray	S R 5	47 68	5,28
Crayford	S Le 4	51 77	2,7
Crofton	S R 8	44 65	5,35
Cudham	S R 13	44 59	5,36
Cuxton	A S 12	70 66	4,10
Darenth	S A 5	56 71	2,3. 5,16–17
Dartford	S A 1	54 74	1,1
Deal[+]	E C 1	37 52	M14(–15);17–19
Dean (Court)	W Ca 5	98 48	D24. 5,167
(Great) Delce	A R 2	74 66	5,91
(Little) Delce	A R 3	74 66	5,90
(Denge)marsh[+]	L La 3	05 18	5,177;179
Denton (near Barham)[+]	E E 22	21 46	5,220
Denton (near Gravesend)	A S 3	66 73	4,11
Dernedale[+]	W W 6	07 47	7,14
Ditton	A La 17	70 58	5,42
Dover[+]	E B 22	32 41	D. (M3). P9–11. (2,2). 5,188; (205. 9,9.)
Each[+]	E E 1	30 58	5,216
Each[+]	E Su 1	30 58	5,212
Eadruneland	L Rm	—	*3,22*
Easole[+]	E E 12	25 52	5,134;217
Eastbridge[+]	L W 1	07 31	9,10
Eastling	W Fa 13	96 56	5,158–159
North Eastling	W Fa 11	96 57	5,156
Eastry[+]	E E 10	31 54	3,17
Eastwell[+]	W W 3	00 47	9,1
Eccles	A La 11	72 60	5,44
Eddintone	S A	—	5,4
Elham[+]	L Lo 1	17 43	5,129
Elmstone[+]	E P 2	26 60	7,24

	Map	Grid	Text
Elmton[+]	E Su E	27 50	5,214
Eltham	S G 7	42 74	5,30
Essella	W Lo	–	9,5
Evegate[+]	W L 6	06 38	9,53
(Temple) Ewell[+]	E B 7	28 44	5,185;192. 9,35–36
Eynsford	S A 14	54 65	2,29
Eythorne[+]	E E 20	27 49	*3,18*
Fairbourne	A E 17	86 51	5,64;87
Fanscombe[+]	W W 8	08 47	5,163. 9,51
(East) Farleigh	A M 6	73 53	3,5
(West) Farleigh	A Tw 3	71 53	5,95
Farningham	S A 11	54 66	2,28. 5,10;13;15
Farthingloe[+]	E B 20	29 40	M22
Faversham[+]	W Fa 6	01 61	1,4
Fawkham	S A 12	59 68	4,3
Finglesham[+]	E E 13	33 53	2,39
Fleet[+]	E Wi 2	30 60	(2,21)
Folkestone[+]	L F 1	22 36	5,128
Fordwich[+]	B Fo 1	18 59	7,10
Frindsbury	A S 10	74 69	4,13;(15)
Frinsted	A E 7	89 57	5,66
Gara[+]	W	–	D24
Garrington[+]	B D 4	20 56	7,6
Giddinge[+]	E E 23	23 46	(3,17)
Gillingham	A C 2	78 68	2,12. 5,88
Godmersham[+]	W Fe 6	06 50	3,13
Goslaches	–	–	D18
Graveney[+]	W Bo 1	05 62	2,35
Gravesend	A To 2	64 74	5,54
Greenwich	S G 3	38 77	5,29
Guston[+]	E B 13	32 44	M5;(18)
Hadlow	A Li 3	63 49	5,60
Halling	A S 13	70 63	4,12
Ham[+]	E E 11	32 54	5,206
Hammil[+]	E E 4	29 55	5,184
Hampton[+]	W W 12	07 43	9,2
Harbilton	A E 11	86 52	5,84
(Lower) Hardres[+]	B Br 3	15 53	5,123;(133)
(Upper) Hardres[+]	B Br 4	15 50	5,120
Harrietsham	A E 12	87 53	5,63
Hartanger[+]	E E 19	26 49	5,202
Hartley	S A 13	61 66	5,3
Harty[+]	W Fa 1	01 66	D18
Hastingleigh[+]	L Bi 1	09 45	5,225. 9,52
Haven	A S 8	74 72	5,111–112
Hawkhurst	W	76 30	P20
Hawley	S A 4	54 71	(1,1). 5,1
Heane? see *Aia*			
Hemsted	L Lo 2	14 41	5,223
Henhurst	A S 11	66 69	5,109
Higham	A S 9	71 74	5,105
Hollingbourne	A E 4	84 55	(2,33). 3,3
Hoo	A H 1	78 71	5,93
Horton[+]	W Fe 1	11 55	D18. 5,162
Horton (Kirby)	S A 9	56 68	5,18
(Monk's) Horton[+]	L Sw 3	12 40	9,25–26;30
Hougham[+]	E B 19	27 39	M23. (5,138)
Howbury	S Le 3	53 76	5,20
Hunton	A M 8	72 49	*3,5*
Hurst (in Chilham)[+]	W Fa 21	06 51	D18. 5,153
Hythe[+]	L St 10	16 34	(2,26;41)
Ickham[+]	B D 3	22 58	3,8

	Map	Grid	Text
Offham	A La 14	65 57	5,47;56
Orgarswick	L Rm 3	09 30	*3,22*
Orlestone	L Hm 2	00 34	9,28
Orpington	S R 9	46 66	2,30. 3,1
Oslachintone	—	—	D18
Ospringe[+]	W Fa 10	00 60	D18. 5,145
Otford	S Co 1	52 59	2,4
Otham	A E 9	78 54	5,83
Otterden	A E 14	94 54	5,76
Otterpool[+]	L St 6	10 36	9,49
Paddlesworth	A La 4	68 62	5,45
Palstre (Court)	L O 1	88 28	5,172–173
Patrixbourne[+]	B Br 2	18 55	5,119
(East) Peckham	A Li 4	66 49	3,2
(West) Peckham	A Li 2	64 52	5,59
Penenden	A M 2	76 57	D23
Perry (Court)[+]	W Fa 7	01 60	D18. 5,151
Perry (Wood)[+]	W Fa 20	03 55	D18. 5,150
Petham[+]	B Pe 1	13 51	2,15
Pett	W Ca 3	96 48	*3,15*
Pimp's (Court)	A Tw 7	75 52	5,94–(95)
Pinden	S A 7	59 69	5,11
Pineham[+]	E B 10	31 45	5,174
Pising[+]	E B 11	32 45	5,174
Pivington	W Ca 7	91 46	5,168
Pluckley	W Ca 8	92 45	2,20
Plumstead	S Le 1	45 78	5,21. 7,1
(North) Ponshall[+]	E B 3	28 47	5,136
(South) Ponshall[+]	E B 4	28 46	5,137
Postling[+]	L Ha 1	14 39	5,169. 9,16
Poulton[+]	E B 16	27 41	9,41
Preston (near Fordwich)[+]	E P 1	24 60	7,23
(South) Preston[+]	W Fa 9	02 60	3,11
Reculver[+]	B Re 1	22 69	2,13
Ridley	S A 19	61 63	5,6
Ringlestone	W Fa 19	88 55	5,161
Ringleton[+]	E E 3	29 57	5,183
Ripe[+]	L La 2	03 19	P6;17
Ripton	W Ct 2	99 44	7,17
Rochester	A R 1	74 68	R. *1,2.* (2,3.) 4,15. (5,44;53; 56;70;93;97;104. 13,1)
Romney[+]	L Rm 2	03 25	2,25;(43). 5,178
Rooting	W Ca 9	94 45	7,16
Ruckinge[+]	L Hm 3	02 33	*3,8.* 9,29
Ruxley	S R 4	48 70	5,22
Ryarsh	A La 9	67 59	5,46
St. Margaret's at Cliffe[+]	E B 15	35 44	M6–13;(14); 21. P8
St. Martin's[+]	B We 3	15 57	*2,16*;24
Saltwood[+]	L Ha 2	15 35	2,41
Sandlings	S R 7	46 66	5,38
Sandwich[+]	E S 1	33 58	D22;24. 2,2. 3,23. 5,198
Schildricheham, see *Cildresham*			
Scortebroc	—	—	P14
Seal	S R 14	55 56	5,26
Seasalter[+]	B Wh 2	09 64	3,10
Sellindge[+]	L St. 4	09 38	9,24
Selling[+]	W Bo 3	03 56	7,15
Sevington[+]	W Lo 4	03 40	9,3
Shalmsford (Street)[+]	W Fe 5	09 54	5,170
Shelborough	A E 18	88 52	5,65
(New) Shelve	A E 21	91 51	5,78
(Old) Shelve	A E 22	92 51	5,77;82

	Map	Grid	Text
Shelving[+]	E E 2	29 54	5,135;219
Sheppey	W T 1	90 72	2,37
Sibertswold[+]	E B 1	26 47	M15–16;20. P12. 7,21
Siborne	L St	–	9,45
Siffleton	A La 18	71 58	5,43
Snodland	A La 3	70 61	4,9
Soles (Court)[+]	E E 16	25 50	5,201
Solton[+]	E B 12	33 45	5,187
'Sonnings'	S A 10	58 68	(5,7)
Sophis	W	–	D24
South Ashford[+]	W Lo 3	00 41	9,4
Southfleet	S A 6	61 71	4,1
Stalisfield	W Fa 18	96 52	5,142
Stansted[+]	L Bi 2	06 37	P4
Stansted[+]	L St 2	06 37	P3
Statenborough[+]	E E 7	31 55	(2,39)
Stelling[+]	B Br 5	14 48	5,121
Stockbury	A E 1	84 61	5,69
Stoke	A H 2	82 75	4,16. 5,92
'Stokenbury'	A Li 5	67 49	3,2. 5,61
Stone	S A 2	57 74	4,2
Stourmouth[+]	B Re 3	25 62	*2,14*
Stowting[+]	L Sw 2	12 41	(2,25)
Stuppington	M M 6	96 59	5,117
Sturry[+]	B Sy 1	17 60	7,7
Sturtune	L Rm	–	*3,22*
Suestone	L F		9,54
Sundridge	S Co 2	48 54	2,5
Sutton (Valence)	A E 24	81 49	5,71
East Sutton	A E 25	82 49	5,73
Swalecliffe[+]	B Wh 3	13 67	5,139
Swanscombe	S A 3	60 73	5,2
Swanton (in Bilsington)[+]	L St 1	02 35	9,46
Swanton (in Lydden)[+]	E B 6	24 44	5,193
Swarling[+]	B Pe 2	12 52	*2,15*
Teston	A Tw 2	70 53	5,99
Thanington[+]	B We 2	13 56	*2,16*
Throwley	W Fa 15	99 55	D18. 5,155
Thurnham	A E 2	80 57	5,86
Tickenhurst[+]	E Su 3	29 54	5,210
Tiffenden	L Bl 1	91 36	9,44
Tilmanstone[+]	E E 18	30 51	2,40
Tinton	L Bl 2	98 31	5,182. 9,8;22
Tonbridge	A Te 1	59 46	4,1
Tonge	M M 4	93 64	5,118
Tottington	A La 12	73 59	5,49–50
Trimworth	W W 2	06 49	12,1
Trottiscliffe	A La 7	64 60	4,8
Tudeley	A Wa 1	62 45	5,62
Tunstall	M M 5	89 61	5,115
Ulcombe	A E 26	84 49	2,32
Upchurch	M M 1	84 67	5,116
Wadholt[+]	E B 5	29 46	7,22
Waldershare[+]	E E 21	29 48	5,215
Warehorne	L Hm 1	98 32	3,19
Wateringbury	A Tw 1	68 53	5,97–98
West Cliffe[+]	E B 14	35 44	5,186
Westerham	S Wm 1	44 54	10,1
Westgate (in Canterbury)[+]	B We 1	14 57	2,16;(24)
Westwell	W Ca 4	99 47	3,16
(West) Wickham	S R 10	38 64	5,25

	Map	Grid	Text
Whitstable[+]	B Wh 1	10 66	2,14
Wic	B We	–	*2,16*
Wichling	A E 8	91 55	5,81
Wickhambreux[+]	B D 1	22 58	(5,67);124
Wilderton	W Fa 12	99 56	7,12
Wingham[+]	E Wi 1	24 57	2,21
Woodnesborough[+]	E E 5	30 56	5,197
Woodnesborough[+]	E Su 4	30 56	5,211
Woolwich	S G 1	43 78	12,2
Wormshill	A E 6	88 57	5,80
Wouldham	A La 2	71 64	4,6
Wricklesmarsh	S G 6	41 76	5,31
Wrotham	A Wr 1	61 59	2,10
Wrotham (Heath)	A Wr 2	63 58	5,103
Wye[+]	W W 7	05 46	D24. 6,1
Yalding	A Tw 5	69 50	11,1

Places not named

P2. 5,140;181;203;205;209;218. 7,25. 9,7–8;11;13–15;17;20–21;23;27;32–34;38;40;43;50.
12,1

Places not in Kent

Elsewhere in Britain
ESSEX ... 5,104. LONDON ... Alstan. OXFORDSHIRE ... Oxford, Wulfric. SUSSEX ... *5,67*.
Battle 6.

Outside Britain
Abbeville ... Walter. Arques ... William. Barbes ... Robert. Bayeux ... Bishop. Brébouef ... Hugh.
Cambremer ... Walter. Colombières ... Ralph, Ranulf. Courbépine ... Ralph. Douai ... Walter.
Eu ... Robert. Ghent ... Abbey. Gironde ... Thurstan. Hesdin ... Arnulf. Le Marais ... Richard.
Mandeville ... Hugh. Montfort ... Hugh. Poitou ... William. Port ... Hugh. Rots ... Ansketel.
St. Ouen ... Bernard. St. Samson ... Ralph. St. Wandrille ... Ralph. Thaon ... William.
Vaubadon ... Ranulf.

MAP AND MAP KEYS

The County Boundary and the boundaries of the Lathes are shown in thick lines, broken where uncertain; Hundred boundaries by thin lines, dotted where uncertain.

The boundaries of the Lowy of Tonbridge, Romney Marsh and *Summerdene* Hundred are not mapped.

The letters of National Grid 10-kilometre squares are shown on the map border. Each four-figure square covers one square kilometre (5/8ths of a square mile).

WEST KENT

Half-Lathe of Sutton

Greenwich (G)
1 Woolwich
2 Charlton
3 Greenwich
4 Lewisham
5 Lee
6 Wricklesmarsh
7 Eltham

Bromley (Br)
1 Beckenham
2 Bromley

Ruxley (R)
1 Bexley
2 North Cray
3 Foots Cray
4 Ruxley
5 St. Pauls Cray
6 St. Mary Cray
7 Sandlings
8 Crofton
9 Orpington
10 West Wickham
11 Keston
12 Chelsfield
13 Cudham
14 Seal

Little (Le)
1 Plumstead
2 Lessness
3 Howbury
4 Crayford

Axton (A)
1 Dartford
2 Stone
3 Swanscombe
4 Hawley
5 Darenth
6 Southfleet
7 Pinden
8 Longfield

9 Horton Kirby
10 'Sonnings'
11 Farningham
12 Fawkham
13 Hartley
14 Eynsford
15 Lullingstone
16 Maplescombe
17 Idleigh
18 Ash
19 Ridley
Eddintone

Westerham (Wm)
1 Westerham
2 Brasted

Codsheath (Co)
1 Otford
2 Sundridge

Aylesford Lathe
Toltingtrough (To)
1 Northfleet
2 Gravesend
3 Milton
4 Nurstead
5 Meopham
6 Luddesdown

Shamwell (S)
1 Cliffe
2 Cooling
3 Denton
4 Chalk
5 Beckley
6 Oakleigh
7 Merston
8 Haven
9 Higham
10 Frindsbury
11 Henhurst
12 Cuxton
13 Halling

Hoo (H)
1 Hoo
2 Stoke

Rochester (R)
1 Rochester
2 Great Delce
3 Little Delce
4 Borstal

Chatham (C)
1 Chatham
2 Gillingham

Eyhorne (E)
1 Stockbury
2 Thurnham
3 Aldington
4 Hollingbourne
5 Allington
6 Wormshill
7 Frinsted
8 Wichling
9 Otham
10 Leeds
11 Harbilton
12 Harrietsham
13 Marley
14 Otterden
15 Langley
16 Broomfield
17 Fairbourne
18 Shelborough
19 Bowley
20 Lenham
21 New Shelve
22 Old Shelve
23 Chart Sutton
24 Sutton Valence
25 East Sutton
26 Ulcombe
27 Boughton Malherbe
Bromfeld

Maidstone (M)
1 Boxley
2 Penenden
3 Maidstone
4 West Barming
5 East Barming
6 East Farleigh
7 Loose
8 Hunton
Burgericistune

Larkfield (La)
1 Nashenden
2 Wouldham
3 Snodland
4 Paddlesworth
5 Burham
6 Birling
7 Trottiscliffe
8 Addington
9 Ryarsh
10 Leybourne
11 Eccles
12 Tottington
13 Aylesford
14 Offham
15 West Malling
16 East Malling
17 Ditton
18 Siffleton
19 Allington

Wrotham (Wr)
1 Wrotham
2 Wrotham Heath

Littlefield (Li)
1 Mereworth
2 West Peckham
3 Hadlow
4 East Peckham
5 'Stokenbury'

Twyford (Tw)
1 Wateringbury
2 Teston
3 West Farleigh
4 Nettlestead
5 Yalding
6 Bensted
7 Pimp's Court

Washlingstone (Wa)
1 Tudeley

The Lowy of Tonbridge (Te)
1 Tonbridge

Half-Lathe of Milton
Milton (M)
1 Upchurch
2 Newington
3 Milton Regis
4 Tonge
5 Tunstall
6 Stuppington

EAST KENT
Wye Lathe
Teynham (T)
1 Sheppey

Faversham (Fa)
1 Harty
2 Luddenham
3 Oare
4 Buckland
5 Norton
6 Faversham
7 Perry Court
8 Macknade
9 South Preston
10 Ospringe
11 North Eastling
12 Wilderton
13 Eastling
14 Arnolton
15 Throwley
16 Leaveland
17 Badlesmere
18 Stalisfield
19 Ringlestone
20 Perry Wood
21 Hurst
Cildresham

Boughton (Bo)
1 Graveney
2 Boughton under Blean
3 Selling

Calehill (Ca)
1 East Lenham
2 Charing
3 Pett
4 Westwell
5 Dean Court
6 Little Chart

7 Pivington
8 Pluckley
9 Rooting

Chart (Ct)
1 Great Chart
2 Ripton

Longbridge (Lo)
1 Kennington
2 Ashford
3 South Ashford
4 Sevington
5 Mersham
6 Evegate
Essella

Wye (W)
1 Beamonston
2 Trimworth
3 Eastwell
4 Boughton Aluph
5 Buckwell
6 Dernedale
7 Wye
8 Fanscombe
9 Ashenfield
10 Coombegrove
11 Brook
12 Hampton

Felborough (Fe)
1 Horton
2 Chartham
3 Shillingham
4 Chilham
5 Shalmsford
6 Godmersham

Bircholt (Bi)
1 Aldglose
2 Brabourne

Hundred not known
Gara
Hawkhurst
'Northborough'
Sophis

Borough Lathe
Whitstable (Wh)
1 Whitstable
2 Seasalter
3 Swalecliffe

Whitstable (Wh) cont'd.
4 Blean

Reculver (Re)
1 Reculver
2 Makinbrook
3 Stourmouth

Chislet (Ch)
1 Chislet

Sturry (Sy)
1 Sturry

Fordwich (Fo)
1 Fordwich

Westgate (We)
1 Westgate
2 Thanington
3 St. Martins
Wic

Bridge (Br)
1 Bekesbourne
2 Patrixbourne
3 Lower Hardres
4 Upper Hardres
5 Stelling

Petham (Pe)
1 Petham
2 Swarling

Barham (Ba)
1 Bishopsbourne
2 Barham

Downhamford (D)
1 Wickhambreux
2 Littlebourne
3 Ickham
4 Garrington

Thanet (Th)
1 Monkton
2 Minster in Thanet
3 Margate

Canterbury (Ca)
1 Canterbury
2 Nackington
3 Northgate
4 Langport

Lympne Lathe
Stowting (Sw)
1 Bodsham
2 Stowting
3 Monks Horton
Bochelande
Lanport

Loningborough (Lo)
1 Elham
2 Hemsted
3 Lyminge
4 Acrise

Folkestone (F)
1 Folkestone
Suestone

Bircholt (Bi)
1 Hastingleigh
2 Stansted
3 Aldington

Hayne (Ha)
1 Postling
2 Saltwood
Belice

Street (St)
1 Swanton
2 Stansted
3 Bonnington
4 Sellindge
5 Court at Street
6 Otterpool
7 Berwick
8 Lympne
Aia
Siborne

Blackburn (Bl)
1 Tiffenden
2 Tinton
3 Appledore

Ham (Hm)
1 Warehorne
2 Orlestone
3 Ruckinge

Newchurch (N)
1 Bilsington
2 Norwood

Worth (W)
1 Eastbridge
2 Blackmanstone

Rolvenden (Rl)
1 Benenden
Belice

Selbrittenden (Se)
1 Newenden

Oxney (O)
1 Palstre

Aloesbridge (A)
1 Brenzett

Langport (La)
1 Langport
2 Ripe
3 Dengemarsh
Afettune

The Borough of Hythe
1 Hythe

In Romney Marsh (Rm)
1* Burmarsh
2* Romney
3* Orgarswick
4* Castweazel
Eadruneland
Sturtune

Hundred not known
Brisewei

Eastry Lathe
Preston (P)
1 Preston
2 Elmstone

Wingham (Wi)
1 Wingham
2 Fleet

Sandwich (Sa)
1 Sandwich

Eastry (E)
1 Each
2 Shelving
3 Ringleton
4 Hammil

Eastry (E) cont'd.
5 Woodnesborough
6 Buckland
7 Statenborough
8 Adisham
9 Chillenden
10 Eastry
11 Ham
12 Easole
13 Finglesham
14 Knowlton
15 Betteshanger
16 Soles Court
17 Barfreston
18 Tilmanstone
19 Hartanger
20 Eythorne
21 Waldershare
22 Denton
23 Giddinge
24 Midley

Bewsborough (B)
1 Sibertswold
2 Coldred
3 North Ponshall
4 South Ponshall
5 Wadholt
6 Swanton
7 Temple Ewell
8 Boswell Banks
9 Appleton
10 Pineham
11 Pising
12 Solton
13 Guston
14 West Cliffe
15 St. Margaret's at Cliffe
16 Poulton
17 Buckland
18 Charlton
19 Hougham

20 Farthingloe
21 Atterton
22 Dover
23 Mederclive
24 Newington
Jaonei
Leueberge

Cornilo (C)
1 Deal
2 Northbourne
3 Great & Little Mongeham
4 Beauxfield

Summerdene **(Su)**
A Each
B Marshborough
C Tickenhurst
D Woodnesborough
E Elmton

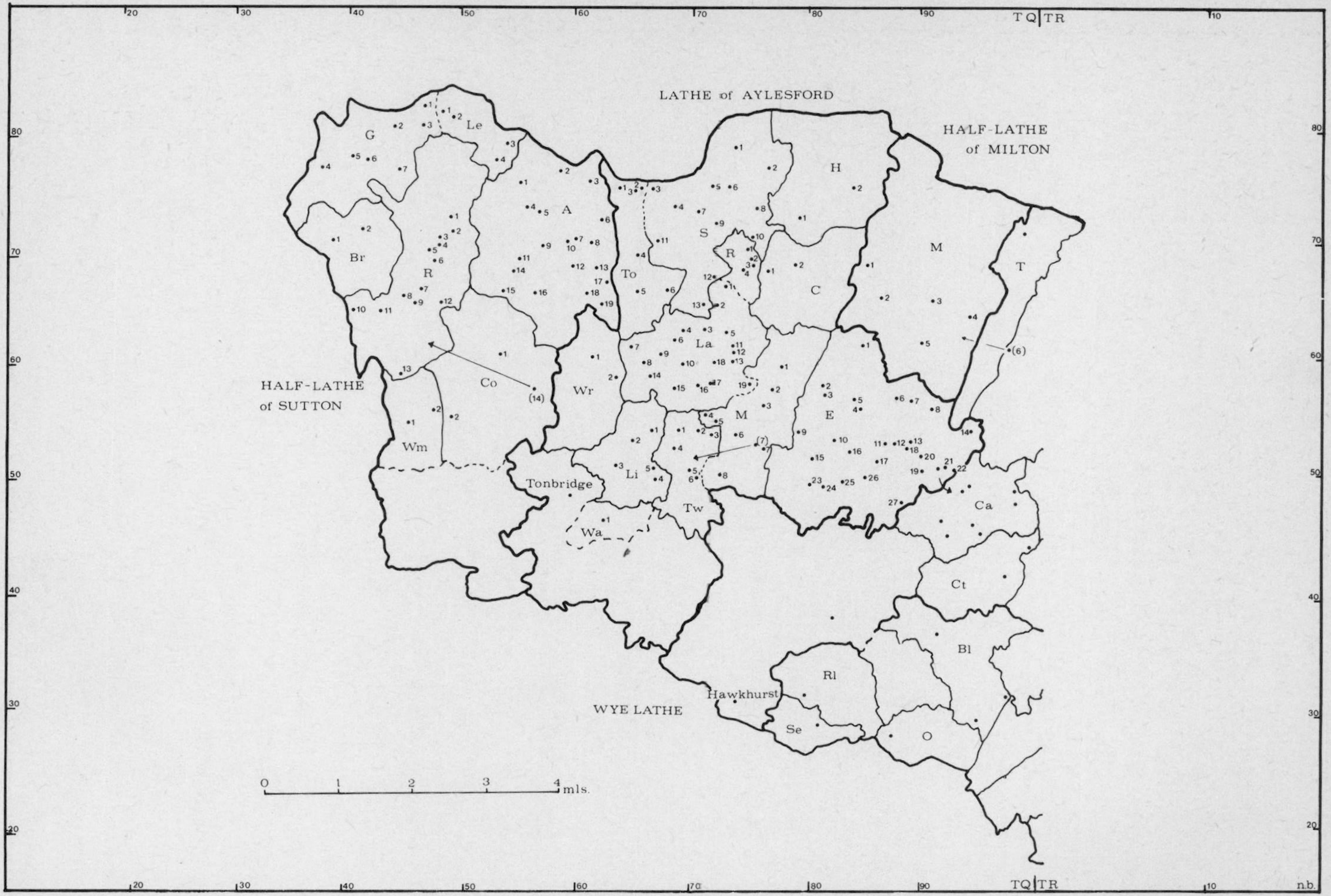

WEST KENT

HALF LATHE of MILTON

LATHE of AYLESFORD

HALF-LATHE of SUTTON

WYE LATHE

TQ|TR

TQ|TR

n.b.

T

M

H

C

E

Ca

Ct

Bl

O

Ri

Se

Hawkhurst

S

R

La

M

Tw

Wa

Li

Wr

Co

Wm

Tonbridge

To

A

Le

R

G

Br

0 1 2 3 4 mls.

EAST KENT

HALF-LATHE of MILTON

WYE LATHE

BOROUGH LATHE

EASTRY LATHE

LYMPNE LATHE

TQ | TR

n.b.

0 1 2 3 4 mls.

Th

Ch

Re

Sy

Wh

Bo

Fa

T

M

E

Ca

Ct

W

Lo

Hm

Bl

O

Rl

Se

Hawkhurst

A

La

N

S

Bi

Sw

Lo

Pe

Fe

We

D

Fo

Ca

Br

Ba

B

C

E

Wi

P

Sa

F

Ha

Hythe

to Eastry Hundred

'a'
'b'

SYSTEMS OF REFERENCE TO DOMESDAY BOOK

The manuscript is divided into numbered chapters, and the chapters into sections, usually marked by large initials and red ink. Farley did not number the sections and later historians, using his edition, have referred to the text of DB by folio numbers, which cannot be closer than an entire page or column. Moreover, several different ways of referring to the same column have been devised. In 1816 Ellis used three separate systems in his indices: (i) on pages i-cvii, 435-518, 537-570; (ii) on pages 1-144; (iii) on pages 145-433 and 519-535. Other systems have since come into use, notably that used by Vinogradoff, here followed. The present edition numbers the sections, the normal practicable form of close reference; but since all discussion of DB for two hundred years has been obliged to refer to folio or column, a comparative table will help to locate references given. The five columns below give Vinogradoff's notation, Ellis's three systems, and that used by Welldon Finn and others. Maitland, Stenton, Darby, and others have usually followed Ellis (i).

Vinogradoff	Ellis (i)	Ellis (ii)	Ellis (iii)	Finn
152 a	152	152 a	152	152 ai
152 b	152	152 a	152.2	152 a2
152 c	152 b	152 b	152 b	152 bi
152 d	152 b	152 b	152 b2	152 b2

In Kent the relation between the Vinogradoff column notation, here followed, and the chapters and sections is

1 a	D1 – D10	6 a	5,1 – 5,8	11 a	5,178 – 5,192		
b	D11 – D24	b	5,9 – 5,18	b	5,192 – 5,203		
c	D25 – M10	c	5,18 – 5,24	c	5,204 – 5,217		
d	M11 – M16	d	5,25 – 5,34	d	5,218 – 6,1		
2 a	C1 – R1	7 a	5,34 – 5,43	12 a	7,1 – 7,8		
b	P1 – P20	b	5,43 – 5,51	b	7,8 – 7,17		
c	1,1 – 1,3	c	5,52 – 5,59	c	7,18 – 7,23		
d	1,3 – 1,4	d	5,60 – 5,70	d	7,23 – 8,1		
3 a	2,1 – 2,7	8 a	5,70 – 5,78	13 a	9,1 – 9,11		
b	2,7 – 2,11	b	5,80 – 5,88	b	9,12 – 9,23		
c	2,12 – 2,16	c	5,88 – 5,95	c	9,24 – 9,35		
d	2,16 – 2,22	d	5,95 – 5,104	d	9,36 – 9,48		
4 a	2,23 – 2,27	9 a	5,104 – 5,115	14 a	9,48 – 10,2		
b	2,28 – 2,35	b	5,115 – 5,124	b	11,1 – 12,4		
c	2,36 – 2,40	c	5,124 – 5,128	c	13,1		
d	3,1 – 3,7	d	5,129 – 5,138				
5 a	3,7 – 3,15	10 a	5,139 – 5,146				
b	3,16 – 3,23	b	5,147 – 5,156				
c	4,1 – 4,9	c	5,157 – 5,166				
d	4,10 – 4,16	d	5,167 – 5,178				

TECHNICAL TERMS

Most of the words expressing measurements have to be transliterated. Translation may not, however, dodge other problems by the use of obsolete or made-up words which do not exist in modern English. The translations here used are given below in italics. They cannot be exact; they aim at the nearest modern equivalent.

AVERA. Provision of draught-horses or mules for the King's use; sometimes commuted to a money payment. *cartage*

BEREWICA. An outlying place, attached to a manor. *outlier*

BORDARIUS. Cultivator of inferior status, usually with a little land. *smallholder*

CARUCA. A plough, with the oxen who pulled it, usually reckoned as 8. *plough*

COTARIUS. Inhabitant of a *cote*, cottage, often without land. *cottager*

DENA. An area of woodland pasture, in Kent mostly associated with land in the Weald belonging to upland manors. *pig pasture*

DOMINIUM. The mastery or dominion of a lord (*dominus*); including plough, land, men, villages, etc., reserved for the lord's use; often concentrated in a *home farm* or *demesne*. *lordship*

FEUDUM. Continental variant, not used in England before 1066, of *feuum* (the Latin form of Old English *feoh*, cattle, money, possessions in general); either a landholder's holding, or land held under the terms of a specific grant. *Holding*

FIRMA. Old English *feorm*, provisions due to the King or lord; a fixed sum paid in place of these and of other miscellaneous dues. *revenue*

GABLUM. Old English *gafol*, tribute or tax to the King or a lord. *tribute*

GELDUM. The principal royal tax, originally levied during the Danish wars, normally at an equal number of pence on each *sulung* of land. *tax*

HIDA. A unit of land measurement, reckoned in DB at 120 fiscal acres; rarely used in Kent, probably in error for *sulung*. *hide*

HUNDREDUM. An administrative district within a shire, whose assembly of notables and village representatives usually met once a month. *hundred*

INUUARD. Provision of a mounted man for the King's use, originally to escort the King when he visited the shire; sometimes commuted to a money payment. *escort*

IUGUM. A unit of land measurement, one quarter of the sulung. *yoke*

LEUGA. An area of jurisdiction, originally a league outside a fixed place; in Kent used of land assigned to the maintenance of Tonbridge castle. *territory*

LEST. A division of the shire peculiar to Kent and containing several hundreds (cf. introduction to the Index of Places). *Lathe*

MANERIUM. A territorial and jurisdictional holding. *manor*

SACA. German *Sache*, English *sake*, Latin *causa*, 'affair', 'lawsuit'; the fullest authority normally exercised by a lord. *full jurisdiction*

SOCA. 'Soke', from Old English *socn*, seeking, comparable with Latin *quaestio*. Jurisdiction, with the right to receive fines and other dues; also the district in which such *soca* was exercised. *jurisdiction*

SOCHEMANNUS. 'Soke man', liable to attend the court of a *soca* and serve its lords; before 1066 often with more land and higher status than villagers; bracketed in the Commissioners' brief with the *liber homo* (free man); see Bedfordshire, Appendix. *Freeman*

SOLIN. The Kentish unit of land measurement, usually reckoned at 200 acres (see note 7,19). *sulung*

TEIGNUS. Person of superior status; originally one of the King's military companions, later often in his service in an administrative capacity. *thane*

T.R.E. *tempore regis Edwardi*, in King Edward's time. *before 1066*

VILIA. Translating Old English *tun*, estate, town, village. The later distinction between a small *village* and a large *town* was not yet in use in 1066. *village* or *town*

VILLANUS. Member of a *villa*, usually with more land than a *bordarius*. *villager*

VIRGATA. A quarter of a hide (40 fiscal acres in DB), rarely used in Kent, often in error for *yoke*. *virgate*